Pearl Cleage and
Free Womanhood

Pearl Cleage and Free Womanhood
Essays on Her Prose Works

Edited by
Tikenya Foster-Singletary and
Aisha Francis

Forewords by Pearl Cleage and Tayari Jones

McFarland & Company, Inc., Publishers
Jefferson, North Carolina, and London

Excerpts reprinted with permission: From *The Brass Bed and Other Stories* copyright 1991 by Pearl Cleage, reprinted by permission of Third World Press, Inc., Chicago, Illinois. From *Flyin' West* by Pearl Cleage, published by Theatre Communications Group, used by permission of Theatre Communications Group. From *Late Bus to Mecca*, in *Playwriting Women: 7 Plays from the Women's Project*, ed. Julia Miles (Portsmouth, NH: Heinemann, 1993): 299–322, by permission of Pearl Cleage. From *Baby Brother's Blues* by Pearl Cleage, copyright © 2006 by Pearl Cleage. From *Deals with the Devil* by Pearl Cleage, copyright © 1993 by Pearl Cleage. From *Some Things I Thought I'd Never Do* by Pearl Cleage, copyright © 2003 by Pearl Cleage. Used by permission of Ballantine Books, a division of Random House, Inc. From *Babylon Sisters* by Pearl Cleage, copyright © 2005 by Pearl Cleage. From *Seen It All and Done the Rest* by Pearl Cleage, copyright © 2008 by Pearl Cleage. Used by permission of an imprint of The Random House Publishing Group, a division of Random House, Inc.

LIBRARY OF CONGRESS CATALOGUING-IN-PUBLICATION DATA

Pearl Cleage and free womanhood : essays on her prose works / edited by Tikenya Foster-Singletary and Aisha Francis ; forewords by Pearl Cleage and Tayari Jones.
    p.   cm.
Includes bibliographical references and index.

ISBN 978-0-7864-6586-6
softcover : acid free paper ∞

1. Cleage, Pearl — Criticism and interpretation.
I. Foster-Singletary, Tikenya S. II. Francis, Aisha.
PS3553.L389Z83 2012
813'.54 — dc23   2012010111

BRITISH LIBRARY CATALOGUING DATA ARE AVAILABLE

© 2012 Tikenya Foster-Singletary and Aisha Francis. All rights reserved

No part of this book may be reproduced or transmitted in any form or by any means, electronic or mechanical, including photocopying or recording, or by any information storage and retrieval system, without permission in writing from the publisher.

On the cover: Pearl Cleage (photograph by Albert Trotman)

Manufactured in the United States of America

McFarland & Company, Inc., Publishers
   Box 611, Jefferson, North Carolina 28640
     www.mcfarlandpub.com

Table of Contents

Acknowledgments — vii
Foreword: These Pages Are My Proof
    PEARL CLEAGE — 1
Foreword
    TAYARI JONES — 3
Introduction — 7

PART I: CLEAGE AS NOVELIST

An "Urban Oasis": Pearl Cleage's West End Imaginary
    MARGARET T. MCGEHEE — 15

Over the Rainbow: Finding Home in West End Atlanta
    RHONDA M. COLLIER — 37

Being Neighborly: Performance in *Seen It All and Done the Rest*
    SHANNA L. SMITH — 49

What Looks Like New: Narrative Call for Social Change
    RASHELL R. SMITH-SPEARS — 63

Critical Thinking Is for Everyone: Social Work as the Praxis of Communal Love in *I Wish I Had a Red Dress*
    AISHA FRANCIS — 78

An Ode to Black Feminism: Reciprocal Empowerment and Anti-Sexism in *I Wish I Had a Red Dress* and *Some Things I Never Thought I'd Do*
    MONICA L. MELTON — 95

Shattering Silence: Pearl Cleage and Black Female Sexual Empowerment
    SANDRA C. DUVIVIER — 110

Part II: Multimedia Cleage: Plays, Essays and the Digital Divide

Teaching Feminist Lessons in *Late Bus to Mecca*
  Ama S. Wattley — 127

Pearl Cleage as a Dirty Realist
  Kelly DeLong — 140

The Blues, Psychosis, and the Black Arts Movement in *Bourbon at the Border*
  Ladrica Menson-Furr — 146

Social Mediation: Pearl Cleage and the Digital Divide
  Sheila Smith McKoy — 154

In Context: Teaching Pearl Cleage in Southwest Atlanta
  Tikenya Foster-Singletary — 166

Backtalk: Respectability as Repression and Pearl Cleage's Incitement to Discourse
  Alexia Williams — 176

A Conversation with Pearl Cleage
  Tikenya Foster-Singletary and Aisha Francis — 182

About the Contributors — 203
Index — 205

Acknowledgments

The editors want to collectively recognize the contributions of several people who have helped to nurse this project from its infancy in their dissertations to its completion in this project. Dr. Sheila Smith McKoy, who has been both friend and mentor since their days in graduate school, was an invaluable guide and resource at every stage. We also want to thank Pearl Cleage herself, who has been so gracious and open for years as we requested her time and energy, all the while, promising that "we're still working on the book about your work!"

Aisha is ever thankful to her family — both close and extended — whose support in her formative years nurtured her dreams before she clearly knew what they were. She is especially grateful to her mother, Judy Lynn Francis, whose unwavering faith has been an unspeakable blessing. Her husband, Clayton Samuels, was patient with all of the late nights, writing weekends and working vacations this project required, and generously lent his proofreading skills when she was too tired to read another line. While working as an independent scholar by night and a fund-raiser by day has not been without its challenges, she is grateful to be a living testimony of the possibilities of an unorthodox career path. The vision for what an academic life could hold unfolded when Aisha became a Mellon Mays Undergraduate Fellow in 1996 at Fisk University. After all of these years, she hopes to have made the following Mellon mentors proud: Dr. Virginia Moran, Dr. Cynthia Neal Spence, Dr. Lydia English, and the late Dr. Rudolph Byrd, who lost his battle with cancer just as this book was being completed. Dr. Byrd's example, in particular, taught Aisha volumes about the importance and process of academic collaboration. One of his most prescient lessons was that any solid working relationship starts with a stellar partner. There could be no greater partner than Tikenya Foster-Singletary, without whom what you now hold in your hands would have remained only as an idea in our heads.

Tikenya wishes to acknowledge her immediate and extended family, especially her husband, Barbary, who believed in her and her ideas without question; her children, Trinity and Barbary Trenton, who were born while this project was coming to fruition and offered both cuddles at opportune moments and the isolated time alone when "Mommy's working, close the door behind you, please"; Dr. RaShell Smith-Spears, who spent countless hours over the phone listening to ramblings, excitement, and complaints as the project and our marriages, children, homes, and careers came together; Dr. Akiba Harper, who established the course that examined Cleage's work, and who has been both supportive and helpful in bringing Tikenya onto the faculty and allowing her to teach that class; the students who participated in those classes, providing valuable opportunities to explore Cleage's work, and feedback both in class and in their writing that helped to conceptualize, in particular, the teaching chapter. Special recognition goes to Alexia Williams for her contributions stemming from that class. Perhaps it goes without saying, but it must be said that Aisha's partnership and friendship held this book together when it was entirely intangible — she is visionary and bright and a believer in the impossible.

Foreword: These Pages Are My Proof

PEARL CLEAGE

I have always known I was a writer. At age two, I told stories from my crib and at four made my older sister, who was six, teach me to read and write so I could record them in a little green notebook provided by my grandfather. I was the kid who gathered long-suffering siblings and unsuspecting cousins together for an original play to be performed after dinner for an audience of turkey-satiated grown-ups, whether they liked it or not.

In fourth grade, I wrote a theatrical adaptation of "Chicken Little," and was allowed to tour the show up and down the halls of the school, with our leading actor gaining confidence and volume with each declaration that "the sky is falling," until we were gently ushered back to our homeroom just in time for Spelling.

In sixth grade, I wrote a poem about a huge jungle snake. If memory serves me, I rhymed the words *wan* and *gone*, but why I was writing about giant reptiles, I can't recall. What I do recall is that my teacher thought the poem was good enough to send me downstairs to read it to the principal, which I did, confounding my schoolmates who saw me, the quintessential goody two shoes, waiting outside the principal's door and assumed I had finally gotten into trouble. It was hard to tell them that I was there for writing a poem about a big snake since that meant I was *still* a goody two shoes, but my mom taught at that school and my dad was a minister. *How bad could I be?*

The thing is I wasn't interested in being bad. I was interested in writing. Always and only: writing. I was fascinated with the complicated overlapping narratives of my own family history and with the mysterious lives of my friends once we left school and walked home to close the doors on our own

1

individual houses. As a child, I eavesdropped incessantly, even going so far as to carry a small notebook on the bus to record the conversations around me. My sister, mortified at this behavior, warned that people would not appreciate being written about by me, but I knew nobody on the Joy Road bus, lurching its way around the west side of Detroit on a workday afternoon, cared about a ten-year-old girl scribbling in a little spiral notebook.

Sometimes when you scribble long enough to build up a body of work that folks find interesting or useful or funny or true to life as they know it, people not only read you, but begin to write about you, too. If you're lucky, some of those people will not only attempt to understand *how* you do what you do, but *why*. If you're very lucky, in addition to loving the writing, they will find a way to love the writer, in all her passionate, messy, missed-another-deadline glory.

The editors of this book, Tikenya Foster-Singletary and Aisha Francis, have given me a gift for which it is impossible to thank them. The only thing I ever wanted to do was live my life as a full-time, straight-up, serious writer. This book is my evidence that I've done it. That I'm still doing it. And that all those hours of scribbling and scowling and pacing around small spaces where only the desk looms large have not been in vain. I am what I say I am: a writer. *These pages are my proof.*

Foreword

Tayari Jones

When I met Pearl Cleage, I was a sophomore at Spelman College, harboring a secret dream to be a writer. I had enrolled in a course simply titled "Creative Writing" and the professor wasn't a full-time faculty member. Forty of us wedged ourselves into a classroom designed to seat maybe twenty-five. The room was not air-conditioned and despite the open windows, the air was thick with the scents of young women — body lotions, singed hair, a hint of sweat, and anticipation.

Pearl arrived looking different from any professor we had seen before. It wasn't exactly that she was younger, although there was something about her that struck us as still growing and evolving. She wore her hair cut close to her head; from her arms dangled a clutch of bangles. She asked us to go around the room and introduce ourselves, but instead of saying our names, classifications, and majors, she asked us to tell the class what we wanted to write about. Spelman is a small school, and everyone pretty much knew everyone else, especially in our major, but when we had to tell what we wanted to write about, it was like we were meeting each other for the first time. That's how Pearl's magic works. It's like she gives you a new set of eyes.

From that very first day she was always "Pearl," not "Professor Cleage." This was unusual at Spelman, where faculty members sometimes addressed even each other as "Doctor." It wasn't that she wanted to be pals with the students. Rather, she connected with us as one human being to another.

One day, Pearl distributed a photocopied page from *Vanity Fair* magazine, a letter to the editor from Aida Chapman, responding to a profile of Miles Davis, the great trumpeter. She complained that the editors of *Vanity Fair* had let go, without comment, Davis's matter-of-fact admission to brutalizing Cicely Tyson. She went on to share her own experiences, alleging that Davis had burned her hands on the electric eye of a stove.

As a class, we were, of course, horrified by this story, but Pearl asked us what we now thought of Miles Davis. We sat quiet, almost afraid to have an opinion. Miles Davis was an icon. Were we allowed to hold him accountable, to say that we didn't give a damn if he was supposed to be some sort of genius? I suspected that we were, but I didn't know what to say about it. But the part of my brain that loves to write thought about it long and hard.

A few weeks later, Pearl invited the class to attend something called Live at Club Zebra. At this time, I didn't have a car and I didn't know anybody with a car. My roommate borrowed an old Ford Escort from a relative and we set off. It didn't matter that we didn't know what to expect. We just wanted to be there. Club Zebra turned out to be a multi-media arts presentation put on by Pearl and her (now) husband Zaron Burnett. In a room decorated to evoke the forbidden atmosphere of a prohibition era speakeasy, attendees of all ages approached the microphone and read poetry, delivered monologues, and I think someone even sang. But the highlight of the performance was when Pearl took the stage and read a piece called "Mad at Miles."

Of course, I had often heard people say "a man should never raise his hand to a woman." But Pearl was the first person I had ever seen take aim at one man in particular, let alone a famous man like Miles Davis. It was brave and fierce in a way that's hard to explain all these years later. What Pearl did that night just wasn't done. But she kept doing it until none of us could imagine ever being silent again.

To this day, no piece of writing has affected me more — and I have read a lot since then. Not even the lyrical styling of Toni Morrison has moved me more than Pearl's brave words. I have friends named Miles, after the great genius. But Pearl stood there and told the world that crimes against black women were major crimes. There was no excuse. She was standing with Aida, with Cicely, and with everyone else who ever feared a man she was sleeping with, who feared she wouldn't be believed, or that she would be blamed.

"Mad at Miles" became part of a collection of essays called *Deals with the Devil*, which included straight talk aimed at young women about protecting themselves against violence. She called this essay "Basic Training," and it was all the advice you could never get from your mother because you couldn't talk to her about desire, about power.

The year I graduated from Spelman, I received a letter in the mail. Pearl was going to publish my first story in a magazine she edited, *Catalyst*. Along with letter of congratulation was a check for $100, which, to this day, remains the best money I ever made. It seems like a long time ago. She likes to joke that she and I now are "two authoresses." One of my favorite memories is of doing a joint performance with Pearl right after my first book came out. I was sitting there with maybe three people in front of me and Pearl's line was all the way around the corner. One of the women had brought Pearl a box of earrings she had made herself. Up on seeing me there with my pen in hand, with nothing to sign, the woman said, "Oh you poor thing! You don't have any fans!" Then to Pearl she said, "Do you mind?" Then she gave me the least ornate pair of earrings. "Here," she said. "Take these."

I put the earrings on, quite happily. Sometimes I tell my friends this story and they say, "Weren't you offended?" But I wasn't. That woman and her earrings are just another way that Pearl leads by example. Pearl writes the books that make people want to make jewelry by hand and it makes that same person want to share with me, a young writer she had never heard of.

There is this false dichotomy in the world of letters — you are either a reader's writer, or a writer's writer. And this means that you are either loved by the people or respected by other writers. Pearl Cleage shows that us that this concept is ridiculous at its core. Pearl Cleage is a people's writer. She writes novels and essays that teach you how to live, that show you who you are. And if who you are is a writer, she shows you how to do it.

Tayari Jones, author of the acclaimed novels Leaving Atlanta, The Untelling *and* Silver Sparrow, *is an associate professor in the MFA program at Rutgers-University, Newark. She was named a 2008 Collins Fellow by the United States Artists.*

Introduction

After decades of actively producing and promoting her own creative work and that of other black women artists, Pearl Cleage enjoyed a heralded heyday of public attention in the 1990s. *Flyin' West*, the most produced new play in the United States in 1994, brought the award-winning Cleage to the attention of national theater-going audiences. She is also a best-selling novelist whose first book of fiction, *What Looks Like Crazy on an Ordinary Day*, was an Oprah Book Club pick in 1999 propelling it to spend nine weeks on the *New York Times* bestseller list. Subsequent novels have been consistent best sellers and perennial book club favorites. *I Wish I Had a Red Dress*, her second novel, won multiple book club awards in 2001. *Some Things I Never Thought I'd Do* was a 2003 *Good Morning America!* book club pick before the show became branded by its abbreviations, *GMA*. Further, almost all of her novels have made *Essence Magazine's* best seller list, and *Baby Brother's Blues* was the inaugural pick of the *Essence* Book Club and an NAACP Image Award winner for best fiction in 2007. Additionally, her three subsequent novels, *Seen It All and Done the Rest* (2008), *Till You Hear from Me* (2010) and *Just Wanna Testify* (2011) have been well-received. Cleage continued to write plays, even as a new generation of readers came to know her primarily as a novelist. Recently produced Cleage dramas include *A Song for Coretta*, set against the backdrop of the homegoing celebration for Coretta Scott King, and her newest play, *The Nacirema Society Requests the Honor of Your Presence at a Celebration of its First One Hundred Years*, which opened in late 2010. Despite her popular success and scholarly appeal, there is surprisingly little scholarship about Cleage's work. Although one volume of essays will not adequately assess the vast output she has produced in decades of writing, this collection of new critical essays begins to fill that void.

One would assume that this level of critical attention would produce a range of written reflection about the meaning and points of intersection in her art. Like many contemporary African American women writers including

Thulani Davis, Angela Davis, Toni Cade Bambara, Sylvia Wynter, Ntozake Shange, Gayle Jones, and of course the powerhouses Alice Walker and Toni Morrison, Cleage's work has been absorbed into the syllabi of courses with titles such as: African-American Literature; Multicultural U.S. Authors; Writing and Gender in the United States; and Southern Women Writers. This volume was conceived because the editors wished plaintively for something like it and finally decided to stop waiting for it to be written. Cleage's work deserves focused theoretical consideration that only a dedicated collection of critical theory can garner. As the publication of critical collections on her contemporaries attests, audiences are ripe for richer considerations of black female authors other than the stalwarts Toni Morrison, Alice Walker and Gloria Naylor, whose work has justifiably yielded literally hundreds of critical essays and several volumes of critical perspectives. Authors with arguably similar levels of name recognition, and as much broad popularity as Cleage, have been the subject of dedicated critical volumes. Consider, for example *Savoring the Salt: The Legacy of Toni Cade Bambara* edited by Linda Janet Holmes and Cheryl A. Wall and *Ntozake Shange: A Critical Study of The Plays* by Neal A. Lester and Ntozake Shange. Given her popularity, acclaim, and longevity, Cleage deserves the critical attention required to unpack the importance of her subject position as both a serious writer who prides herself on placing black women at the center and one who has garnered mass appeal with a cross-over audience.

Pearl Cleage texts are squarely focused on the significance of black women's cultural work and its role in perpetuating a specific code of conduct for African American women. Her unequivocal objective is to encourage and empower black women in their struggle against covert and overt forms of victimization. Through artistic expression, Pearl Cleage has carved a niche for her voice that connects her with sentiments expressed in her work. Her oeuvre includes journalism, plays, novels, and essays. Accordingly, Cleage has made monumental contributions to the cannon of contemporary African American literature. We believe that this book's content will be immensely valuable to both the general reader and to scholarly audiences who hold particular interest in the critical implications and cultural context of Pearl Cleage's literature. Because of the range of topics and genres the author has broached throughout her long career, the essays published herein also intersect with many of the focus areas: American and Southern literature; African American Studies; American and Southern history; popular culture; American studies; women's studies; cultural criticism; and criticism of literary nonfiction.

This collection also intentionally draws attention to the many practical applications of Pearl Cleage's work. Her work can and should be applied in the classroom and outside of it as a tool to enhance critical thinking and in the community as a tool to enhance social justice. It should probably go without saying that on another level, beyond our appreciation of Cleage from a scholarly point of view, it's likely no surprise that we both happen to be longtime fans of her work. Tikenya was introduced to Pearl Cleage as an undergraduate student at Spelman College. She had the great pleasure of taking a master playwriting course with her. Elements of that class found their way into the teaching essay included. The class had a small group of students and demonstrated both Cleage's personal openness and the level of craftsmanship that goes into her work. It began a decades long relationship with Cleage and her work. For her part, Aisha's first encountered Cleage's *Flyin' West* and *Deals with the Devil* as a Women's and Gender Studies minor at Fisk University in an effort to make sense of what it meant to be a practicing black feminist. She recalls her parents' excited response when she shared her college reading list with them. As it turns out, they were familiar with Cleage and her first husband, Michael Lomax, their time at the Atlanta University Center having overlapped by a few years.

Framed using the critical rubric of Free Womanhood — which we position as Cleage's own particular brand of feminist theory — this text is as broad in scope as Pearl Cleage is expansive in her aesthetic. Cleage's artistry maps the cultural and political intersections of critical challenges facing African America and the border Diaspora. These inflection points include: the consequences of apathy; the post civil rights movement; charting the landscape of the new South; the affects and international implications of cultural epidemics (i.e., HIV/AIDS; domestic violence, substance abuse; and the international sex trafficking trade); and the difficulty of maintaining healthy romantic relationships in the post-modern world. The tenor of her work demands an in-depth, scholarly response to the breadth and scope of sociopolitical ideas it engages. Thus, another purpose of this collection is to respond to this call.

The Free Womanhood concept that anchors Cleage's novels — and indeed all of her writing — is central to setting up a viable paradigm for women's self-actualization. Her written record reveals that she first began to shape this idea years before her first novel was published. The 1995 convocation speech she delivered at Spelman College demonstrates just how indelibly ingrained this Free Womanhood concept is to Cleage on a personal and professional level. She begins the talk, which took place on the heels of both the O.J. Simpson trial and the Million Man March, by stating that she wanted to talk to and about black women:

> I didn't really want to talk about the brothers. I wanted to talk about us. About finding us in the middle of all the confusion. About loving us in the middle of all the encouragement not to. About saving us in the middle of these strange, strange days. So I decided to talk about love and to share

with you several pieces about different kinds of love and how they are capable of healing and sustaining us. But then I realized that the place we have to start with all that love and sweetness is with ourselves [Cleage, "Convocation"].

In addition to centering her talk on love Cleage importantly introduces the term "Free Womanhood" in this oral context. It is a phrase and theme carried forward from her seminal play *Flyin' West*. Originally commissioned and produced in 1992 by the Alliance Theater Company in Atlanta, Georgia, the sisters at the heart of this story of black homesteading share a beautiful bonding ritual in the First Act that reads in part: "Because we are free Negro women.... Born of free Negro women.... Back as far as time begins.... We choose this day to declare our lives to be our own and no one else's" [Cleage, *Flyin' West* 44]. Cleage also outlines an early version of this paradigm in the 1993 essay collection, *Deals with the Devil and Other Reasons to Riot*. Here she lists "The Other Facts of Life," to map out wordly dangers specific to womanhood. They include sexism, violence, and rape. This list of life-skills predates and prefigures the one that appears in both *What Looks Like Crazy on an Ordinary Day* and *I Wish I Had a Red Dress*. The accounting of "Ten Things Every Free Woman Should Know" as outlined in Cleage's first two novels, not only advises young women and girls to set achieving "Free Womanhood" as a goal, but it also compels older women to commit to embodying this specific set of skills for their own protection and preservation, too. The list proposes a basic skill set that includes growing flowers, nutrition, self-defense, elementary health care, spirituality, and money management. By consciously and carefully constructing a life based on Free Womanhood, Cleage manages to create an ideology that can stand the test of time and offers awareness to women in a way that invites exploration of themselves, each other, and men. Just as with Cleage's writing, the ideology of Free Womanhood is flexible enough to function as a framework for this entire volume.

The essays in this book are linked by their careful consideration of how the author treats and lays claim to complex contemporary articulations of neighborhood and community, familial and romantic love, health and wholeness, feminism, freedom and the pursuit of happiness. For Cleage, writing is a form of resistance that has taken multiple generic forms. To reflect the breadth of genres Cleage tackles with alacrity, this compilation is organized into two parts: one covering novels and the second on plays, essays, and short stories. As revealed in an interview with the authors, Cleage has signaled the conclusion of the West End novel series through which so many readers have come to know and appreciate her work. At least in the near term, she will focus on her first love of playwriting. Whatever comes next, readers expect to be challenged by the themes and uplifted by the content in ways that will keep audiences engaged for years to come. Cleage wouldn't have it any other way.

This volume includes essays focused on many of the genres that Pearl Cleage has mastered. There are several considerations of Cleage as dramatist, essayist and novelist. (However, her inspiring poetry has been left for another occasion because of the difficulties entailed in receiving permissions to reprint her verse.) Taken together, these essays demonstrate the intersection of activism and art that has maintained Cleage's following among a broad audience. The contributions were chosen for their particular perspective of her voice, which deftly combines admonition and enlightenment with power and pragmatism. By including essays written both from a scholarly perspective and geared toward a lay audience, we hope that this collection will be a timely resource for students from the college through graduate level, librarians, scholars, journalists, writers and an enthusiastic fan-base of the general public as well. In fact, we included a essay on teaching Cleage, precisely because we thought it would serve as a useful reference for high school and college teachers who are inclined to incorporate Cleage into their curriculum.

The first seven essays deal with Cleage as novelist. In "An 'Urban Oasis'" Margaret T. McGehee examines the role of place and home in Cleage's recent novels and considers how Atlanta's West End functions as a character in these texts. More than a setting or backdrop, the woman-centered "urban oasis" of the imagined West End represents an idealized urban environment and utopian relations between African American men and women. By the measure of its difference from that which lies beyond its borders (e.g., drugs, prostitution, crime, domestic abuse), this utopian place functions, in part, to point out the dystopic qualities of contemporary urban environments.

Rhonda M. Collier explores the concepts of globalization, community building and homes real and imagined in "Over the Rainbow." Her position is that *Seen It All and Done the Rest* demonstrates modern possibility for a functioning twenty-first century community when black women are no longer misunderstood and displaced but rather feel recognized and "at home" notwithstanding their geographic location.

In "Being Neighborly," Shanna L. Smith positions *Seen It All and Done the Rest* as the embodiment of the concept of "spoken work" which involves oratorical skill that utilizes performance specifically to address social issues and engage in social justice. That work involves coalition building and activism sparked by "the word"—a verbal call to action. This essay explores Cleage's novel as a response to that call, and as black women's way of recording and tracking social justice action. The essay argues that while spoken work involves a variety of means and a multitude of ways for transmission, in this particular novel Cleage interrogates orality for justice through internet technology.

"What Looks Like New," by RaShell R. Smith-Spears, explores the ways in which Cleage's first two novels frame problematic aspects of three major institutions in the African American community — the church, the school, and social welfare. It positions the primary roadblock to progress within these institutions as the inability of the individuals representing them to move beyond the traditional methods of operation particularly in terms of gender identity and sexuality. This reading of Cleage demonstrates how she re-envisions gender roles as a way to achieve social change in the black community.

Aisha Francis' "Critical Thinking Is for Everyone," in positioning critical thinking as central to community redemption, considers how Cleage's *Red Dress* presents grassroots social work as a possible solution to mend the fraying social fabric confronting African American communities in the twenty-first century. In so doing, Cleage adroitly presents *Red Dress* as a collective teaching moment for her audience at large. This essay interrogates the practical value of putting a premium on accessibility when going about the difficult work of translating society's most complex and important ideas a younger generation.

In "An Ode to Black Feminism" by Dr. Monica L. Melton, the protagonists of Pearl Cleage's *Some Things I Never Thought I'd Do* (2003) and *I Wish I Had a Red Dress* (2001) are examined for their representations of black feminist epistemologies. Melton positions these characters as role models for African American communities who rely on feminist standpoint theory to create a space for black folk to see images of black feminism in action. In so doing, they bring to life a space in which women and men embrace black feminist thought, images that are sorely lacking in popular culture today. In so doing, Cleage's novels work to bridge the gap in popular culture of empowering images of Black women and create representations of how life can be for African Americans instead of reifying historical negative stereotypes and scripts.

Silence and respectability politics surrounding black female sexualities have allowed black communities to challenge pervasive stereotypes of black female bodies as lascivious and hypersexual, thus creating a counter narrative that places blackness within the realm of morality and equality. Nevertheless, silence has failed to not only eradicate these misrepresentations of black female sexuality but also provide a discourse on black female sexual agency and empowerment. Pearl Cleage acknowledges the necessities of this discourse in her delineation of empowering black female sexualities in her understudied novel *What Looks Like Crazy on an Ordinary Day* (1997). "Shattering Silence," by Dr. Sandra C. Duvivier, then, explores the ways Cleage shatters silence, thus providing an empowering narrative of black female sexualities. In so doing, it also examines her exposure of the ramifications of silence — including HIV and teenage pregnancy — which thus illuminates the need for a more progressive discourse of black sexualities, particularly black female sexualities.

The essays in Part II analyze Cleage's plays, essays, and social media. "Teaching Feminist Lessons in *Late Bus to Mecca*" by Ama S. Wattley looks at the themes of abuse and exploitation of women in the portrayal of two black female characters who are oppressed and victimized in society, one through the sex trade industry. Watley argues that this play advocates many of Cleage's womanist positions including her exposure of oft-dismissed sexist oppression within the black community. Finally, it considers how Cleage, as playwright, breaks boundaries in her characterization of the female protagonist, Ava, a prostitute who challenges the myth of the black superwoman.

Kelly DeLong in "Pearl Cleage as a Dirty Realist" views Cleage's short collection *The Brass Bed and Other Stories* through the lens of dirty realism as defined by *Granta* magazine's special issue. Examining the minimalist nature of the pieces in her brief volume, he argues that Cleage is rightly included in this group of writers. Her focus on the lives of black women interrupts initial boundaries that limit the framing of these writers. Cleage's coupling of minimalist writing with gritty domestic concerns elevates her short fiction.

In "The Blues, Psychosis, and the Black Arts Movement in *Bourbon at the Border*," Ladrica Menson-Furr highlights Cleage's appreciation of history, activism, and the psychological impact of the civil rights movement on the contemporary moment as dramatized in her play. The author positions this play as a work of experiential and historical memory that illustrates both the blues, as a vernacular tradition that enabled African Americans to exist on the border of reality and pain, and Toni Morrison's concept of "rememory" as a cultural imperative.

"Social Mediation" will consider the specter of orality and intimate communication methods as re-framing tools in Cleage's work and consider how social media plays an important role in *Seen It All and Done the Rest*. Through an engaging reading of the West African cultural concept of *ayan*—literally and figuratively a language and the language of the talking drum—Sheila Smith McKoy's essay analyzes the subversive and powerful role of in-group communication in various forms including drumming, codes of conduct, and social media within African American communities. Ultimately, the novel acknowledges and embraces alternate communication systems to transmit language and ideas. These alternate methods require an ability and willingness to "hear" that hearkens to African and Afrocentric notions of communication.

Tikenya Foster-Singletary's "In Context" explores useful methods for teaching Cleage's novels, plays, and essays. Unique to this approach will be the perspective of teaching Cleage's work in West End Atlanta, where a number of her novels have been set. Also unique is the experience of teaching at Spelman College, Cleage's alma mater, where she is frequently on campus. This essay will examine the many intersecting strands that are present in her work: violence against women, feminism, gender relationships, love.

"Backtalk," an insightfully composed student essay by Alexia Williams, serves as an example of the kind of work produced in a course designed and focused on Cleage's work. The essay examines *What Looks Like Crazy on an Ordinary Day* and *Baby Brother's Blues* with an eye towards their use of sexuality and transgression. Discourse and the conversation become tools for social progress.

To wrap, we offer "A Conversation with Pearl Cleage." Between the spring of 2010 and the spring of 2011, Cleage generously agreed to meet with students in the course focused solely on her work. In 2011, she also granted an interview to the editors on the campus of Spelman College. The interview explored her work over the years, her time as a student at Spelman, and the intersections between Cleage and other artists.

WORKS CITED

Cleage, Pearl. "Convocation Speech." Sisters Chapel, Spelman College, Atlanta, GA. 12 October 1995.

———. *Deals With the Devil and Other Reasons to Riot.* New York: Ballentine, 1993.

———. *Flyin' West and Other Plays.* New York: Theater Communications Group, 1999.

———. *I Wish I Had a Red Dress.* New York: HarperCollins, 2001.

———. *What Looks Like Crazy on an Ordinary Day.* New York: Avon, 1997.

PART I:
CLEAGE AS NOVELIST

An "Urban Oasis": Pearl Cleage's West End Imaginary

MARGARET T. MCGEHEE

Petite, quietly forceful, and prolific, Pearl Cleage (pronounced Cleg) has emerged in the past two decades as an author critically aware of Atlanta's past and present. She has lived and worked in Atlanta for over thirty years, residing for most of that time in the southwestern section of the city, about a mile from the neighborhood of West End. Throughout the 1970s and 1980s, Cleage wrote columns for various Atlanta-based publications. She founded a literary magazine called *Catalyst* while teaching creative writing at Spelman from 1986 to 1991 (Cleage, "Re: questions"; Cleage, "Catalyst" 15).[1] During the 1990s, Kenny Leon, artistic director of Atlanta's Alliance Theater, commissioned her to write three plays. In that decade, four collections of her writing and her first novel, *What Looks Like Crazy on an Ordinary Day*, were published (Giles 709). (*Essence* editor Susan Taylor suggested this book to Oprah Winfrey, who then chose it as a selection for her book club, ensuring its status as an instant bestseller and garnering Cleage national recognition.[2]) Cleage followed this novel with a sequel, titled *I Wish I Had a Red Dress* (2002), and then six more novels in quick succession. Her published works include fifteen plays, a book of poetry, four collections of columns and essays, and eight novels, as well as numerous magazine articles.[3] Cleage is well-known in Atlanta, frequently reading to a packed house at the independent feminist bookstore, Charis Books, or to large audiences at Spelman or at the annual Atlanta-based National Black Arts Festival. With that said, it is surprising that she has received such little critical attention from scholars.[4]

This essay examines the imagined Atlanta and imagined West End neighborhood within the city that serve as the setting of her six most recent novels. *Some Things I Never Thought I'd Do* (2003), *Babylon Sisters* (2005), *Baby Brother's Blues* (2006), *Seen It All and Done the Rest* (2008), *Till You Hear From Me* (2010), and *Just Wanna Testify* (2011) all take place in Atlanta, a city known within popular culture as the home of numerous contemporary R&B, rap, and hip-hop groups and artists, including Outkast and Ludacris. Cleage has characterized Atlanta as a "completely different world" from Los Angeles or New York City. She finds Atlanta to be of "a perfect size"—more accessible and manageable from a writer's vantage point than other urban spaces—and, having lived in the city for over thirty years, she is more familiar with its contours (Paige 241). While Atlanta's song imagines "the ATL" as a place where one can fulfill dreams, Cleage also thinks of Atlanta as "an urban laboratory for black folks" in which anything is possible:

> We have all the opportunities here to make a perfect urban American environment. We do not have to be controlled by race or gender, so I am free to let my imagination roam around and explore ways we might make the kind of community we want to live in. Atlanta removed the problem of being a racial minority and of being marginalized because of gender. Black women in Atlanta can go as high as we want to go, so my characters are never confined by their sex or their race ["Re: questions"].

Cleage's novels and her non-fiction (newspaper columns and essays) comprise a literary geography that reveals the limitations of the dominant narrative of the city as racially "progressive" and foregrounds the discrepancies between the city's image and its social realities. In this way, Cleage is reminiscent of urban-focused writers such as Gwendolyn Brooks, whose novella *Maud Martha* brings to life Chicago's South Side in the late 1940s/early 1950s while also pointing out the social restrictions confining working-class African American women in the pre–civil rights era. Out of Pearl Cleage's fictional re-construction of a utopian, all-black, southwest Atlanta neighborhood emerges the dystopian nature of Atlanta and, more broadly, the challenges facing many African American communities and populations across the country.

At first glance, the utopian construction of West End offers a hopeful vision of neighborhood revitalization and of positive, productive gender relations between African American men and women. However, Cleage's version of West End is limited. Combining in essence her feminist politics with the ideas of black nationalism espoused by her father, the late Reverend Albert Cleage, founder of black liberation theology, Cleage's work falls into familiar patterns of utopian fiction that contradict her feminist leanings. Her imagined West End is characterized by boundaries and exclusivity challenged by the progressive models of utopia and place offered by contemporary feminist scholars, especially as her imagined West End is sustained primarily by the vigilance and the vigilantism of a single patriarchal figure.

Cleage creates that utopia in reaction to Atlanta's historical development over the last fifty years. Atlanta's historians have provided detailed examinations of spatial segregation within the city from the post–World War II period forward, segregation that resulted in part from the white business elite's attempts to transform the downtown area into a central business district that would attract more businessmen, tourists, and conventions.[5] Their efforts led to poorer African Americans being pushed into areas south and west of downtown (with whites living primarily to the north and east) that remain predominately black areas today. The "South Side" is the area of metropolitan Atlanta that is home to Hartsfield-Jackson International Airport, Fort McPherson, and the Lakewood Fairgrounds, an area "characterized by manufacturing concerns, warehouses, and light industrial facilities" as well as all the "ancillary functions" of the airport (Gournay, Beswick, Sams, and AIA 325). But this part of metropolitan Atlanta also includes at its northern edges portions of two areas bifurcated by Interstate 20, commonly referred to as West End (located immediately southwest of the central city and downtown) and South East Atlanta (which includes Grant Park, Cabbage Town, and the Oakland Cemetery area).

Pearl Cleage has lived in southwest Atlanta for most of her almost thirty years in the city. She resides about a mile from West End in the neighborhood planning unit defined as "Cascade Road." (The City of Atlanta map shows West End as demarcated by a northern boundary of Westview Drive, Lucile Avenue, Park Street, and West End Avenue, an eastern boundary of West Whitehall Street, a western boundary of Cascade Avenue and Langhor Street, and a southern boundary of Beecher Street and Donnelly Avenue [City of Atlanta].[6]) Once home to Joel Chandler Harris, author of the Uncle Remus tales and editor of the *Atlanta Constitution* during the late nineteenth century, historic West End now borders the Atlanta University Center comprised of several historically black colleges and universities, including Spelman and Morehouse. In recent years, West End has experienced some renewal due to the efforts of its residents and other local organizations to restore it to its pre–World War II vitality (Crimmins 33–50; Gournay 325; National Park Service). Population demographics available through the *Atlanta Journal-Constitution*'s Homefinder website show West End (ZIP Code 30310) as having a population of 36,118 and a median household income of $29,935. Of that population, 6.9 percent has no high school degree; 15.8 percent has some high school education; 38.4 percent holds a high school degree; 16.6 percent percent has some college education; 4.2 percent holds an associate's degree; 11.8 percent holds a bachelor's degree; and 6.3 percent holds a graduate degree. Of that population, 78.8 percent of the workforce is white collar. The majority of adults are between the ages of 35 to 54. There is an almost even split between the number of homes owned and homes rented with the median home sale price at $73,500, significantly lower than in other parts of the city (OnBoard Informatics).

As historian Kevin Kruse reveals in his impressive account of white flight in Atlanta from World War II to the present, Atlanta's "West Side" served as the battleground for segregationists immediately following the war. Prior to the 1940s, "nearly 40 percent of the city's black population lived [in the Ashby Street region], making the enclave's name synonymous with 'black Atlanta.'" Working-class whites living in the areas just to the west of "black Atlanta" feared that African Americans would soon "encroach" upon their neighborhoods. Ashby Street, Kruse claims, "became the central place where blacks and whites battled over their relative positions and places in the postwar world," and three white segregationist groups — the Columbians, the Ku Klux Klan, and the West End Cooperative Corporation — arose in the area during the 1940s and '50s to combat residential integration (Kruse 43–44).[7] These fringe groups eventually failed to keep out African Americans, in part due to their reliance on violent tactics which were frowned upon by city officials.[8]

Atlanta historian Timothy Crimmins credits the West End Business Men's Association, a group formed in 1927, with expanding the business activities of the intersection of Gordon and Lee streets. (Kruse does not mention this group.) In the mid–1950s, the Association pushed, in part, for the construction of I-20; the businessmen felt that exit ramps at Lee and Ashby "would bring droves of shoppers to their satellite business district" (Crimmins 47). Promoted as "a barrier to protect [white West Enders] from the intrusion of blacks living around the Atlanta University complex," the construction of I-20 resulted in the creation of a "gulch" in West End that "obliterated a half dozen blocks of housing on the northern perimeter of the community" (Crimmins 47). The barrier did not keep out African Americans. In the 1960s, many African Americans moved to West End because of "newly accessible housing." In 1970, the income level was below the city median, Crimmins points out, and by 1976, the majority (86 percent) of "West Enders were black" (Crimmins 46–47).[9] Since 1974, the organization known as WEND (West End Neighborhood Development, Inc.) has served as a neighborhood association geared towards promoting the neighborhood's revitalization and improving the "quality of life and the perception of that quality of life" for West End residents and property owners (West End Neighborhood Development, Inc.).

But as mentioned earlier, while West End with its lovely Victorian homes ("gingerbreads," as Cleage calls them) has experienced some renewal in recent years, many neighborhoods in southwest Atlanta continue to face the same problems found in lower-income and working-class, urban neighborhoods across the country. Cleage, for example, wrote in 1996, "I can't remember my neighborhood without crack. I have forgotten how it feels to walk in the park with Zeke [Burnett, Cleage's husband] unarmed. I understand. But understanding doesn't make it alright. I miss the safety. The freedom" (Cleage, *Dreamers* 20). Cleage began to see her neighbors move away in the '90s, and she has mentioned occasions when she heard looters rifling through the abandoned house next door.

It's against this real-life backdrop that Pearl Cleage imagines a utopian neighborhood in her fiction. Clearly, the place Cleage calls home and the potential that she sees within it have greatly influenced her fictional vision of the area. The West End of the six novels bears some resemblance to its real-life counterpart in terms of the landmark institutions within the area, its general racial and class composition, and its residents' commitment to their community. But this essay is not interested in comparing and contrasting the real and the represented geographical areas as it is in examining the ways in which Cleage "makes place," specifically the version of utopia that she imagines and the elements of that utopian vision that re-work or reinforce utopian conventions.

The woman-centered "urban oasis" of West End in Cleage's latest novels represents an idealized urban environment and idealized relations between African American men and women. By the measure of its difference from that which lies beyond its borders (e.g., drugs, prostitution, crime, domestic abuse), this utopian place functions, in part, to point out the dystopic qualities of contemporary urban environments (including "real-life" southwest Atlanta). But this imagined place also brings together — and is shaped by — elements of *feminist* politics (of which Cleage became increasingly aware from the 1970s) and of *black nationalist* thought long familiar to her. In the imagined West End, Cleage constructs a black nationalist collectivity that is committed to women's rights and to African Americans' efforts to establish self-supporting, relatively separatist communities. Cleage infuses gender concerns into an ideology concerned with issues of race and class. As she has said, discussions of gender had no place in her father's home or pulpit, thus leading her to take up such discussions in her writing (Cleage, Interview by Paula Gordon).

At the same time, although she offers a model of productive and nonviolent relations between men and women, traditional gender roles of woman as nurturer and man as protector are reinforced, not challenged or exploded. For the most part, Cleage's West End remains faithful to the patriarchal nature of traditional utopias, with the vigilante Blue Hamilton as the man-in-charge of maintaining social harmony within the neighborhood. (His role is also reminiscent of that of the Shrine of the Black Madonna's primary leader, known to followers as the "Holy Patriarch" (Shrine of the Black Madonna). Furthermore, circumscribed by boundaries of class and caste, this essentially working- and middle-class enclave, absent of the poor and the "undesirable," embodies the exclusivity of utopia that limits its viability — even as Cleage shows West End's dynamism and connection to a city, nation, and world beyond its borders. And although Cleage wants to offer readers a hopeful vision of what could be, the blueprint for getting there is absent.

Plot Overview

The utopian vision that Cleage presents in her novels and the limitations of that vision will be the focus of what follows later in this essay. First, a brief plot summary of each novel seems necessary for understanding the later analysis. This essay considers five of her most recent works; *Till You Hear From Me* is not considered because of the absence of in-depth discussions of the West End community and Blue Hamilton therein.

Narrated in the first person, *Some Things I Never Thought I'd Do* (2003) tells the story of Regina Burns, a journalist fresh out of a six-month stint in rehab for cocaine addiction. She comes to Atlanta after Beth Davis, a popular motivational speaker and bestselling author, hires her to organize a tribute to Beth's late son and Regina's former lover, Son Davis. Up on arriving in West End, Regina discovers a thriving, middle-class African American community where crime and violence are entirely absent, a neighborhood where women can feel safe on the streets at night, and a place where men treat women respectfully. In this place, Regina also finds romantic love and a new start on life.

Babylon Sisters (2005) takes place in the same West End of *Some Things I Never Thought I'd Do*. Characters from *Some Things* make brief cameos in this work: the recently married Blue and Regina (Burns) Hamilton; Senator Precious Hargrove; an expectant Aretha and her new husband Kwame Hargrove, Precious's son; and Flora Lumumba and her husband Hank. *Babylon Sisters* introduces Catherine Sanderson, a single mother living in West End with her daughter Phoebe in a house left to them by Catherine's parents. After years of part-time freelance consulting, Catherine realizes she needs to find full-time employment to finance Phoebe's college education. Phoebe is in her senior year at a private, northeastern boarding school and has plans to enter Smith the following year.

Baby Brother's Blues (2006), the first of Cleage's novels to be written in third-person, follows several old and a few new characters' narratives, interweaving a story that is more complicated and well-developed than her earlier novels. Blue and Regina are expecting their first child. Aretha and Kwame Hargrove have a child, and rumors circulate that his mother Precious will be the city's next mayor. Minor characters from earlier novels play significant roles and become more developed: Kwame, who struggles with his bisexuality while trying to maintain a healthy relationship with his wife, further his career as a promising architect, and protect his mother from scandal; Regina's postmenopausal, visionary aunt Abbie from D.C. who has established a relationship with Blue's longtime friend, Peachy; General Richardson, Blue's chauffeur, bodyguard, and childhood friend who we learn had a long-term affair with Blue's mother, Juanita; and Brandi Harris, who works as a stripper at a nearby club and who General thinks represents a sign from the late Juanita. New characters and villains make their way into the story as well, including Wesley "Baby Brother" Jamerson, a soldier who has gone AWOL from the war in Iraq, and Lee Kilgore, a corrupt female police officer.

Her most recent novels also return to West End. In *Seen It All and Done the Rest* (2008), actress Josephine Evans returns home to Atlanta after many years in Europe, only to find that her late mother's home, located outside of West End, has essentially become a crack den. Greer Woodruff, the head of the rental company that was to manage the property in Josephine's absence, has let the house become rundown in an effort to buy it at a low price and turn it around to developers for a quick profit, developers who want to build a prison in the area. The villain of the story is once again a woman in search of power and money, but Josephine and members of the West End community, where she temporarily resides as her granddaughter Zora housesits in the neighborhood, resist her threats by creating a web program documenting their renovation of the house, which they in turn use to expose Ms. Woodruff and her nefarious ways.

Perhaps capitalizing on the recent vampire obsession in popular fiction, Cleage turns to the supernatural in *Just Wanna Testify* (2011). While the vampire tale that comprises the majority of the book turns out to have been merely a dream on Regina's part, the depiction of West End and of Blue's role within the frame narrative is quite compelling. When a group of five models arrive in West End for a photo shoot, Blue quickly discovers they are vampires in search of men to further their ancestral line. Bent on recruiting the most attractive and smartest African American men they could find, these women had recruited a group of Morehouse freshmen four years prior to help them in the process of procreation. The vamps had promised to fund the young men's college education with the understanding that upon graduation, the Morehouse men would come live on the island for an unspecified amount of time where they would be required to have sex with the vampire women and would have access to unlimited pornography. When Blue learns of the women's plan to kill the men once they have served their purpose, his instinct is to kill the vampires. But killing women, as Regina reminds him, is not part of his code. They devise an agreement with the head vampire that if Blue can make her feel the possibility of love, then she will take her gang and head back to their island. The plan works.

Cleage's Imagined West End

Described in *Some Things I Never Thought I'd Do* as "a model for African American urban communities" (27), Cleage's imagined West End represents an urban neighborhood largely absent of violent crime, drugs, prostitution, poverty, substandard housing, and unemployment. "Gone were the boarded-up crack houses and overgrown vacant lots," Regina tells us. "The streets were clean of litter, homes and lawns were uniformly well tended, and garden plots ... were fenced off and identified with signs proclaiming their membership in the West End Growers Association" (27). In West End, drivers appear to obey, if not drive below, the speed limit (Cleage, *Some* 36). In *Baby Brother's Blues*, Regina and Blue live in a "beautifully restored Victorian house with a huge vegetable garden out back and roses out front that seemed to bloom all year long" (5). In West End, "a peaceful oasis in a sea of neighborhoods plagued by guns and crack, desperation and despair," the "biggest challenges were youthful predators, middle-aged desperadoes, wannabe gangsters of all ages, and domestic bullies who preyed upon the women and children trying desperately to love them" (6). "In response to these ever-present threats," the narrator tells us, "what Blue promised was that in the twenty-odd square blocks under his control, women would be safe, men would be sane, and children would act like they had some sense" (6). Although Regina and Blue have a pact not to discuss his work, she knows intuitively that his work involves physical punishment, if not murder, of perpetrators, men only. He is repeatedly referred to as "the godfather," even dressing in *Godfather*-esque attire, suggesting the authority of big-screen gangsters.

In Cleage's West End novels, the area's viability as a utopian collectivity depends in part on its female residents' investment in the neighborhood, as shown through the community gardens and the Growers Association. Comprised primarily of women, this group is responsible for the intergenerational gardens that provide food to local restaurants and that depend upon the labor of West End's residents, particularly senior citizens. (These gardens are reminiscent of Albert Cleage's efforts to establish Beulah Land Farm, a self-sustaining collectivity in South Carolina, or Fannie Lou Hamer's backing of the Freedom Farm cooperative in Sunflower Country, Mississippi, during the early 1970s.) The Growers Association also serves as a neighborhood watch organization, keeping an eye out for trespassers or activity that might threaten residents' safety and the safety of their children. This grassroots group has the ear of local state senator Precious Hargrove, who helps to ensure the sanctity of West End. In Cleage's most recent novel, the Growers Association has grown to include one hundred community gardens. The gardens represent the abundance and vibrancy of the neighborhood, a vitality that matches the neighborhood's own:

> Abernathy Boulevard, still the commercial heart of West End, was alive with shoppers and street vendors, all pursuing their small bit of the area's commerce with great enthusiasm. The West End Mall had as many people sitting on the pedestrian-friendly benches outside as it did window-shopping, but nobody seemed to mind. The twenty-four-hour beauty shop next to the West End News was full of patiently waiting women who knew their rare humidity-free moment would allow them to toss their freshly done hairdos around fearlessly for at least the next forty-eight hours.
>
> There was a line inside and outside the Krispy Kreme.... The Jamaican jerk-chicken specialists were in full swing next to the African clothing store where merchandise had been hung outside to flutter up some paying customers [Cleage, *Baby* 148–49].

In this neighborhood, local businesses thrive like gardens.

Cleage sets many fictional works (all of her novels, a few of her plays) in all-black areas. Her 1992 play *Flyin' West* takes place in Nicodemus, Kansas, an all-black town founded in 1877 by former slaves and children of slaves who left the South to escape post–Civil War oppression and violence. The small, all-black town of Idlewild, Michigan, was the setting for Cleage's first two novels, in part because she says she did not have the nerve to "tackle" the big city of Atlanta (Cleage, "Re: questions"). All-black settings are common in Cleage's works because she has, in fact, always lived in all-black environments — the west side of Detroit, Howard University, and southwest Atlanta. Those places, she admits, are clearly what she knows best. And, as Cleage states, "It is too easy to make 'white folks' the enemy in black fiction. I remove the white folks so that the moral questions are all occurring within our own group. This makes the questions more complex and more dangerous. You want to kill evil Klan members, but what do you suggest we do about young black men the age of our sons?" (Cleage, "Re: questions"). Moreover, in her own life, "the Good Guys, the Bad Guys and all those in between are all black folks" (*Paula Gordon Show*).

Cleage places the burden of community development on African Americans within the community. Cleage claims to "take responsibility as a person who lives [in West End] for making this environment the way I want it to be. I don't spend a second of time saying, you know, 'If the white folks would do this and if the white folks would do that.' They don't live here. It's us" (Cooper 45). Such sentiments echo her father's urging that African Americans take control of their environments, environments that were not separatist by deliberate choice but as a result of history. As Pearl Cleage explains in an essay in *Deals*, urban nationalists believe in fixing problems within their areas — or, as she puts it, taking care of the "nation" within (Cleage, *Deals* 15–17). This type of community-centered civic responsibility is a crucial component of the Atlanta-based collectivity that Cleage imagines in these novels, the emphasis being on change that comes from within rather than from without.

West End's sanctity is equally dependent upon the implicit code of gender relations that gird the utopia. When men pass women on the street, Regina tells us, "they touch their brims and say 'Good morning.' They don't actually say 'ma'am,' but it's clearly implied" (Cleage, *Some* 75). Furthermore, men are "in motion all over the place," repairing cars and screen doors or raking leaves. "I realized how good it was to see men around visible and working. *And how rare*," Regina emphasizes (Cleage, *Some* 30, emphasis in original). She describes the men of West End as "invariably engaged in doing something constructive or walking like they got someplace to go and a certain time to get there." These descriptions of the utopian West End as a safe space are nearly identical to those in *Babylon Sisters*: "Here, women could walk around without fearing for their lives," Catherine Sanderson tells us. In other words, "good-for-nothin'" men are remarkably absent from the West End of Cleage's novel. At night, Catherine notes, the only word to describe West End's streets is "peaceful" (26).

The presence of industrious, kind men (and the absence of shiftless, violent ones) is clearly due to the efforts of Blue Hamilton, a vigilante-like resident who is primarily responsible for West End's initial transformation into a safe space. After a girl was brutally raped and murdered by two men seeking her lunch money for drugs, Blue burned down the crack houses in the area. He then bought the properties, tore down what remained of the houses, and offered the land to his friend Flora who started the community garden project and the Growers Association. Blue played a role in establishing a code of conduct for the neighborhood's men, although how he went about this is never fully explained. All we know from Aretha is that in West End, "Mr. Hamilton doesn't let the men act a fool" (Cleage, *Some* 35). Catherine further explains in *Babylon Sisters* that West End was not always the safe haven it appears: "A few years ago it went though a period of economic transition that left it fragmented and newly vulnerable to the same crimes that plague poor communities from Los Angeles to Washington, D.C. Rape, robbery, street crime, domestic violence, and child abuse were rampant, and then crack came and the situation became almost intolerable" (27). Crimes against women began to increase and became more visible; women were discovered dead in area dumpsters, and one woman was found dead on the train tracks, after having been raped and murdered. Then, Blue Hamilton stepped in and "transformed our ordinary African American urban community into a peaceful, crime-free zone where women could walk unmolested any hour of the day" (27). In other words, thanks to Blue, West End morphed into a picturesque neighborhood: "The woman across the street was watering her lawn while her husband played a game of catch with their son in the driveway. It looked like a scene out of some mythical small-town America, and that's exactly what it felt like" (93).

The presence of the powerful male figures of Blue Hamilton, his henchman General Richardson, occasional accomplice Zeke, and other male employees clearly signal a patriarchal quality to this utopia. Blue plays the classic role of "godfather," though of a benevolent kind (at least benevolent to those who don't "cross the line" in West End). Women are by no means repressed in the contemporary utopian scheme offered by Cleage. Blue Hamilton is present not to subjugate but to assist the women of West End in securing their liberation from danger. However, he is clearly in control and assumes a traditionally masculine role as protector.

Feminist Utopia?

Although Cleage offers a more forward-looking model of utopia in terms of gender dynamics and although she identifies as a feminist, her imagined West End cannot really be understood as a "feminist utopia." Women remain subordinate to benevolent patriarchal rule within the area's borders. Moreover, the imagined West End falls into familiar patterns of what Erin McKenna calls an "end-state" model of utopia, or a utopia that lacks "any notion of, or room for, evolution and change within the vision" (McKenna 3). McKenna sees the possibility of utopia as "an ongoing task rather than a resting place" and argues that a "process model of utopia seeks to create and sustain people willing to take on responsibility and participate in directing their present toward a better, more desirable future" (McKenna 3). While Cleage's West End does have an active citizenry engaged in the constant betterment of their neighborhood, they seem to be engaged in the "ongoing task" of keeping "bad" people out and, for the most part, they are not able to extend their borders to include failing neighborhoods nearby. Angelika Bammer has described traditional utopias as representative of "a static and, in the most literal sense, reactionary stance: a place which, being 'perfect' does not need to — and will not — change" (Bammer 2). These utopias, she continues, "tend to reinforce established ways of thinking even as they set out to challenge them" and "are actually not very utopian" (2–3). Cleage's work falls into that pattern with characters reacting when someone (usually not from West End) does something that might disturb the community's inner harmony; their actions in turn are geared towards preserving the status quo. In this way, Cleage's vision remains locked within the boundaries of a traditional utopian framework.

The residents of West End have strong attachments to the place they call home in part because of their involvement in the making, surveying, and maintaining of that place and because of the peace and safety that come with their living there. Because of those attachments, a notion of understood membership, or belonging, contributes to the sense of the utopia as contained and set apart from the city within which it exists. Feeling like she has "fallen through the rabbit hole," Regina comments that in West End, "we stood in the safe oasis and clucked over the presence of crime somewhere *out there*" (Cleage, *Some* 137). West End may be a part of Atlanta, but Regina regularly contrasts it to the city: "It really did have the feel of a small town, even though you could look over your shoulder and see the skyscrapers of downtown Atlanta less than ten minutes away" (27).

Cleage's utopia further contrasts with the dystopia of Atlanta. Differentiating West End from other metropolitan sections, such as Stone Mountain to the east and Buckhead to the north, helps distinguish and demarcate the neighborhood. Buckhead stands as a bastion of the white elite and as a site of violence. When Flora asks Zeke, the owner of a West End club, if the reason behind his not wanting to move his business to Buckhead's booming club scene is because he "love[s] black folks too much," Zeke responds that "'Loving black folks ain't in it.... They got too much crime out there!'" (Cleage, *Some* 137). Similarly, in *Baby Brother's Blues*, the narrator makes reference to a "stabbing incident" that occurred at a Buckhead club and which resulted in a "celebrity murder trial" (Cleage, *Baby* 162). Here, Cleage indirectly makes reference to the real-life incident in which Ray Lewis, a linebacker for the Baltimore Ravens, was accused (and later found innocent) of stabbing to death two people outside of the Cobalt Lounge in Buckhead during the Super Bowl in 2000 (Pilcher). Cleage portrays the Buckhead nightlife scene as one of potential danger and violence; crime, she suggests, does not just occur in black neighborhoods.

Cleage only occasionally discusses other black, much poorer areas of Atlanta "out there." In *Babylon Sisters*, for example, Cleage depicts the once-vibrant African American section of Auburn Avenue as economically depressed in contrast to the thriving and bustling West End. "Every black mayor since Maynard Jackson had tried in vain to come up with a plan to bring back the glory of what had been preintegration black Atlanta's main commercial strip," Catherine tells us, "but the lure of huge, upscale malls like Lenox Square and Phipps Plaza had made the small storefronts of Auburn Avenue seem quaint reminders of a time that was as gone with the wind as Scarlett O'Hara's plantation" (Cleage, *Babylon* 15).[10] Similarly, Vine City, where the Haitian women are held, is described as an "economically depressed neighborhood" filled with slum housing (148). Josephine Evans' rental property in *Seen It All* is located northwest of West End (north of I-20), on Martin Luther King Drive, near Washington High School and the Mozley Park area. Josephine offers the following contrast between the two areas: "From the litter-strewn parking lot outside the grocery store, to the overflowing trash can in front of the gas station, on past the hard-eyed young men in their oversize pants who seemed to be gathered on every corner, this was clearly a neighborhood in distress" (Cleage, *Seen* 89). Blue knows he can only handle a limited area of people and commerce, even as he had once hoped that the neighborhoods nearby would change based on the model near them. However, "many of the neighborhoods were getting worse. Unemployment was rampant. Drug addiction was epidemic" (Cleage, *Just* 63). Through these descriptions, Cleage distinguishes West End more directly from other black neighborhoods and communities in class- and caste-based terms. It is depicted as superior to such areas by virtue of its revitalization. Such a vision evokes what Larry Keating describes as "the growing economic inequality between middle-class blacks and poor blacks" in Atlanta (Keating 8).

But West End is not closed off from the city and world beyond its borders. All of Cleage's West End-set novels lend credence to feminist geographer Doreen Massey's and others' understandings of place as open and dynamic, even as the borders and boundaries of Cleage's imagined West End show it as closed and static. But the neighborhood is clearly porous: people, goods, and public transportation move in and out of the area; there is no gate to keep people from entering or exiting; Regina travels outside to shop at Lenox Mall in Buckhead or eat at restaurants scattered around the city; the presence of international newspapers at the coffee shop-newsstand reveals connections to, interest in, and awareness of the world beyond; the looming presence of the Iraq War in *Baby Brother's Blues* connects West End to global events; and the international popularity of Josephine and Zora's web-based documentary reveals the area's place within a virtually connected "global community" (Cleage, *Seen* 205). West End is not removed from Atlanta or the nation or the world and therefore not impervious to infiltration, thus why problems do arise within the community from time to time.

Yet the borders are under constant surveillance. When potentially troublesome characters enter West End, their presence is quickly noticed and addressed. In *Some Things*, when the not-so-subtly named DooDoo and his buddies begin to trespass into the yards of two Association members who live one street beyond the border of West End, those members ask for help from Senator Hargrove, who agrees to see what she can do. After she leaves, they ask what Blue could do to help. Flora, the meeting's leader, responds that their block is not technically within West End, that Blue has only "committed his assistance" to West End proper, and if these trespassers would just "stay on their side of Stewart Avenue —," she trails off (Cleage, *Seen* 115). Association members who live on the same "side" as the trespassers immediately react to Flora's statement — "'Their side? ... So now I live on *their side?*" (115) — and to their implicit relegation to the "outer" realm inhabited by the villains. The instant division between those who belong and those who do not reveals the artificial limits of this seemingly bounded community. The need to address constant threats and to negotiate the ever-changing social relations that constitute place reminds us of West End's porous-ness and dynamism, even as the utopia appears contained and sanitized.

Though Cleage's feminist views seem to gird her utopian vision, the villains within her narratives are most often assertive, power-hungry women who are literally and figuratively independent from West End. Well-to-do motivational speaker Beth Davis, Regina's employer who resides in Stone Mountain, reinforces the fact that West End's boundaries are never as solid as they might seem. She is exposed near the end of *Some Things* as the person behind the violent threatening of a woman claiming to be the mother of her late son's child. Similarly, in *Babylon Sisters*, Ezola Mandeville, "a former Buckhead maid who "got sick and tired of being sick and tired and started organizing other maids and cleaning women to demand better wages and more humane treatment" (Cleage, *Babylon* 12), emerges as the unexpected villain. In the final pages of the novel, we learn that she reaps much of her profits from her involvement with a prostitution ring between Miami and Atlanta that traffics in young Haitian women, particularly virgins. Catherine eventually confronts Mandeville, to be told that "Some people need maids. Some people need cheap whores. It's all the same to me" (266). Although able to infiltrate West End through her connection to Catherine, she nevertheless exists outside of it. In *Seen It All*, Greer Woodruff— a business woman with an undergraduate degree from Howard and a Harvard MBA — turns out to be in business with cocaine dealers and has no regard for the older generations trying to hold onto their homes in the midst of the crack neighborhoods she has helped create and sustain. Though ultimately revealed to be part of Regina's dream, the collective of female vampires in *Just Wanna Testify* also poses a threat to the sanctity of West End. Perhaps Cleage's consistent use of female villains is not incompatible with feminist ideology, and having all male protagonists would see a bit heavy handed and unrealistic. Yet her portrayal of African American corporate businesswomen in only a negative light does seem a bit limiting.

Those Within and Those Without

Villains are not the only folks kept out of West End's metaphorical gates. The neighborhood is circumscribed by boundaries of class, caste, and sexual orientation as well. The poor, the queer, the troubled, and the potentially troublesome are absent. At one point, Regina notices a homeless man asleep on the steps of a church in West End, but his inertia makes him a non-threatening presence in a neighborhood that does not make room for such "untouchables." Instead of panhandlers or "dope fiends" on the street corners, she tells us, one finds "three young brothers in dark suits and bow ties offering *Muhammed Speaks* or bean pies, depending on whether you were looking to feed your head or your face" (Cleage, *Some Things* 28). One does not find "street predators" or "loitering groups of hopeless, hard-eyed men" in West End: "Around here, even the liquor store had a clean parking lot and nobody outside looking crazy and trying to beg a beer" (75).

The commercial and residential areas, as Cleage imagines them, are safe spaces for black women and men of a working- to middle-class level of financial and social capital. West End's imagined boundaries keep out not only potentially dangerous criminals but the African American underclass — surprising given Cleage's 1996 reactions to the ways in which Atlanta Committee for the Olympic Games (ACOG) ignored and erased Atlanta's poor populations while primping the city for the event. These absences beg the question of what West End's class restrictions say about intra-racial relations.

The borders of Cleage's imagined West End delimit the area in terms of a bourgeois identity, but the borders further delimit the neighborhood in terms of sexuality and heteronormativity. The romantic relationships that exist and thrive within West End are between straight men and women, husbands and wives, boyfriends and girlfriends. There are clear limits as to what counts as legitimate relationships for the community members. For example, the women of the community are depicted as enjoying healthy sex lives, but they are not licentious sexual predators. When there is such a threat — as in the case of the vampire group "slinking around in their tight black clothes and their bright red lips" (Cleage, *Just* 11) — Blue and his assistants must find a way to remove them from West End.

What seems an even more significant threat is homosexual activity, which always occurs beyond West End's borders — whether in a parked car on a nearby street, in Club Baltimore in Buckhead on DL Night, in a loft just outside of West End, or between male soldiers in Wes Jamerson's platoon in Iraq. None of the main characters identifies as gay or bisexual, implying that West End has no room for either homosexual *behavior* or homosexual *identity* even as Cleage takes on the (now more openly discussed) phenomenon of "the down low" in *Baby Brother's Blues*. While she has repeatedly voiced concern over the growing epidemic of HIV/AIDS within African American populations, this book suggests that her concern primarily lies with the women who are infected by lovers or partners who, for whatever reasons, have not disclosed their sexual histories. In *Baby Brother's Blues*, Kwame is a straight, married man when he is within West End's borders and while working for Blue Hamilton. Beyond the neighborhood, Kwame is on the "down low," seeking out sexual encounters with men while remaining married and seemingly in love with his wife Aretha. Although his sexual practices suggest a bisexual identity, he does not identify as anything but heterosexual because of his professional ambitions, his mother's political career, and his desire for "that respectable Atlanta *lifestyle*" (Cleage, *Baby* 66). His ambition leads him to a position in a highly respected architectural firm as well as a chance to move from West End to a modern home located in Midtown's Ansley Park. Those opportunities mean escaping from the scrutiny of Blue. That might explain why Kwame already owns a loft outside of West End, "just over the line," as he tells Teddy one evening when he is in town on business:

> Teddy chuckled as they headed for the door.
> "What?"
> "Nothing. Just the way you said that. *It's just over the line.* That Hamilton Negro has got a serious hold on y'all."
> *You have no idea*, Kwame thought, opening the door for Teddy and glad all over again for a night outside the gates of Hamilton city [Cleage, *Baby* 73].

In the end, we infer that Kwame does not belong within West End because he has cheated on his wife, putting her at risk because of his exploits "outside the gates." Bisexuality and homosexuality are not necessarily *un*acceptable in this utopian place, but sexual behaviors and acts that might threaten others, especially women, are.

Cleage wants to point a finger here at the homophobia rampant within many African American collectivities in the United States. But while she seems intent upon bringing these issues to readers' attention, her depiction indicates that utopian West End, where latent homophobic attitudes are alive and well, is by no means an idyllic environment for all. The lack of a clear stance on homophobia points to a broader problem of superficiality within Cleage's utopian vision. Her imagined West End offers an alternative model for urban life, but the pressures at work within Atlanta's real-life, African American neighborhoods — the pressures that lead to crime, drugs, prostitution, or homelessness, for example — do not receive much in-depth examination. Nor does Cleage offer a plan for realizing the kind of change she advocates. With the exception of the Growers Association, Blue is the only blueprint. Vigilantism — and the violence and fear that accompany Blue's gangster-like rule — becomes the imagined foundation on which to create a peaceful "oasis."

So why does this matter if, as some might argue, her works of popular fiction are merely meant to entertain the reader? The novels are "just books," right?

Not exactly. Cleage has always intended her work to go beyond entertainment to educate and inspire her predominately African American readers.[11] Working from her personal experiences as well as current events, she seeks to come to grips with — and help others work thorough — the gender and racial relations that have contributed to making places dystopian. As Bammer reminds us, utopian literature "is always meant to have not just an aesthetic, but a political effect on the reader" (Bammer 157). Cleage's novels are no exception.

Part of her effort seems to be to counter the reality of how Atlanta has failed to live up to the promise it seemed to have under the leadership of Maynard Jackson, and even later under Mayor Shirley Franklin (who adopted a slogan of "Every Day Is an Opening Day" to capture Atlanta's business spirit). In *Seen It All*, Josephine Evans asks:

> What happened to the idea we had about being a community of people on the move? Atlanta was a magnet once for every bright young black person with a willingness to work hard and a desire to share the vision of a city where we were the decision makers, the visionaries, the leaders, the ones who could already see that future where everybody got a slice of the seemingly inexhaustible pie. We walked proud and we felt free. We were free! [Cleage, *Seen* 148].

Those who tried to maintain racial boundaries, she claims, were "overwhelmed by the voices of men and women determined to change the face of business as usual *forever and ever, amen*" (148). She continues, "But all that seemed like a cruel joke now. All those dreams dovetailed into a community-wide nightmare where casual violence is the order of every day, vandalism is a spectator sport, and a strange sense of entitlement allows those unwilling to work at anything to still feel they have the right to kick in somebody's door to get the things they want" (148). Her novels thus offer an alternate grassroots vision of what the city could be if citizens committed themselves to effecting change, one neighborhood at a time.

But her works also speak to issues facing African American populations nationwide. After working in many genres during her writing career, Cleage chose the popular novel as a vehicle for reaching "as many women as possible" (Cleage, "Re: questions"). "My target audience of readers or theatergoers," she states, "is always black women. We read a lot of novels. Many of us don't ever go to the theater, so I can reach more people with fiction than I can with plays" ("Re: questions"). Cleage is invested in crafting a form of consciousness-raising for black women *through* her writing and their reading. As Cleage puts it, "I am not a violent person. I own no weapons and have never been in a fight in my life. I am not an organizer and I have no troops to marshal with marching songs and battle plans. What I do is write about what I see and what I feel and what I know in the hope that it will help the people who read it see more and feel more and know more" (Cleage, *Deals* 6). Moreover, she uses the formulaic and the familiar to talk about serious topics — domestic violence, child prostitution, international prostitution rings, HIV/AIDS— as well as issues of race and gender relations among African Americans, including "the down low." She bends the medium of popular fiction to her purpose of making women, especially black women, aware of everyday sexism and racism. If Cleage's early essays and columns provided straightforward commentaries on racism and politics, her later novels cloak critiques of the issues confronting African American women within the guise of appealing stories. Her prose is direct and her tone familiar, a style that carries over into her novels and contributes to making complicated ideas revolving around race and gender accessible to a lay audience. June Akers Seese in the *New Georgia Encyclopedia* captures it best when she claims Cleage's "trademark" to be a "highly readable style that imparts a sense of immediacy."

Pearl Cleage admits that her novels follow patterns characteristic of romance fiction, but at the same time, she distances herself, labeling them "revolutionary romances":

> Because the people are always very much grounded in real life, they're dealing with real problems. They're trying to figure out how to be in love in the middle of the real world, rather than those stories where everybody's at the beach, everybody's rich, everybody's healthy, everybody's hair and clothing blows so beautifully in the wind and all of that. My heroines ... live in the West End, they've got to deal with crack heads, they've got to deal with garbage on the street. But what they do is fall in love in the midst of all that [Cleage, Interview by Paula Gordon].

In effect, the problems around Cleage's "heroines," rather than distracting them from love and romance, inspire them to make their neighborhood a place where romance can thrive. Cleage claims that her novels are "grounded in what I really want in real life. Which is for people to be able to have a neighborhood where they can raise their children, where they can grow old, where they can sit on the porch and wave at their neighbors across the street" (Cleage, Interview by Paula Gordon). Cleage uses her fiction to show readers the potential for such a space. "By creating a zone that is crime free ... I can make readers consider how it might be to actually live in a neighborhood like that one where there is no predator crime," Cleage claims (Cleage, "Re: questions").

From Cleage's reflections on her work, we can better understand her construction of West End as a self-sustaining, utopian place — an urban oasis — intended to present to female readers the possibility of city life as liberating and to suggest a model of urban renewal that comes from within rather than from without. In fictionalizing a neighborhood's revitalization and in showing women's roles (apart from that of Blue) in "growing" something positive within their communities, Cleage provides a vision of a small-scale, on-the-ground reworking of socially-troubled urban spaces that does not involve movement away from or abandonment of that space. She intends that vision to provide hope of safety — safety in one's home, neighborhood, and city, not to mention in a geographical region with a long history of racism and violence towards African Americans. Yet questions remain: Whose revolutionary romances are allowed to thrive in this imagined West End? Who is included in the safe zone, and who remains outside its gates? What role does violence, or vigilantism, play in securing freedom?

NOTES

1. In 1995, Cleage asked the Fulton County Arts Council, who had helped fund *Catalyst* since its inception, to discontinue their support since Republican council members had "questioned the magazine's frank sexual references and overall value to the community." Cleage further claimed that the council's chair had attacked her personally and argued that "such attacks were 'distressingly similar' to [Jesse] Helms' criticisms of the federal NEA" (Campos). Cleage has taught at Spelman College, where she was Atlanta writer Tayari Jones' first mentor (Jones). For an exchange between the mentor and mentee concerning their experiences as writers struggling to effect change, see Jones and Cleage, "Which Comes First, Our Paychecks or Our Principles."

2. Most recently, Oprah Winfrey commissioned Cleage to write a poem in honor of African American women who have been for her a "Bridge to Now." Oprah invited these women, as well as forty-five younger women, to come to her home for a weekend-long celebration during which the "young 'uns," including Cleage, read the poem. See "The Legends Who Lunch." Cleage's poem, *We Speak Your Names: A Celebration*, was published by One World/Ballantine in 2006. Interestingly, twenty years earlier, Cleage had written a column titled "Small-Town Attraction" in which she expressed disdain for Oprah and her talk show: "All of a sudden it seemed Oprah was everywhere, smiling and squealing and being grateful for the fame and fortune that had suddenly come her way. I still didn't like her style. She was a little too aw-shucks for me.... There is already around the edges of Oprah's mouth the increasing cynicism of one who finds the rewards of playing down much more readily accessible than the prize for reaching higher" (Cleage, "Small-Town Attraction" 15).

3. Giles makes mention of *puppetplay* (1983) and cites the following plays: *Hospice* (1984), *Porch Songs* (1985), *A Little Practice* (1985), *Essentials* (1986), *Come and Get These*

Memories (1986), *Late Bus to Mecca* (1992), *Chain* (1992), as well as *Banana Bread* (1982), *Hymn for the Rebels* (1974), *The Sale* (1972), and *Duet for Three Voices* (1968). More recent plays include *Flyin' West* (1992), *Blues for an Alabama Sky* (1995), and *Bourbon at the Border* (1997) (Giles 709-12).

4. See Giles and Paige articles.

5. See, for example, Larry Keating, *Atlanta: Race, Class, and Urban Expansion* (Philadelphia: Temple University Press, 2001); Ronald H. Bayor, *Race and the Shaping of Twentieth-Century Atlanta* (Chapel Hill: University of North Carolina Pfress, 1996); and Kevin Kruse, *White Flight: Atlanta and the Making of Modern Conservatism* (Princeton: Princeton University Press, 2005).

6. The West End Historic District actually appears to be more narrowly defined. City of Atlanta, "West End Historic District."

7. For more information on the Columbians in Atlanta, see Weisenburger.

8. However, as Kruse so thoroughly illustrates, such experiences led segregationists in Atlanta to develop new strategies, such as homeowners' associations, that would lend an air of "respectability" to their efforts and "legitimize their cause" (Kruse 77).

9. The association also pushed for a shopping mall "to replace the 'unsightly' and 'deteriorated' businesses and residences north and east of Gordon and Lee streets" (Crimmins 47). Eventually, Crimmins points out, commercial development "accelerated the disappearance of the nineteenth-century residences that had lined the old trolley line. The asphalt of gas stations and fast-food drive-ins soon replaced the lawns of Victorian houses" (47).

10. Catherine's comments in the novel echo Cleage's comments on Auburn Avenue in an essay from *Dreamers and Dealmakers* in which she describes the area during its heyday as "something to see," an area rooted in the black nationalist teachings of "self-reliance, self-sufficiency and self-love." "Packed into that bustling downtown commercial strip were all the things that a community needed to take care of itself. A bank, a police precinct, a drug store, financial and real estate institutions, newspapers, doctors, lawyers, political leaders, civic leaders, geniuses, fast talkers, race women and race men." However, the area, at the time of Cleage's writing in 1996, was "struggling for simple survival" as a result, claims Cleage, of integration and African Americans' movement away from the area's retail and financial establishments (Cleage, *Dreamers* 13-15).

11. Although there are no statistics readily available on the racial composition of her readership, various indices suggest that black women represent the majority of her readers. Her novels, for example, are published by Ballantine's One World Press, an imprint devoted to publishing "multicultural titles" with a particular focus on African American writers. Furthermore, at the readings and book signings that I attended, the majority of attendees were, by my rough count, black women (with the exception of her readings at Charis Books, which were relatively equally divided between white and black female audience members). These events included two readings at Charis Bookstore in Atlanta in 2004 and 2005; a reading at the 2004 National Black Arts Festival in Atlanta; a conversation with Charlene Hunter-Gault at the 2006 National Black Arts Festival; "An Evening with Pearl Cleage" at Spelman College, February 4, 2006; a reading at the Margaret Mitchell House in Atlanta, March 21, 2006; and "Mentoring Young Writers," a reading and conversation with Tayari Jones at the 2006 North Carolina Festival of the Book, held at Duke University, April 30, 2006.

WORKS CITED

Bammer, Angelika. *Partial Visions: Feminism and Utopianism in the 1970s*. New York: Routledge, 1991. Print.

Bayor, Ronald H. *Race and the Shaping of Twentieth-Century Atlanta*. Chapel Hill: University of North Carolina Press, 1996. Print.
Bondoc, Anna, and Meg Daly. *Letters of Intent: Women Cross the Generations to Talk About Family, Work, Sex, Love and the Future of Feminism*. New York: Free, 1999. Print.
Campos, Carlos. "Editor Asks Fulton to Stop Funding Literary Journal." *Atlanta Journal-Constitution* 1 March 1995: 4C. Print.
City of Atlanta. "Neighborhood Planning Units." *City of Atlanta Online*. Web. 30 Jan. 2007.
_____. The Atlanta Urban Design Commission. "West End Historic District." *City of Atlanta Online*. Web. 30 Jan. 2007.
Cleage, Pearl. *Baby Brother's Blues*. New York: One World/Ballantine, 2006. Print.
_____. *Babylon Sisters*. New York: One World/Ballantine, 2005. Print.
_____. "Catalyst: An Introduction." *Southline* [Atlanta] 10 Sept. 1986: 15. Print.
_____. *Deals with the Devil: And Other Reasons to Riot*. New York: Ballantine, 1993. Print.
_____. *Dreamers and Dealmakers: An Insider's Guide to the Other Atlanta Games*. Roswell, GA: The Atlanta Tribune, 1996. Print.
_____. Interview. *L-I-N-K-E-D: The Spelman College Online Literary Journal*. n.p. Web. 1 Dec. 2005.
_____. Interview by Paula Gordon. *The Paula Gordon Show: Conversations with People at the Leading Edge*. 23 August 2004. Print. Transcript.
_____. *Just Wanna Testify*. New York: One World/Ballantine, 2011. Print.
_____. *Mad at Miles: A Blackwoman's Guide to Truth*. Southfield, MI: Cleage, 1990. Print.
_____. "Re: questions." Message to Margaret T. McGehee. 31 January 2005. E-mail.
_____. *Seen It All and Done the Rest*. New York: One World/Ballantine, 2008. Print.
_____. "Small-Town Attraction," *Southline* [Atlanta] 5 November 1986: 15. Print.
_____. *Some Things I Never Thought I'd Do*. New York: One World/Ballantine, 2003. Print.
_____. *Till You Hear From Me*. New York: One World/Ballantine, 2010. Print.
Cooper, Monet. "Cleage's Revolution: A Conversation with a Renaissance Woman." *Atlanta Tribune Magazine*. September 2003: 45. Print.
Crimmins, Timothy J. "West End: Metamorphosis from Suburban Town to Intown Neighborhood." *Atlanta Historical Journal* 26.2–3 (1982): 33–50. Print.
Giles, Freda Scott. "The Motion of Herstory: Three Plays by Pearl Cleage." *African American Review* 31.4 (1997): 709–12. Print.
Gournay, Isabelle, Paul G. Beswick, Gerald W. Sams, and American Institute of Architects. *AIA Guide to the Architecture of Atlanta*. Athens: University of Georgia Press, 1993. Print.
Jones, Tayari. "Sweet Pearl Cleage." *Tayarijones.com*. 29 March 2005. Web. 26 April 2005.
_____, and Pearl Cleage. "Which Comes First, Our Paychecks or Our Principles?" *Letters of Intent: Women Cross the Generations to Talk About Family, Work, Sex, and Love and the Future of Feminism*. Ed. Anna Bondoc and Meg Daly. New York: Free, 1999. 33–41. Print.
Keating, Larry. *Atlanta: Race, Class, and Urban Expansion*. Philadelphia: Temple University Press, 2001. Print.
Kruse, Kevin M. *White Flight: Atlanta and the Making of Modern Conservatism*. Princeton: Princeton University Press, 2007. Print.
Massey, Doreen B. *Space, Place, and Gender*. Minneapolis: University of Minnesota Press, 1994. Print.
McKenna, Erin. *The Task of Utopia*. Lanham, MD: Rowman, 2001. Print.
National Park Service. "West End Historic District." *National Park Service*. n.p. Web. 1 December 2005. <http://www.cr.nps.gov/nr/travel/atlanta/whd.htm>.
OnBoard Informatics. "West End in Fulton County (30310)." *AJC HomeFinder*. Atlanta

Journal-Constitution. Web. 19 July 2011 <http://neighborhoods.ajchomefinder.com/Fulton/West%20End/30310?id=1#tab>.

Paige, Linda Rohrer. "Southern Women Playwrights and the Atlanta Hub." *Southern Women Playwrights: New Essays in Literary History and Criticism*. Ed. Robert L. McDonald and Linda Rohrer Paige. Tuscaloosa: University of Alabama Press, 2002. 230–45. Print.

Pilcher, James. "Pro Bowl Linebacker Ray Lewis Charged with Murder." *Associated Press State and Local Wire*. Associated Press. 31 January 2000. Web. 22 July 2011.

Seese, June Akers. "Pearl Cleage." *The New Georgia Encyclopedia*. Georgia Humanities Council and the University of Georgia Press. 15 September 2008. Web. 20 July 2011.

Shrine of the Black Madonna Cultural Center and Bookstore. "Holy Patriarch." Web. 2 February 2007.

Weisenburger, Steven. "The Columbians, Inc.: A Chapter of Racial Hatred from the Post–World War II South." *The Journal of Southern History* 69.4 (2003): 821–60. Print.

West End Neighborhood Development, Inc. "About Us." *West End Neighborhood Development, Inc*. Web. 30 January 2007.

Winfrey, Oprah. "The Legends Who Lunch." *O, The Oprah Magazine* Aug. 2005: 174+. Print.

Over the Rainbow: Finding Home in West End Atlanta

RHONDA M. COLLIER

Imagine an encounter between two great Harlem Renaissance figures Josephine Baker (1906–1975) and Zora Neale Hurston (1891–1959). But replace Josephine Baker with Josephine Evans who is fleeing Paris under the auspice of preventing her fictional granddaughter Zora Evans, not Josephine Baker's contemporary Zora Neale Hurston, from running away from her problems in Atlanta. The scenario could happen in a magical place where time and space do not matter: perhaps in a dream, a movie or even, a Pearl Cleage novel. In *Seen it All and Done the Rest* (2008), Pearl Cleage gives modern readers another possibility for a place that exists over the rainbow and how after some twenty-first century *technicolor*[1] there is a place in America for our often misunderstood and displaced sisters. Cleage's title *Seen it All and Done the Rest* asks the reader to revise America and the place of black women in America: the key word is "seen." In the globalized context of a post–9/11 world, the novel's main character Josephine Evans must see herself as an American. Likewise, in a more localized context of a post–9/11 world, Zora Evans must see evil in her community and confront the aftermath of war. "Only in the movies" are viewers allowed to sit back and see themselves through Pearl Cleage's eyes; audiences are enthralled as they identify with characters who teach them life lessons. In *Seen it All and Done the Rest,* the legendary American film icon of Dorothy from the 1939 Academy Award nominated classic *The Wizard of Oz* emerges as a new way to articulate Cleage's theory of Free Womanhood. According to Aisha Francis,[2] whose work provides readers with the genesis for Cleage's term "Free Womanhood": "The knowledge Cleage imparts first to her specific audience and then to the general reader — is offered as "a 'workbook' of tangible socio-political and economic trials of being black in an unjust society that is nonetheless full of possibility and hope" (33). The character Dorothy personifies the American image of the free woman: a young girl who battles the forces of good and evil and emerges as a woman who not only saves herself but her friends too. In *Seen it All and Done the Rest*, the Dorothy paradigm serves two-fold to embrace all readers in the American concept of freedom, and to reinstate black women in a place that is not usually seen as home – the United States of America.

Wicked Witches and Wild Women

In her epigraph, Cleage summons diverse notions of freedom for all women in America. Using Isadora Duncan's (1877–1927) words, "You were wild once. Don't let them tame you," Cleage reminds readers of the social, physical and geographical boundaries society places on women who fail to fit the mold. In the classic film, the initial problem of Dorothy is that she refuses to give up her dog Toto, who is considered to be "a menace to the community," but mainly to Miss Gulch. Toto is accused of biting Miss Gulch and destroying her garden. If Aunt Em and Uncle Henry refuse to hand over Toto, Miss Gulch threatens to sue them and take the farm. Aunt Em exclaims: "Almira Gulch, just because you own half the county doesn't mean you have the power to run the rest of us! For twenty-three years, I've been dying to tell you what I thought of you! And now — well, being a Christian woman, I can't say it!" The socio-political systems of Miss Almira Gulch, who is later transformed to the Wicked Witch of the West in Oz; and Ms. Greer Woodruff, who wants to strong arm Josephine Evans out of her duplex in Cleage's novel; require that Dorothy/Josephine Evans give up something that is of great value — her dog, her red shoes, and yes, even her house. The Wicked Witches have more money and more influence in the community, but Josephine Evans proclaims, " I don't care how much you offer me.... Nobody is going to run me off" (246). But the little girl Dorothy decides to escape with Toto to "somewhere over the rainbow." Once they arrive, the house lands on the Wicked Witch of the East and Dorothy immediately wants to return home — but before she leaves has one more witch to conquer. Cleage's life lesson is that a house is not a burden; instead it is the journey home that contains the keys to self-discovery. Josephine Evans claims:

> The idea of being rooted on a little corner of Atlanta, Georgia never had been my intention. I was a citizen of the world, just passing through on my way back to the life I'd created for myself in a place where nobody ever dumped trash on my lawn.... What was it about this house that was starting to pull at my heartstrings in a way I had never intended and didn't really understand? [223–4].

Recalling Josephine's free life in Paris and Isadora's advice on being wild, it seems likely that the character Josephine Evans would find it puzzling to feel a sense of "rootedness" in the very place she seeks to escape.

Speaking of Rainbows

Similar to Josephine Baker and Josephine Evans, Isadora Duncan represents the American woman who leaves the United States of America to pursue her dancing career and breaks societal conventions. Duncan is credited with the invention of modern dance and the integration of more natural movement into traditional ballet. She refuses to be American, heterosexual, tame, classical, and she discovers many places "over the rainbow" as she professes her freedom. Ironically, in modern-times, the rainbow also represents the freedom to define one's own sexuality and gender. For many Americans, the rainbow flag[3] stands as emblem of pride, activism and safety for Lesbian Gay Bisexual Transgender (LGBT) individuals around the world — urban legend attributes this to the popularity *The Wizard of Oz*. Resembling many of his historical predecessors, Josephine Evans' best friend Howard experiences freedom as a gay man in Paris. Howard is Josephine's partner in crime as he encourages her to be free: free to leave Paris and free to return to Paris. While Howard has a minor role in the novel, he acts as a reminder of the diversity that exists "over the rainbow." Reminiscent of Isadora Duncan and Josephine Baker, Josephine Evans embraces freedom in Europe: "For the first time, there were no forces, seen or unseen, attempting to put me in a box or another because I was a woman or because I was black. Nobody in Amsterdam gave a damn" (17). Josephine Evans delights in her connection to Josephine Baker; she comments on her performance of Ntozake Shange's play *For Colored Girls Who Have Considered Suicide When the Rainbow is Enuf*: "The reviews were rapturous, and everywhere we went, the ladies who made the cast were treated like the reincarnation of Josephine Baker — five times" (16). For many this was a false freedom, a freedom based on being a spectacle and being exotic. Her friend Denise warns, "Right now, we're still exotic to them ... you wait until we aren't superstars or jazz musicians and see how much they love us" (17). But Josephine Evans finds her freedom in Europe in spite of her friend's warnings. Other American sisters embrace Europe, like Isadora Duncan who rejects her American citizenship to become a Soviet citizen and Josephine Baker who becomes a French citizen. Europe becomes fatal for Duncan and she dies a tragic death chasing after a scarf. In contrast, Josephine Baker emerges as a French national hero, who also participates in the American Civil Rights Movement. She even adopts her own "rainbow tribe": literally becoming a mother to children of various cultures.[4] In a historic twist of events, Duncan rejects jazz music and feels that it does not express America but " it expresses the primitive savage" (qtd. in Needham 198). That is to say that Isadora Duncan, who is an iconic representation of female freedom, negates an original manifestation of Americanness, one that incorporates both African and European artistic expressions — jazz music. Yet, perhaps, Duncan is another misunderstood sister. One the one hand, she critiques "negro convulsions" in jazz music, but on the other she calls for true American dance that incorporates Walt Whitman and Abe Lincoln (qtd. in Needham 198). This contrast in definitions and perspectives on freedom separates the experience of black women in America and white women in America. Isadora Duncan seems to be waiting for a fulfillment of an idealized freedom while ignoring a freedom that has been carved out, "improvised," in a constantly evolving music and jazz rhythm that she fails to acknowledge as American. Embracing that rhythm, Cleage creates a place where the character Josephine Evans is historically connected to both of these arguably free women. However, Josephine Evans remains rooted to her corner in Atlanta.

In her essay "Rootedness: The Ancestor as Foundation," Toni Morrison describes the essential presence of the ancestor in African-American writing: "There is always an elder there. And these ancestors are not just parents, they are sort of timeless people whose relationships to the characters are benevolent, instructive, and protective, and they provide a certain kind of wisdom" (62). In Cleage's *Seen it All and Done the Rest* the ancestral connections are numerous — Isadora Duncan, Zora Neale Hurston, Josephine Baker, Josephine Evan's mother Doris Evans, and a life-size brown mermaid — to name a few.

No Place Like Home — House?

To understand how the character Josephine revisions America as "home," her connection to her mother and her own history in the contested house/duplex must be seen on widescreen as directed by Cleage. As other black American writers such as Alice Walker and Toni Morrison have also shown readers, literature is a space that allows black women a place in America. In another essay "Home," Morrison argues that "home" is a place that is only available in fiction (3). For Morrison, "'Home' seems a suitable term because it allows [her] to make a radical distinction between the metaphor of house and the metaphor of home and helps clarify [her] thoughts on racial construction" (4). Applying Morrison's concept to Cleage's work, "house" may be seen as a socio-political structure built to exclude black women thus pushing our misunderstood sisters into exile. In contrast, "home" is the creative space that women create to interrogate those structures. Cleage creates an Atlanta West End community where women are safe and beauty shops are open twenty-four-hours a day. A blue-eyed godfather named Blue Hamilton maintains the peace. Cleage claims, "One of the things I'm always trying to do in my books is to create the kind of neighborhood I want to live in.... I try to make readers remember how it feels to be safe and happy and loved and free" (306). In this creative space, we encounter the exiled Zora and Josephine in a Victorian home once owned by a rich white family. *Technicolor* allows readers to access the wonderful magic available to Cleage's main characters. The colorful house is full of magic and is a place for reflection. Josephine is immediately drawn to the swimming pool, and both leading ladies are mystified by the life sized brown-mermaid. With her cinematic gaze, Cleage sets the scene:

> The area around the pool was tiled in the same shades of deep blue as the painting over my bed, and at the bottom there was indeed a beautiful, life-size, brown mermaid whose long black hair curled around her face and spread over the floor of the pool in tendrils that conch shell and with the other, she covered her pubes delicately, demure for all her nakedness [41].

Like Josephine Evans, minus the long hair, the brown mermaid is an exotic black woman. She is on display, but she is also an ancestor full of wisdom and magic. Josephine wonders if the mermaid has a story and "if she ever disengaged herself from the bottom of the pool when nobody was looking and did a few languid laps in the moonlight"(41). If one considers the brown mermaid as a salutation to the African Diaspora, she might be read as the *orisha* Yemanjá, the Yoruba goddess of the sea, and the mother of all the *orishas*. Yemanjá embodies motherhood, fertility, beauty and creativity: she protects the fishermen so she is often represented as part human and part fish. Many African American writers have invoked her presence, most notably Ntozake Shange and Audre Lorde. In the poem "From the House of Yemanjá," Lorde describes her mother as having two faces, one light and the other dark (235). In this poem, Lorde refers to not being the perfect daughter and not being seen by her mother. The poem asks for the mother's "blackness" (235). The house and the pool are healing spaces for Josephine and Zora; and Josephine as a grandmother heals in a unique way. There is nothing the two cannot work out together. The presence of brown mermaid offers a sense of rootedness and wisdom that is connectedness with our ancestors.

Ever the producer, director and the writer, a Dorothy is at the center of Cleage's brown-mermaid story. In one scenario, Zora and Josephine reflect on Dorothy Dandridge as the real star of the mysterious mermaid story (156). The pool allows the ladies to reflect on beauty, power, and race, issues that set the stage for their exile. Josephine rewrites history:

> Think how differently the whole crowd could have gone down in history if they had all jumped in the pool when he insulted Dorothy to show their support for another human being. Then Dorothy would have jumped in too, and they would have had the great pleasure of seeing one of the most beautiful women in the world laughing and playing in the water with all of her new friends [156].

The brown-mermaid becomes more than a set of tiles from Morocco or a misplaced brown-mermaid that disturbed the white lady of the house, she serves as an ancestral-figure of resistance and defiance. In reimagining Dorothy Dandridge's experience at a Las Vegas pool, where the pool was emptied and scrubbed after Dandridge defiantly dipped her toe in the water, Cleage highlights Morrison's house/home construction where Dorothy is literally an alien at "home." The brown-mermaid signifies, using Henry Louis Gates' Jr. definition of the term, on the idea of an alien being. The mermaid is the wrong color, in the wrong place, and in the wrong nation.

Are You a Good Witch or a Bad Witch?

Where is home anyway? For Zora Evans, "home" should be West End Atlanta and Spelman College, but the media hounds her for her involvement in a scandal with a murdered vet — she is accused of being a deadly antiwar activist. *Dig It!* headlines proclaim *Scandal takes its tolls!* as the ensuing article details the changes in Zora's physical appearance from hair, breast, to "booty" (74). Zora claims, "Because I want to do what you did, Mafeenie! I want to leave all this bullshit behind and go far enough away to start a life where nobody knows who I am or what I've been" (82). "Home" for Josephine is France. She claims: "I found freedom in a place I stumbled upon by the grace of the goddess, and I had enough sense to stay there and be the woman I was born to be. I wasn't running from anything and I never had the slightest intention of constructing a life where nobody knew who I was or what I'd been up to" (83). Josephine is an aging actress who exiles herself from her "home" in Paris because of her unbelievable Americanness: she is truly surprised by anti–American sentiments directed at her. What Josephine Evan discovers in the United States of America is a house in desperate need of repair, a granddaughter who needs her help, and a set of new friends. The novel's second epigraph quotes Alice Walker, "Remember, that you, yourself, are, America." Through the character Josephine, Cleage reinforces the idea that black women have forgotten their place in America. Josephine claims her black Americanness, but seems confused by her American identity. Her friend Howard exclaims, " Oh, excuse me missy. We're *Negroes*, okay? African Americans. *Jigaboos*! Take your pick! All I'm saying is, we're not *real* Americans!" (4). The two friends negotiate their American identities while being exiled from their circle of friends in Paris. Howard never accepts himself as an American man. He is gay, he is black, but he is not American! But Josephine is rooted to the United States because of her granddaughter Zora. To those who accept it, Cleage's lesson is that black Americans are indeed Americans regardless of their physical location.

Josephine Evan's return home as a concerned grandmother is a sharp contrast to her onstage role in Paris as the monstrous Medea, the classical Greek mother who kills her children on stage to avenge her husband Jason. It seems intentional that Cleage, a playwright, would cast Josephine Evans as Euripides' Medea, a woman in Greek mythology who left her country and her family to marry a man in a foreign country, so perhaps Medea is another misplaced and misunderstood female character. But without a doubt, Josephine Evan's starring role is that of Zora Evan's Mafeenie — who is anything but a bad witch. In Atlanta, Josephine stars as a "shero" in her own YouTube series produced by the novel's other good witch: "Zora leaned closer when I came on the screen, listening intently. I was listening, too, but mostly looking. I assumed I'd hate myself on camera the way I looked this morning, but I didn't. I actually liked the way I looked and the way I sounded" (150). On her journey fighting for her mother's house and for her granddaughter's future, Josephine Evans sees herself and likes what she sees. As the novel progresses, the project of saving the house and planting community peace gardens goes YouTube viral. The gardens represent the house of Josephine's childhood and the care and attention her mother gave to her beautiful roses. Alice Walker, in her essay "In Search for Our Mothers' Gardens," notes "I notice that when my mother is working in her garden she is radiant, almost to the point of being invisible — except as the Creator: hand and eye" (241). Doris Evans is an artist and leaves a powerful legacy for our leading ladies — a creative spark along with economic freedom. The house is also a part of a community and as Josephine realizes that she too is America, the significance of her story becomes tantamount. Her story is America's story: "Because you left your glamorous life in Europe to reclaim your granddaughter's inheritance and bring back beauty to this one small corner on a street named for an American hero" (168). Everyone enjoys a good story and Cleage offers many layers and levels as we search for happy endings — for our selves, our families, and our communities.

The cultural icon of Dorothy from *The Wizard of Oz* serves as a reminder of all the possibilities available to free women. Cleage notes, "She was already endowed with the qualities that her traveling companions desired" (105). Dorothy has brains, a heart and plenty of courage. Dorothy is an American woman who may be played by iconic figures such as Dianna Ross, Josephine

Baker, Zora Neale Hurston, but in Cleage's "screenplay," she is played by Zora and Josephine Evans. These displaced leading ladies play a large role in the construction of black women's identity in America. They are women like Zora Neale Hurston, whom Alice Walker also writes about *In Search for Our Mothers' Gardens*. Cleage's Zora is linked to Hurston by the connection to the American South and the mutual rejection they experience by communities they try to observe. Zora Evans attempts to observe and help the post-war soldiers, but instead becomes the subject of observations. She is photographed and becomes the subject of gossip. Zora Neale Hurston, the classic cultural anthropologist, dies unappreciated and poor. The one who sees so much goes unseen. To give a few contemporary examples, Diana Ross is the sister who plays Dorothy with Michael Jackson as the Scarecrow, marries a white European man, and lives abroad to raise her children. Similarly, Josephine Baker is the sister who escapes St. Louis to pursue her dancing career in Europe only to be accused of acting white and isolating herself from the black community. Josephine Baker and Cleage's Josephine Evans are linked by their names and their need to escape America to pursue their crafts. In each case, these black American women experience the dynamic of spectator versus spectacle, but Cleage's "seeing" approach attempts to relocate these sisters in a very focused way. They are in the position of being watched and watching themselves from the outside: the crystal ball effect. However, each woman is capable of saving herself and someone else. The power of Dorothy is her ability to see her reflection and change the story: escape the box. The free black woman is the author of her destiny wherever she lands, and as Alice Walker puts it, she is America. In *Seen it All and Done the Rest*, we see the power of the brown mermaid and the water. We know that the power to be one's self and overcome one's fears can defeat evil. When you encourage others to join the party, you can melt a Wicked Witch or you can launch a movement. Zora is no longer mystified by evil and the presence of cruelty. Instead, she has the tools to fight them.

Ignore the Man Behind the Curtain

When Zora decides to use technology in her favor, her depression ends. She goes from watching war 24/7 to broadcasting her grandmother's *Rescue on MLK*. She refuses to be intimidated by photographs and decides to live free. *Dig It!!* goes from incriminating enemy to righteous mouthpiece for the protest: "Burned Out Actress Vows to Rebuild" (285). For Josephine, technology represents freedom in the Isadora Duncan sense of the word, "A wild woman with wild eyes, a wild face, a wild gypsy heart that finally found a home where she least expected it. *Is that what I look like now?*" (297). Josephine must tell her friend Howard, who mistakes Josephine's live video for an amazing performance and not her actual life, that she will not return to Paris. As the women increase their use of technology, their online fans increase. They eventually plan The Sea to Shining Sea MLK Rescue Tour around the United States of America (284). "They been watching you live it on their little computers, in their little individual rooms, now they want to be part of the story, not just observers," Abbie says (279). Modern day technology is embodied as a character in novel serving as a hero and trickster figure: technology is in essence the "man behind the curtain" directing the characters reactions in both positive and negative ways. Before the MLK Rescue Project, Josephine worried that "Zora was channeling other people's nightmares for a living" (46). While Zora's expertise in technology was admirable, she lacked the background to confront the issues facing soldiers; she was listening to war stories all day through a website interface. In the end, Zora and Josephine use the Wiz to find their way home. In the midst of a war in Iraq, Josephine's crusade to save her home and honor Martin Luther King, Jr. with peace gardens around the world is a welcome respite for internet viewers around the globe. Internet viewers are captivated by Josephine's rendition of "This Little Light of Mine," as she vows to rebuild her burned down duplex.

Follow the Yellow Brick Road

Likewise, the song "Over the Rainbow," which won the Academy Award for the Best Song in 1939, was later coined as a World War II theme song to encourage American troops in the struggle for freedom against domination and fascism abroad. The song's lyrics idealized a place (Langley 40). Soldiers conjured the optimism of the American dream, the bravery of Dorothy and her friends, and perhaps the beauty of the lyrics and the leading lady Judy Garland. Many contemporary artists including Patti LaBelle and the now-deceased Hawaiian singer Israel Kamakawi'wo have rendered amazing versions of the song, but what holds is the feeling of "home" that the song invokes. The listener knows that whatever place is "over the rainbow" it is enough to inspire dedication, determination, and yes, even defiance. It is a place and a dream worth protecting: risking one's life for. It is a safe, happy and free place: like Cleage's West End community. For U.S. troops during World War II, "Over the Rainbow" was the United States of America. Thus, through Josephine experience as the lady in red, Cleage evokes Ntozake Shange's *For Colored Girls Who Have Considered Suicide/When the Rainbow is Enuf*, to reiterate that in the twenty-first century "somewhere over the rainbow" belongs to American black women as well. In Paris some of Josephine's most notable roles are misunderstood, even crazed mothers — Euripides's Medea and Shange's lady in red — who risk their children's lives. However, the female goddess role that she improvised is "probably what made [her] reputation as much as anything else. It ended with Halima finding somebody who would let us use their beautiful horse, and me riding around Paris claiming my opinion through the persona of a fictional Amazonian warrior woman" (Cleage 114). What is at stake when "over the rainbow" is not available to black women in America? The journey to Oz was not only a journey for personal freedom, but Dorothy was introduced to the economics of the farm and the power of industrial Oz. One of the film's many catch phrases, "follow the yellow brick road," takes Dorothy on her path to discovery as she meets the farmer worker, "the Scarecrow"; the industrial worker, "the Tin Man"; and the politician, "the Cowardly Lion." A little girl conquers an empire and kills two witches. The *technicolor* present in the film *The Wizard of Oz* shows that art is an investment and a risk. Ironically, MGM made very little money on the box office release of the film, but it was a risk that paid off as the film is considered a national treasure. The emergence of *For Colored Girls* in the 2010 Hollywood Box Office shows the financial stakes are high, but black women need to be seen on the big screen. Timeless works like Ntozake Shange's *For Colored Girls* need to be a part of the national fabric. Audiences must support culturally relevant works. As Langston Hughes might say, black women "too sing America." The song "Over the Rainbow" is still relevant because it still inspires audiences.

Is there truly, as Dorothy phrases it, "no place like home?" The following excerpt from the film begs this question:

> TIN MAN: What have you learned, Dorothy?
>
> DOROTHY (thoughtfully): Well, I ... I think that it ... that it wasn't enough just to want to see Uncle Henry and Aunt Em ... and it's that if I ever go looking for my heart's desire again, I won't look further than my own back yard. And if it isn't there, I never really lost it to begin with. (timidly to Glinda)
> Is that right?
>
> GLINDA: That's all it is.
>
> SCARECROW: But that's so easy!! I should have thought of it for you!!
>
> TIN MAN: I should have felt it in my heart!
>
> GLINDA: No — she had to find it out for herself. And now those magic slippers will take you home in two seconds!![5]

As Glinda notes, Dorothy had to find the answer for herself. All journeys home may not begin in our backyards as Dorothy suggests, but they may begin in our dreams and in the continual reflection of our past that like magic allow us to travel over the rainbow. "Home" could be Oz or Kansas, both or neither. Home is in the stories we pass on from generation to generation. Doris Evan's duplex on Martin Luther King, Jr. Blvd did not become "home" until Josephine gave it her story. Josephine Evans is a free woman who is rooted to Atlanta, but is still a citizen of the world. Cleage invents a West Atlanta that her readers believe in, want to live in and definitely visit through reading her wonderfully crafted stories. Salman Rushdie, famed author of *Midnight's Children* (1980) and *Satanic Verses* (1989) argues that the secret to the magic slippers is that "there is no longer such a place as home; except, of course, for the home we make, or the homes that are made for us, in Oz: which is anywhere, and everywhere, except the place from which we began."[6] (57). In *Seen it All and Done the Rest*, like the film *The Wizard of Oz*, Cleage take readers to the next realm of possibility through time and space. Cyberspace creates a wonderful possibility for Zora and Josephine as they tour America, the hybridity of face-to-face contact and YouTube interfaces mirror Frank L. Baum idea creating the thirteen volume series featuring Dorothy Gale and her many returns to Oz. The story was always to be continued....

Notes

1. Technicolor(r) is a twentieth-century trademark for a film technique specific to super-imposing primary colors on black and white film. *The Wizard of Oz* (1939) is famous for this technique. For this essay, I will use the nomenclature *technicolor* to emphasize the author's ability to bring a very cinematic approach to her writing style.

2. By examining Cleage's speeches and earlier works, Aisha Francis summarizes Cleage's theory of Free Womanhood in "In Search of Free Womanhood: Black Conduct Literature, Contemporary Cultural Production and Pearl Cleage." *Obsidian* Spring–Summer 2009. 32–47.

3. The Rainbow Flag was actually designed by Gilbert Baker in 1978 for Gay Pride in San Francisco after the death of Harvey Milk as a symbol of resistance and activism for those advocating for the Gay Rights.

4. After World War II, Josephine Baker had the dream of bringing children of all races together and did so by adopting twelve children of different nationalities. They lived in Les Milandes, Frances during the early 1950s. The experience was financially crippling and put a strain on Baker's marriage to Jo Bouillon (Schroeder 86).

5. Noel Langley, Florence Ryerson, and Edgar Allan Woolf, *The Wizard of Oz: The Screenplay*, 128.

6. Salman Rushdie, *The Wizard of Oz*, 57.

Works Cited

Brice, Carleen. "A Conversation with Pearl Cleage." *A Reader's Guide*. New York: Random House, 2008.
Cleage, Pearl. *Seen It All and Done the Rest*. New York: One World, 2009.
Francis, Aisha. "In Search of Free Womanhood: Black Conduct Literature, Contemporary Cultural Production and Pearl Cleage." *Obsidian* (Spring–Summer 2009): 32–47.

Gates, Henry Louis. *The Signifying Monkey: A Theory of African-American Literary Criticism*. New York: Oxford, 1989.
Langley, Noel, Florence Ryerson, and Edgar Allan Woolf. *The Wizard of Oz: The Screenplay*, 128.
Lorde, Audre. "From the House of Yemanja." *The Collected Poems of Audre Lorde*. New York: Norton, 2000. 235.
Morrison, Toni. "Home." *The House that Race Built*, ed. Wahneema Lubiana. New York: Pantheon, 1997. 3–12.
_____."Rootedness: The Ancestor as Foundation." *What Moves at the Margin: Selected Nonfiction*.
Ed. Carolyn Denard. Oxford: University Press of Mississippi, 2008. 56–64.
Needham, Maureen. *I See America Dancing: Selected Readings, 1685–2000*. Chicago: University of Illinois Press, 2002.
Salman Rushdie. *The Wizard of Oz*. London: Palgrave Macmillan, 1992.
Schroeder, Alan, and Heather Lehr Wagner. *Josephine Baker*. New York: Infobase, 2006.
Walker, Alice. "In Search of Our Mothers' Gardens." *In Search of Our Mothers' Gardens: Womanist Prose*. New York: Harvest, 2004. 231–243.
Young, William, and Nancy. K. Young. *Music of the World War II Era*. Westport, CT: Greenwood, 2008.

Being Neighborly: Performance in *Seen It All and Done the Rest*

SHANNA L. SMITH

> They understood intellectually and intuitively the meaning of homeplace in the midst of an oppressive and domineering social reality, of homeplace as site of resistance and liberation struggle.—D. Soyini Madison, "That Was My Occupation"

> There she was, Citizen Evans, reporting for duty.—Pearl Cleage, *Seen it All and Done the Rest*

Preface

    A menagerie of new residents moved next door, beginning a heightened understanding of the difference between having neighbors and being neighborly. Neighbors dwell together in the nearby locations; being neighborly involves acts of agency. The new residents began to mark their territory by trashing the shared grounds of our apartment building before setting up a drug selling lounge in their unit. Our new residents were now bad neighbors, moving from unknown figures to known abusers of collective territory and peace of mind. The bad neighbors fought loudly with their hollow-eyed customers, whom they invited to trudge up their steps all through the night and day. The bad neighbors recruited teenaged boys to sell for them and teenaged girls to party with them. They danced to music blasting from the trunks of their cars in the daylight while surveying the timing of the school buses from their balcony. No one knew exactly who lived there, but a *number stayed in their unit, including four pit bulls. However, even as these residents revealed themselves as bad neighbors, the neighborly began to announce themselves as well.*

Our neighborliness was activated similarly to the ways that Pearl Cleage demonstrates in her works of fiction, including Seen It All and Done the Rest. Neighborliness, for us, was eye contact and communication. A couple of neighbor friends, adjacent neighbors, and I formed a loose neighborhood watch group while sharing updates and looking out for each other's property. We were each other's "all seeing eye."[1] *I see you, our eyes said as we spoke, acknowledging our wayward neighbors and subtly correcting them when safe to do so. "How are you?" I greeted while picking up discarded fast food bags and moved stolen dirt bikes from the sidewalk. Sometimes the younger men sprang into action, offering to take care of the mess. The interaction, and others, demonstrated that not only do I care about our property, but was willing to act to maintain it. This posture of respect was consistent. What I learned most about neighborliness, and the performance of it, was that it is present. Presence is an active response that can be subversive. It says: I will not look away and do nothing. It involves what Ruth Behar calls "getting down into the mud" (1–2), which involves coming out from the safety and distance of the observer's position. Presence in this instance is being an active and engaged witness.*[2]

Introduction

In Pearl Cleage's novel, *Seen it All and Done the Rest*, neighborliness performs functions of citizenship, co-performative witness[3] and social action. *Seen it All's* collection of neighbors includes an expatriate actress, an artist, a visionary, an anti-war activist, a homeless former crack addict, and a displaced Hurricane Katrina survivor, to name a few. As a means for urban renewal, these neighbors battle a home management company for the right to revitalize and retain their own property instead of being forced to sell their homes at an undervalued price. Cleage signifies on an image of the old black neighborhood, where neighbors correct children, black businesses thrive, and where grassroots civil rights efforts address community needs. These images hearken back to efforts of race men and women,[4] inside and outside of early twentieth century black club movements. In Cleage's contemporary texts, they serve as markers to "turn the ships around"[5] to a utopian image of a black neighborly heyday. This image is imperfect; however, Cleage embraces imperfections and uses flawed characters to address them. She complicates the idea that black neighborly values are lead and modeled solely by the black middle class by portraying artists, activists, and addicts engaged in proving solutions for social problems. They, along with the elderly and the working class, are proactive participants in neighborhood revitalization.

Neighborliness and neighborly performance[6] are recurring themes throughout the body of Cleage's literary work, and its social activism drives the development of her plots. These performances are captured in the urban landscapes of Cleage's West End series, primarily discussed in this essay. Yet, neighborliness is also significant to her small town Idlewild works of fiction and within her historical plays, particularly *Flyin' West*. Neighborliness expresses care and concern for neighbors, but acts especially as investment in the upkeep, safety, and governing of neighborhoods. Neighborly performance is collective social action among neighbors. It is an intervention strategy, and at times, a performance of resistance. Neighbors participate in ways that contribute to the feeling of belonging. However, there is also an element of policing the behaviors and actions of residents who may or may not choose to act in ways that are neighborly. Ultimately, neighborliness and neighborly performance captures the way residents identify as citizens and demonstrate citizenship within their home sites.

Background

Pearl Cleage signifies on the names of Josephine Baker and Zora Neale Hurston, and adds traces of their real lives to her fictional narrative. Cleage often uses historical elements in her work, and bridges them with contemporary issues. Generations come together to build futures, and in this way wisdom and innovation are respected. In *Seen It All*, she reclaims Baker and brings her "home" through the character of Josephine Evans, taking the opportunity to re-establish citizenship for each of them. Cleage also offers Hurston, through the troubled Zora Evans, reconnection with a community that values her. It is interesting that Cleage characterizes these women in particular, who are known to transgress boundaries. Her choice validates her use of the international gaze as co-performative witness, demonstrates orality as a subversive tactic, and establishes a new tribe as community. Both Hurston and Baker offer a platform for Cleage to consider performances of possibility.

In *Seen it All*, Josephine Evans is a reluctant activist. She is a theatre star in Amsterdam who returns home to Atlanta to see about her troubled granddaughter, Zora, and to check on the property she inherits from her mother. Both her granddaughter and childhood home are in an extreme state of disrepair: Zora has become a recluse and alcoholic after a media scandal and Josephine's home has become a battered crack house occupied by squatters. Josephine enjoys being an ex-patriate but is encouraged to reconsider the significance of home and citizenship by her friend Abbie Browning, whom she respects as a sister sojourner. The West End of Atlanta is home for Josephine, and she depends on Abbie, who employs herself as a visionary healer, to help re-imagine herself as a citizen there and to re-conceptualize the home she inherits and neglects. On board with the home repair and reclamation project, albeit reluctantly, is Victor Causey, a former addict who lives in the abandoned property. Family friend, Aretha Hargrove, is a local artist known in her neighborhood to paint doors blue in an African tradition to ward off the evil eye. Louie Baptiste, a Hurricane Katrina survivor, is also a displaced chef who helps the crew develop Abbie's vision of a peace garden. Zora decides to film the project, called "Rescue on MLK," which she uploads to YouTube and attracts a wide viewership.

While Cleage's offers a romantic view of black life, there is an undercurrent of dissatisfaction among neighbors within the text. In *Black on the Block*, Mary Patillo notes, "The most earnest political battles are played out when (residents) face threats to their neighborhoods or try to fashion a new kind of neighborhood" (2). *Seen it All and Done the Rest* presents the story of two neighborhoods: the one where Josephine spends the summer with her granddaughter, Zora, and the one where her matrilineal home is located. Her summer home, belonging to a middle-class couple for whom Zora house-sits, is under Blue Hamilton's protection. Her matrilineal home is in an adjacent working class neighborhood outside of Hamilton's jurisdiction, and does not have the same protection. Both neighborhoods had fallen into urban decay, but only one has the resources to make and sustain change. Cleage offers a literary representation of black middle class urban renewal efforts in black working class neighborhoods, and the conflicts that arise. Josephine, Zora, and several of their friends take a middle class revitalization mindset with them into the old neighborhood, and begin their rebuilding efforts. However, it is not until collaboration with long-time residents, like the Causeys, that neighborliness takes effect and proves successful. According to Patillo, "Homeowning new comers and their old-timer allies translate their economic power into political voice" (15). That collaboration in *Seen it All* is successful.

Neighborliness acts to restore Josephine's lineage and legacy, *and* to infuse dignity into a crumbling neighborhood and its afflicted residents. Her home is a site of rupture; crime is an open sore that blights what was once a tight-knit neighborhood. The disrepair is indicative of ruptures in personal responsibility, familial relationships, and social involvement among characters in the novel. Pearl Cleage uses neighborly performance as social action; marginalized residents are restored as engaged citizens and their actions are a demonstration of participatory citizenship. Other neighbors witness the destruction to their neighborhood and "Rescue on MLK's" efforts to rebuild. That witness helps build the social activism in neighborly performance, particularly as Josephine and Abbie rally elderly neighbors to fight for their own homes. Josephine hires Greer Woodruff to manage her property while away, not realizing Woodruff's company applies financial pressure and encourages criminal activity to force the low sell of homes and acquire property. Woodruff seeks to benefit from local businessmen and politicians interested in acquiring the land to build a prison. However, neighbors trust what they have seen through "Rescue on MLK" and join in neighborly performances of their own. Thereby, neighbors begin to establish a new vision for the neighborhood.

Performances of Possibility

Atlanta's West End, Pearl Cleage's adopted hometown, is where she imagines possibilities. Cleage's particular signature is the rounding up of ordinary folk to activate and enforce change. She allows the visions and voices of those who have been marginalized, stigmatized, and addicted to be heard. Several of her works, including *Babylon Sisters*, *Some Things I Thought I'd Never Do*, *Baby Brother's Blues*, and *Seen it All and Done the Rest*, are set in the West End, which is wrought with the crime and lack of care that claims urban neighborhoods everywhere. Perhaps her fictive story lines offer trial runs of solutions to the problems that she sees and experiences within her very real community. By creating a "godfather" in Blue Hamilton, who develops an alternative police sub-station of black men, and who enlists residents to organize an effective neighborhood watch and cultivate abandoned grounds into gardens, she puts to work the wish lists of countless block associations. D. Soyini Madison calls this "putting to work" a performance of possibilities which, she argues, takes a stand and is charged to do something in the world ("Performance" 278). Activism is at the heart of the neighborliness portrayed in *Seen it All*, and in Cleage's series of other West End texts. *Seen it All* is a performance of such neighborliness, and as such, performs the value of home place and enacts a performance of possibilities for the residents of it.

Josephine Evans has the unique position of being an "inside" former resident with far reaching "outside" status. Her past performance as an international theatre star has equipped her to perform as a neighborhood agitator who rallies to reclaim her home on her own terms. She uses performance to encourage neighbors to re-imagine their landscapes — their home spaces. Josephine's talent is her oratory skill, which she uses to press her granddaughter, Zora, Victor, and other members of "Rescue on MLK" into service. The restoration project transforms, transgresses, and interrogates in the way that Madison describes to activate a sense of neighborliness. It places power back into the hands of the residents, who will determine whether to stay or sell their homes at a higher rate of return. Together, they not only refurbish Josephine's property but restore agency to the elderly and working class home owners. Their collaborative work, flash mobs, and ritual celebrations demonstrate that present *and* future worlds are possible. These actions are a response to housing developer Greer Woodruff, who frightens homeowners into selling their homes to her cheaply. Restoration is demonstrated as a rebuke, made even more so when Zora decides to film the process and stream it live on YouTube.

Restoration does not come without vision and hard work, which are essentially the bare bones aspects of a performance of possibilities. D. Soyini Madison coined this term in an activist sense, defining it as action that "centers on the principles of transformation and transgression, dialogue and interrogation, as well as acceptance and imagination to build worlds that are possible" ("Performance" 278). The performance of possibilities is intended to be a structure for resistance, and neighborly performance utilizes this as its foundation. Its collective effort builds and establishes networks that engage in social action. Josephine's neighbors have little but their memories of how their neighborhood once was. After enlisting Zora, Aretha, and Abbie, Josephine and the other residents are able to re-imagine possibilities their homes. As well, a larger internet and international audience becomes invested in the success of the restoration. Josephine is surprised to learn that workers at her local grocery store watch her progress by internet daily. Her friend, Howard, in Amsterdam, where she formerly resided, proudly tells her of fans cheering her on from the Netherlands. During the course of "Rescue on MLK's progress, and despite its setbacks, Zora comes to believe, "It's more about all of us working together, about seeing the house go from what it as, to what it could be" (274). The entire process does more than rebuild homes; it signifies on the restoration of relationship in families, communities, and nations in unique and innovative ways.

West End Citizenship

The context for *Seen it All* is citizenship and what it means to be a full, participating citizen. Cleage's scenarios in the text suggest that citizenship is tied to personal responsibility. At the start of the text, Josephine does not particularly identify as an American citizen, having lived abroad for many years. Conversations with Abbie remind her that citizenship involves seeing oneself as a functioning part of a whole. Josephine can embrace a world view and act on a local level. If those conversations nudge her into participation, her initial confrontation with Victor propel her directly "into the mud" (Vulnerable, 1–2). Though he is homeless and living in her abandoned home, he is a citizen of it — neatly caring for his personal space within it and running off intruders. At her return, she reacts in horror at the condition of her childhood home. He feels Josephine has abdicated her responsibility for the property, and demands of her:

> "Who are you?"
> "Who are *you*?"
> "I own this place."
> "You do?"
> "Yes, I do."
> "Well, where have you been?"
> "What?"
> "Look at it! How could you let it go like this?'
>
> This was becoming more surreal by the second. Now the homeless squatter was going to reprimand me for being an absentee landlord? What next? A citizen's arrest? [91].

Citizenship has become messy, complicated, and difficult to manage. Josephine is now mired in a struggle with an opportunistic management company, the tedious effort to reconstruct her home, and deal with the criminal elements that threaten those efforts. She must also face the rebuke Victor issues and the fear that paralyzes her elderly neighbors. She is in the mud. Neighborly performance allows her to see her way through while she is still in it with them. Victor's challenge insists that she face her responsibility to her property, and eventually, the shared responsibility for the neighborhood. Their exchange opens a space for contestation and collaboration, as neighborly performance is rarely achieved without dissention and compromise.

Pearl Cleage's belief in the effective power of active citizenship is developed throughout each of her West End novels. In *Some Things I Thought I'd Never Do*, "activism was the kind that required (leaders) not to propagate the latest theoretical approach to activating the masses, but to have actual exchanges with real people confronting real problems" (15). Cleage establishes a pattern of problem solving on a local level. Her analysis of citizenship is mostly placed in neighborhood settings and nearly always paired with aspects of gardening. In the midst of urban predators who make simple acts of gardening difficult, Betty Causey, an elderly resident in *Seen it All*, demands impatiently, "We still have a right to live, don't we? We still have a right to grow collard greens" (227). Home invasions imprisoned many of Betty's longtime neighbors behind their barred windows and locked doors. Much like her son, Victor, she insists on basic rights of citizenship including the right to venture safely onto her property. Betty recalls with pride how Josephine's mother encouraged women to own property, and rallied wives to add their names onto deeds alongside their husbands. How do collard greens and citizenship work together in the minds of the elderly? In Pearl Cleage's texts, it is a matter of consumption. Collard greens can be grown, shared, and preserved. Crops can bring nourishment and be marketed as a product, which both sustains life and provides an economic base. However, vandalism is the context of Betty Causey's observation. She and her neighbors have lost the freedom of being full participants — citizens — in their own yards and neighborhood. Their proximity to the West End Grower's Association demonstrates to them the possibilities for an economic base. Betty Causey understands that the association turns vacant lots into community gardens, provides jobs, and serves loosely as a block watch organization. Without this for her block, their lives and homes are vulnerable to consumption by vandals and outside property buyers.

Setting a new vision for this neighborhood, Abbie establishes a peace garden as part of the "Rescue on MLK" project. Abbie is the "visionary healer" and considers, among other things, that viewing self as a functioning part of home, whether home country or hometown, is an important aspect of citizenship. She explains to Josephine that touring the country and seeing it for herself lead her to this view. Her character is the most impassioned about citizenship: she readily takes the microphone to complain about United States participation in wars waged "in her name" during anti-war gatherings (237). Abby makes citizenship personal, envisioning it as simply as peaceful coexistence in her neighborhood. During her peace garden ceremony, she explains:

> This garden is a part of a street and this street is part of a community where Miss Betty can take an evening walk with Victor and Miss Thelma can braid her grandbaby's hair on the front porch and me and Peachy can sit on Jo's back steps and eat some watermelon he brought from the island while Zora tells us what the rest of the century is going to look like.... There should be gardens like this on every street and boulevard and byway in this country that carries the name of Martin Luther King, Jr., because we owe him that much [261].

Abbie connects gardening, evening strolls, and porch sitting with citizenship because of the basic ordinariness of these actions. Pearl Cleage uses the ordinary to make salient points in her themes. Multi-generational activism is demonstrated throughout her work; the above passage suggests that it is a legacy that has been passed down. The home set on Martin Luther King Boulevard is representative of the disrepair of neighborliness and activism, and of how citizenship has been taken for granted. "Rescue on MLK" goes from being one woman's story to a collective witness. "It's their story, too" Zora tells Josephine. "We're still telling the same story, right?" (247–48). Zora's point establishes a framework for a discussion of co-performative witness.

Citizen Witness

Josephine Evans' decision to reconstruct her home impacts more than her own interests. Others are watching. Betty Causey, Daisy Turner, and other elderly neighbors peer through their windows and are encouraged. They move from watchfulness to activeness while lending their voices to the video documentation and tooting their car horns as part of a flash mob rallying against Greer Woodruff. Their participation reinforces Cleage's belief that leadership and activism is only self serving if it does not meet basic needs and does not include ordinary folk. In fact, the performance of possibilities considers "the audience as citizens with the potential for collective action and change and ... reinforces to audience members the "web" of citizenship and the possibilities of their individual selves as agents" (Madison, Performance 281). Witness in this instance is a necessary function of neighborly performance and the social action it produces.

Co-performative witnessing, according to Dwight Conquergood and D. Soyini Madison, allows for local audiences to have a stake in the outcomes of social action. As stakeholders, they hold the social activists accountable for their work. In their unique position as participant/observers, they form the web of community that Madison describes which reinforces their identification as change agents. In context with neighborly performance, co-performative witness is a corroborative element that allows for full participation as world citizens. Technological advances have made possible a digital witnessing, which is demonstrated in *Seen it All and Done the Rest*. Pearl Cleage melds together a (g)local community of neighbors that take part in restructuring what it is means to be a neighbor-as-citizen.

Zora Evans' use of technology to record and stream her grandmother's narrative to the virtual public is a reversal of the media gaze that has consistently plagued her. Her commitment to co-performative witnessing is an act of defiance. "Absolute defiance," Abbie, insists, "in the face of all the madness, and the meanness" (177). She now controls a particular gaze and operates it as a strategy for resistance. Orchestrating the flash mob that dismantles the corporate interest in her family's property, Zora participates in preserving her matrilineal legacy. Her co-performance advances the narrative into the new millennium through the use of technology.

The most interesting co-performative witnesses are members of the internet audience. This non-direct audience benefits from the visual performance as participating eye-witnesses to Josephine's present reality. D. Soyini Madison acknowledges this type of performance, suggesting, "These listeners and observers are, then, affected by what they see and hear in ways that motivate them to act/think in forms that now beneficially affect (directly or indirectly) either the subjects themselves or what they advocate. At this point, the audience moves from the performance space to the social world of the interrogative field" ("Performance" 280). Therefore, the renovation project benefits from the unknown host of watchers who encourage and critique it. Like those who come to the aid of Josephine as an amen corner while she confronts Greer Woodruff, the internet audience can act as a quasi flash mob virtually engaged in social change.

Social Action

Neighborly performance as social action does not necessarily call for an agreeable outcome; it calls for empowerment. The premise for Pearl Cleage's novels is that everyday folk can have an impact on their local communities, and that the collective raising of their voices can effect change. In *Seen it All*, home place becomes the site for galvanizing neighbors and enacting the neighborly performance involved in social action. Social critic bell hooks accurately locates home place as a site of resistance and liberation struggle (*Yearning* 45, 146). For Josephine Evans, home place is the site that rearticulates for her the meaning of citizenship. Social action is the "tankling agent" that Elin Diamond describes ("Introduction" 1) through which neighborly performance can protect and defend the neighborhood, and to help continue shared cultural traditions.

In Pearl Cleage's series of texts located in West End, Blue Hamilton is godfather, a home place activist who controls the policing of the neighborhood to deter domestic abuse, drug and sex traffic, ill kept property, and the listlessness of (mainly) men that stirs an atmosphere of crime and hopelessness. Policing is provocative, perhaps even romanticized somewhat, by the portrayal of black men in suits and hats quietly warning, then dispensing hard justice to those who threaten the well-being of residents. There is an ominous air that surrounds Blue Hamilton and his men, their means of transport, and way of disposing of troublemakers. The methods are not discussed, but the outcomes are respected and supported by West End residents. Cleage creates tension in the narrative by not detailing *how* sexual predators and violent offenders are disposed of, but *that* the violence has ended.

In Cleage's literary world it is the responsibility of women and men, with the cooperation of youth, to maintain peace and order. Her characters consider this responsibility an act of citizenship, and they measure it through the effectiveness of neighborliness. Evidence for its success is the presence of twenty-four hour hair salons, community gardens, and the simple act of a woman walking alone, with her child or her lover, undisturbed at any hour of the day. In several of her texts, Cleage's female protagonists note the actions of men they encounter in this "new" West End neighborhood:

> There seemed to be brothers in motion all over the place.... Several of the men inclined their heads slightly to acknowledge my passing by, but otherwise they were all about whatever task lay before them. I realized how good it was to see men around visible and working. *And how rare* [*Some Things* 29–30].

Cleage offers mundane tasks and behaviors in everyday life to stand in as a socially active response to criminal activity.

Outrage is the determining factor that propels the women in Cleage's texts into home place activists who confront social issues directly. Women who speak out and who take a stand for justice are depicted as empowered and sexy. Feminist social critic bell hooks argues for vocal empowerment for women, insisting that "for us, true speaking is not solely an expression of creative power: it is an act of resistance, a political gesture that challenges politics of domination that would render us nameless and voiceless. As such, it is a courageous act—as such, it represents a threat" (*Talking Back* 8). Sass is one of three communicative devices Cleage uses to promote care among black women. Sass is a woman-truth, according to the work of Joni Jones and Terri L. Varner, in which they cover issues of health, etiquette, gender performance, childrearing, personal style, interpersonal relations, aesthetics, food preparation, career development, and sex ("Take Care of Your Sisters" 150). These woman-truths mirror Pearl Cleage's concept of Free Womanhood, which are skills and knowledge she believes women must have in order to be independent and assertive. Cleage insists that women ask themselves, "What would a Free Woman do?" in the face of personal challenges and difficult decision making.

Pearl Cleage spends time developing her character's critical response to social problems, and shows them navigating their way through various and difficult decisions and reactions. When Louie realizes he has no "home" to return to in New Orleans—his family, friends, restaurant, and residence all displaced or destroyed by Hurricane Katrina—he makes a return to Atlanta with an offering of soil. He mourns his conception of home, which includes his relationships with friends and family, and the spaces that gathered the members and nurtured those relationships. Without the people or locations that recall the heritage of those relationships, New Orleans is no longer home. Yet, Louie becomes a home place activist. The container of soil he brings to Atlanta represents his conception of home and allows him to plant it in a new location. The band of neighbors he assists in creating a peace garden accepts his offering while mixing it in with newly turned over soil. In return, the garden represents a substitution of memory for all involved.

Joseph Roach understands these actions to be surrogation, a substitution of representation and memory. In *Cities of the Dead*, Roach examines the fruitfulness and failures of ritualized collective memory in New Orleans and other circum–Atlantic cities. He argues, "The process surrogation does not begin or end but continues as actual or perceived vacancies occur in the network of relations that constitutes the social fabric" (2). He also notes that the "fit" is never exact. Cleage angles the act of surrogation in *Seen it All* differently; she utilizes the flaws of imperfect individuals while offering opportunities for grace. The workers gathered for "Rescue at MLK" are misfits. None of them have particular skills in home renovation, but each use their abilities to make change. As an actress, Josephine's use of orality commands attention and holds those who disrupt progress accountable. The home they renovate is in a declining neighborhood. City planners and administrators are not in support of the project. Criminals are paid to destroy rebuilding efforts. However, in the spirit of grace, the act of rebuilding restores pride and dignity and becomes a testament for a performance of possibilities.

Neighborliness does not occur when Josephine has coffee with Abby at Paschal's Restaurant or West End News. Neighborliness occurs during moments of conflict: while challenged by Victor or angered by the unneighborly acts of Greer Woodruff and her minions. Those incidents provoke a response to rally people around her for change. Abbie's mantra is "You have to do some things you might not do otherwise, just because it is your country, too" (194). The first moment of realization for the redemptive element of neighborliness is found during an anti-war demonstration:

> Almost nobody seemed to notice. Nobody except those of us who showed up like the good citizens Abbie keeps telling us we have to be and spoke up for peace. In public. In the company of our neighbors. One by one until we all stood together. Stronger, even if just for the moment. A little stronger [239].

It is interesting to observe what Cleage does by involving Victor, Louie, and Zora in a restoration crew along with Josephine, Abby, and the talented artist, Aretha. Each of them needs the redemption of neighborliness in spite of various flaws and shortcomings. Redemptive performance allows each to serve and become an active member of a community. Cleage redeems them by re-casting their identities as productive, capable citizens.

Being Neighborly

The participatory experience of neighborly performance is restorative. In Pearl Cleage's *Seen it All and Done the Rest*, the performance restores the citizenship of marginalized individuals, neighborly relations in a fractured neighborhood, and social action that opens possibilities for continued collaboration. However, the novel is not as neatly packaged as this description suggests. The unlikeliest of neighbors perform, and their futures are uncertain ... until Cleage revisits them in succeeding novels as she often does in her work. The impact of neighborliness in the way Cleage narrates comes from Elin Diamond, who writes, "As soon as performativity comes to rest on a performance, questions of embodiment, of social relations, of ideological interpretations, of emotional and political effects, all become discussable" (5). Neighborliness begins with a dialogue whether it is collaborative or contested in its nature.

Cleage uses these places of rupture to enact strategies for healing and social action. She demonstrates through fiction the opportunities that citizens have for making progress in ruptured situations. Patillo argues, "Choosing participation over abdication and involvement over withdrawal, even and especially when the disagreements get heated and sometimes vicious, is what *constitutes* the black community (3). I would argue that this choice is what constitutes most communities, certainly mine, once our bad neighbors made the decision to move in drugs and crime along with their belongings. Choosing participation, involvement, and *presence* allowed for all of us to have a stake in refashioning our home space. Like the crew members of "Rescue on MLK," we had also seen it all and done the rest, gaining a new appreciation of being neighborly.

Notes

1. Reference to Michel Foucault's panoptic eye as a surveillance tool for the carceral system in *Discipline and Punish: The Birth of a Prison*. New York: Random House, 1975.

2. Ruth Behar references an Isabel Allende in *The Vulnerable Observer*. Boston: Beacon Press, 1996.

3. Term is defined by Dwight Conquergood as involving matters of the heart, putting the self on the line, and engaging in political action as a shared experience, elaborated upon by D. Soyini Madison in "Co-Performative Witnessing," *Cultural Studies*, Vol. 21. No. 6, 2007.

4. Term refers to black women and men engaged in racial uplift as leaders and through benevolent organizations during the late nineteenth through the first quarter of the twentieth century.

5. From Pearl Cleage's "Good Brother Blues," *The Bluelight Corner: Black Women Writing on Passion, Sex, and Romantic Love*, Rosemarie Robotham, ed. New York: Random House, 1998.

6. Neighborliness and neighborly performance are not solely specific to Pearl Cleage's work, or within African American literature; however, Cleage's pattern of neighborliness and neighborly performance as social action throughout the body of her literary work that bears investigation.

Works Cited

Behar, Ruth. *The Vulnerable Observer: Anthropology That Breaks Your Heart*. Boston: Beacon, 1996.

Cleage, Pearl. *Baby Brother's Blues*. New York: One World/Ballantine, 2007.
_____. *Babylon Sisters*. New York: One World/Ballantine, 2005.
_____. "Good Brother Blues." *The Bluelight Corner: Black Women Writing on Passion, Sex, and Romantic Love*. Rosmarie Robotham, ed. New York: Random House, 1998.
_____. *Seen It All and Done the Rest*. New York: One World/Ballantine, 2008
_____. *Some Things I Thought I'd Never Do*. New York: One World/Ballantine, 2006.
Conquergood, Dwight. "Of Caravans and Carnivals: Performance Studies in Motion. *The Drama Review* (Winter 1995). Vol. 39, No. 4
Diamond, Elin. "Introduction." *Performance and Cultural Politics*. New York: Routledge, 1996.
Griffin, Farah Jasmine. "*Who Set You Flowin'?*": *The African-American Migration Narrative*. New York and London: Oxford University Press, 1996.
hooks, bell. *Yearning: Race, Gender, and Cultural Politics*. Cambridge, MA: South End, 1999.
Jones, Joni L., and Terri Varner. "Take Care of Your Sisters." *Centering Ourselves: African American Feminist and Womanist Studies of Discourse*. Marsha Houston and Olga Idriss Davis, eds. Creskill, NJ: Hampton, 2002.
Langellier, Kristen M., and Eric E. Peterson. *Performing Narrative Storytelling in Daily Life*. Philadelphia: Temple University Press, 2004.
Madison, D. Soyini. "Co-Performative Witnessing." *Cultural Studies* (November, 2007). Vol. 21, No. 6.
_____. "Performance, Personal Narrative, and the Politics of Possibility." *The Future of Performance Studies: Visions and Revisions*, Sheron Daily (ed). National Communication Association, 1998.
_____. "That Was My Occupation: Oral Narrative, Performance, and Black Feminist Thought." *Exceptional Spaces: Essays in Performance and History*. Della Pollock, ed. Chapel Hill: University of North Carolina Press, 1998.
Patillo, Mary E. *Black on the Block: The Politics of Race and Class in the City*. Chicago: University of Chicago Press, 2007.

What Looks Like New: Narrative Call for Social Change

RaShell R. Smith-Spears

In 2004, comedian Bill Cosby angered many people in the African American community when he called for poor blacks to assume greater responsibility in their social situations. He criticized the use of foul language, the conspicuous consumption of parents, as well as the assignment of specific names to their children and the lack of academic achievement on the part of low-income black people. Cosby's perceptions of the problems facing black Americans may have angered some, but in addition to what he said, many had contention with where he said it. Although the comments were spoken at the NAACP conference on the academic achievement gap, mainstream media was present, allowing a wider audience to hear the shortcomings of the black community. Historically, black people have worked to maintain a certain positive public image and in speaking of the problems within the community, Cosby broke an often unspoken rule to remain silent in public. In short, Bill Cosby was airing dirty laundry.

Confronted with high drop-out rates, teenage pregnancy, youth delinquency, rising HIV/AIDS rates and poverty, African Americans are loathe to reveal the problems that are, nevertheless, discussed among themselves with those outside of the community. In a constant struggle to wrest its image from the mainstream and reshape it into something positive, or at the very least, diverse, it is imperative for many that the negative aspects of the culture remain in house, so to speak. This struggle has plagued the black community for countless generations, causing actors, artists, and writers to contend with the politics of presenting their art in addition to the artistry. The debate surrounding this culture of silence even prompted Langston Hughes to declare in "The Negro Artist and the Racial Mountain" that "We know we are beautiful. And ugly too. The tom-tom cries and the tom-tom laughs" (1271). So regardless of white or black critics, he would present the Negro in all his/her beauty and ugliness.

Writer Pearl Cleage identifies with Langston Hughes whom she says "was utterly devoted to writing about *real* black folks" (Carroll 54). Like Hughes, Cleage believes in speaking truth about the community, even its ugliness. Speaking these truths is necessary because it is the first step in addressing its problems. Perpetuating and even tolerating a culture of silence around issues that are detrimental to the community in order to maintain a pristine image proves to be even more harmful to the community and its individual members. In much of her drama, essays, and fiction Cleage proves that silence is unacceptable. In her first two novels in particular, *What Looks Like Crazy on an Ordinary Day* (1997) and *I Wish I Had a Red Dress* (2001), Cleage boldly illustrates and critiques the problems facing the black community as she sees them. In *What Looks Like Crazy*, she tells the story of Ava Johnson, an independent black woman who has been diagnosed with HIV and is on a journey that takes her back home to the once-idyllic small town of Idlewild, Michigan. At home with her sister Joyce, Ava finds that city problems such as crime, drugs, and domestic violence, have affected her small hometown. As she confronts these issues, she also finds a sense of spiritual healing.

Similarly, in *Red Dress*, Joyce discovers healing at home. A widow who has also endured the death of her two children, Joyce has buried herself in working with teen mothers. She discovers, through her mentorship of the young women, and a blossoming new romantic relationship with a good man, that there can be safety and healing within the community. In both novels, Cleage demands that the silence be broken so that truth can bring change and healing to the individuals and the community they comprise.

A child of the 1960s and '70s, Cleage brings her activist ideology to her writing, seeking to improve the world. Like the writers of the Black Arts Movement of the 1970s, Cleage insures that her work has an ethical purpose as well as aesthetic one. Beth Turner's "The Feminist/Womanist Vision of Pearl Cleage" reports that Cleage explains the energy behind her writing as her determination to participate in the global struggle against the oppressive forces in the world, racism, sexism, classism and homophobia (99).

Cleage's determination results in the production of plays like *Bourbon at the Border* that takes something as sacred in the black community as the civil rights movement and examines its darker side. It results in the penning of essays such as the ones in *Mad at Miles* that recognize the community's love for the musician and his art, yet reveals the reasons we should expect more of him. And it results in the creation of *What Looks Like Crazy* and *Red*

Dress, novels that present a once utopic black community plagued by the problems not only of the big city, but the problems that black folks would prefer weren't mentioned, at least not in the view of the outside world. Cleage's determination, however, insists that she does place these problems in view of everyone. In this way, readers are challenged to reshape their view of the community. In particular, Cleage calls on audiences to reframe their traditional and exclusive visions of spirituality and sexuality in order to create new and effective solutions to the problems of the community.

Shifting Views of Spirituality

The black church has historically been the epicenter of the black community, producing many of its political and cultural leaders as well as being the source of the civil rights movement of the 1960s. In *Righteous Discontent*, Evelyn Higginbotham explains that the black church, due in large part to the fundraising efforts of its women, was able to provide a great many social services to the community that would otherwise have been lacking. Such services included building schools, orphanages, and nursing homes as well as providing food and clothing (2). In addition to these provisions, the church also offered the black community a sense of relevance within a racist nation that denied black significance and even humanity. According to Higginbotham, the black baptist church adopted a social teaching that claimed equality for all humans, a principle of liberation that distinguished them from their white spiritual counterparts (121).

In more recent times, for reasons such as integration and suburbanization, the black church has lost much of its primacy in the lives of African Americans. Cleage argues in *What Looks Like Crazy* that the church has also lost its effectiveness because it has maintained a gendered hierarchal structure and the social agenda of past eras, making it irrelevant in the present. She illustrates the ineffectiveness of this structure and agenda by juxtaposing two images of the church in both of her novels and points to a purer spiritual ideal in the process.

In her *Essence* article, "When Preachers Prey," Marcia Dyson claims that over 70 percent of the black church's membership is female, but these women are often excluded from "the central station of power, the pulpit." This denial of power is problematic because it limits women's talents and potential and it restricts them from full participation in the life of the church and their own spiritual lives. Quoting her husband and preacher/scholar, Michael Eric Dyson, Marcia Dyson writes that the church's denial of feminine power results in "ecclesiastical apartheid." She goes on to assert that "Black churches will suffer as long as a double standard prevails for males and females."

Cleage reveals the manner in which the church as an institution suffers through the church presented in *What Looks Like Crazy*, which functions under a very traditional system. Not only does it insist on the male-as-leader construct, and deny the agency of female leaders in the process, but it also proceeds with the notion that the old ways of addressing social issues is the best and only way.

The church, ironically called *New Light* Baptist Church, is led by the Reverend Anderson. He is assisted by his wife, Gerry Anderson, who seems to do all of the legwork. She is the one who makes face-to-face connections with the congregation and monitors the activities of the church, in particular, the activities of the Sewing Circus, a group for the young women at the church that Joyce leads. Several letters addressed to and about Joyce, bearing the pastor's name, reveal that Joyce's leadership of the Sewing Circus is one of great consternation for the religious couple. Her intimate knowledge of the trials and triumphs of the young women of the Sewing Circus makes little difference in her ability to righteously lead them, according to the Reverend and Gerry Anderson. After discovering Joyce's intention to discuss HIV/AIDS with the group, Gerry advises Ava, "You tell Joyce *the Good Reverend* is not happy about this. Your big sister's been a bad girl" (53). She defers the responsibility to her husband although clearly she is the one who has the problem with Joyce. However, the disapproval must come from the man, the "head" of the church, even if it is only in name. For Gerry, the power and authority is resident in the man-as-leader. It's also worth noting that in this instance, Gerry also de-legitimizes Joyce as a leader by infantilizing her, calling her a girl and reprimanding her as a parent does a child.

The Andersons' disapproval of Joyce results because she refuses to adhere to the traditional ways of thinking that has been a part of church culture for generations. Describing what she terms the "politics of respectability," Higginbotham explains how turn-of-the century church women, representing the church as a whole, advocated moral and refined behavior in the struggle against racial oppression: "By claiming respectability through their manners and morals, poor black women boldly asserted the will and agency to define themselves outside the parameters of prevailing racist discourses" (192). These women demanded that their parishioners, male and especially female, be polite, demure, thrifty, clean, and sexually pure. This prescribed behavior was meant to work against the dominant image in white America of the black race as degenerate and the black woman as the cause of such degeneracy.

As a part of an overall campaign of racial uplift that argued black people could be just as civilized as white people and therefore deserved social and political equality, the church's emphasis on the politics of respectability experienced some of the same complexities as racial uplift, namely the internalization of some of the racist ideologies it sought to refute. In fact, "[c]ultural patterns that deviated from those of white middle-class Americans were viewed as retrogressive" (Higginbotham 201). Also, by calling for specific public and private behavior, the church placed blame on the individual who did not or could not adhere to such behavior. In 1904, S. Willie Layten, the president of the Black Baptist Women's Convention, declared that "the tendency of the age is to relaxation and frivolity which will develop loose and morally weak character: our young people are inclining this way"(qtd. in Higginbotham 199). Inherent in this statement was the admonishment of the youth for doing what most young people do, as well as an admonishment of the mothers who were responsible for the morals and characters of their children. Also under attack were jazz music, dance, and women's fashion. While jazz music was thought to be animalistic, young women's fashions were considered too revealing and thus "lower[ed] man's respect for woman and open[ed] her to sexual advances" (Higginbotham 200). The latter placed the responsibility of sexually questionable behavior on women, and overall these critiques of youth culture did not take into account the uniqueness of African American ingenuity nor consider the need for youthful amusement.

The contemporary church has not evolved much past its Victorian predecessor. It is still attempting to adhere to the politics of respectability that blames the individual who does not wholly observe them as well. It also offers these prescribed behaviors as answers to the problems faced by its youth, believing that such complexities can be addressed by maintaining an approach of politeness and demureness. This approach, while somewhat beneficial in a different era, only manages to make the church irrelevant today. New Light Baptist Church in *What Looks Like Crazy* evinces the irrelevancy of this method.

Joyce is working with teenage mothers who must confront abusive boyfriends, sexual pressure and assault as well as HIV/AIDS, among other issues. While Joyce wants to discuss and confront the problems the young women must face, the church's response is to teach them "old-fashioned lessons in how to say *no*. All that other just confuses them. We need to teach them how to cross their legs and keep their dresses down" (Cleage 52). When Joyce rightly understands that the girls are way past those lessons and decides to teach them how to use a condom, Gerry decides that the group no longer serves the "vision" of this particular church. In fact, Joyce is admonished for not returning the group to its original name (the Women's Sewing Circle) and its original purpose (sewing and placing flowers on the altar); clearly, these are activities that are much more in line with traditionally gendered religious behavior. The pastor and his wife are less concerned with the real needs of the younger church members than they are with propriety and some old-fashioned sense of decorum and respectability.

For Cleage, this propriety and decorum fosters a culture of silence that ultimately leads to judgment and complicity. Because the church refuses to address the sexual realities of its members and communities, believing instead that one's sexual complexities can be contained by just saying no, it can more easily judge those who do not say no. As it foregoes the principles of love and acceptance in favor of secular concepts of judgment and prejudice, it absolutely does just that. Ava, who is infected with HIV, is judged and ostracized by Gerry Anderson and her circle. At one point, she even declares Ava to be a harlot. In "Why Can't We Flip the Script?" Ayana Weekly states that society divides individuals with HIV/AIDS into categories of those who are innocent victims and thus deserving of sympathy and those who are culpable in their acquisition of the disease and should thus be ostracized. In this way, HIV "continues to be contextualized as a disease of the other." By adopting this secular view of human worth, the church fails not only to distinguish itself from the world, but it also fails in its mission to provide healing to those who are most in need. Instead of creating an environment that is encouraging and communal so that they can better minister to the people, the church creates an environment of judgment that drives away potentially vital and active members like Ava and Joyce, who leaves the church and takes the Sewing Circus with her.

Cleage explains in her play *Late Bus to Mecca* that "we cannot allow class distinctions, superficial moral judgments and personal prejudices to divide and conquer us" (Turner 105). We become counterproductive to our goals of achievement when we do. She was speaking of a different character in her play who, ironically, is also named Ava Johnson, but she maintains this philosophy in both *What Looks Like Crazy* and *I Wish I had a Red Dress*. In *Red Dress*, she offers a corresponding picture of how successful the church can be when it eliminates judgment and class distinctions. In this novel, time has moved forward and the Andersons are no longer the leaders of New Light. Instead, they have a female pastor, Sister Judith, who is open to the possibilities of change. Her presence in the primary leadership role as a woman immediately reveals a significant change that argues for the potential equality of all people. Furthermore, she prefers not to be called "reverend," which she says carries "the undeniable scent of the patriarchy" (Cleage 24). Instead she is called "Sister" which invokes a sense of respect but also speaks of connection. Through Sister Judith as representative of the church as it should be, Cleage argues for more one-on-one relationships between the leaders and the people. She illustrates the potential for real community change that this approach to ministry has through the friendship of Joyce and Sister Judith. Joyce says, "I kept waiting for her to be more 'ministerial,' whatever that means, but Sister acts just like any other fortyish female except that on Sunday mornings, she stands up in front of everybody and calls the spirits in" (26). Sister is not demanding and dogmatic, insisting that the way it has to be is the way it has always been. She does not lord her power over the parishioners under her. Instead, she encourages Joyce and others to make their own decisions. Cleage believes, as she writes through her protagonist, that learning to make one's own choices and developing the "capacity for critical thinking [is] part of the overall process of becoming a free woman" (*Red Dress* 12). Both women and men must be free in order for the community as a whole to be free.

Shifting Views of Sexuality

In Cleage's novels, she explores the role of spirituality in the black community because it is so essential to our history and survival. But there is another issue that is just as central to survival and that is also becoming destructively paramount: sexuality. As evidenced by the Reverend and Mrs. Anderson, sexuality is a topic the church would rather tacitly ignore, but in doing so, the church becomes complicit in perpetuating sexual oppression. According to Lee Butler in "The Spirit is Willing and the Flesh is, Too" sexuality is viewed by the church as wholly separate from and inferior to spirituality. Consequently, those who are poor in spirit are considered the most worldly and the most sensual (117). The church then regards the body as evil and those who indulge in its pleasures as the evil "other." Such attitudes lead to an adherence to concepts such as the Madonna/Whore dichotomy (the belief that women can either be a pure mother-figure or a promiscuous harlot but not both) which, like the secular community, the church embraces. In this way, it contributes to spiritual repression. By maintaining the separation of the spiritual and the physical, Butler argues that we deny our humanity (117). Furthermore, this separation contributes to sexual oppression. Christian ethics scholar Katie Cannon concurs, stating that "Church traditions keep the vast majority of women living in a dichotomous state of binary opposites, a mind-body split of conflicted fluctuation. And yet ... within each of us, there are reservoirs of erotic power that know no boundaries" (17). Cleage reframes the trope of the separated body and spirit, the whore and the Madonna, however, to reveal the flaw in such thinking and the danger it carries.

On first glance, Ava is the whore. She has slept with so many men that once when she attends an event in Atlanta, she realizes that she has seen every man in the room naked. She has slept with married men, men with girlfriends, and men for whom she had no feelings. As long as her promiscuity is unknown, no one has any judgment for her. Nevertheless, when she contracts HIV and it becomes public knowledge, she is ostracized by the Atlanta community and the religious community in Idlewild. It is like she is the biblical

Woman at the Well. Reflecting on how her standing in the community has changed since her diagnosis, Ava states, "All those folks who had been giving me those African-American Businesswoman of the Year awards and Mentor of the Month citations and invitations to speak from the pulpit on Women's Day stopped calling me" (Cleage 10). Like the woman who functions on the outskirts of her community, people avoid Ava and in running away to San Francisco, she is attempting to avoid them.

Cleage complicates the simple assessment of Ava as whore by problematizing the relationship between Ava's body and her sexuality. Prior to contracting the disease, Ava uses her body capriciously, having sex for her pleasure or even only to avoid hurting her date's feelings at the end of the night. But once she is diagnosed, she must be more thoughtful about her sexual choices. In quiet contemplation she thinks about all the sex she has had in the past; now she worries not only that there won't any more sex in her future, but that she will never get the chance to make love (Cleage 48). She believes she will never be able to truly experience the connection between the spiritual and the sexual as the church sanctions it. Internalizing the community's sexist and gendered ideas about the sexual woman and the diseased as "other," Ava sees herself as punished when she encounters Eddie Jefferson and the possibility of a traditional romantic relationship arises. She is still the same unmarried woman she was prior to the disease, but after contracting HIV, she realizes she must be purposeful in the use of her body, preferring it to be a part of a love pact. Ultimately, through her relationship with Eddie, she is able to view her body not as evil, not as the punished, not even as an entity of bad smells, night sweats and decay, but as a unification of the physical and the spiritual. She sees her body as a site of healing. Butler asserts that healing is "the transformative process necessary for integrating the spirit and the body. Healing restores us to life by restoring us to relationship with God and one another" (118). When Ava is able to dismiss the dichotomy of the spiritually pure versus the sexually perverse, she finds wholeness.

As Ava learns to see herself in a transformative way, readers are also forced to see her in a different light because the world is observable through her eyes. She has learned to re-evaluate her life because of her new understanding of her body, in much the same way Weekly claims that HIV/AIDS has forced homosexuals to reprioritize. Ava finds different measures by which to assess her life and because she is no longer an objectified "other" for readers — who now know her and empathize with her — they are called on to do the same.

Ava is not the only example of the complication involved in oversimplifying and judging women's sexuality. The young women of the Sewing Circus would probably be assessed as whores by the church community and the mainstream society who views them as black baby mamas. This assessment draws on not only the good spirit-evil body split, but it also reveals the internalized racism inherent in the racial uplift of the early twentieth century. Because racist ideologies associated black people with the body, with the black body being seen as an exoticized "other," Butler explains that black people were and are considered inherently sexual and thus evil (116). These teenage mothers are denied the possibility of wholeness by the church because as women — as black women — they have expressed their sexuality outside of the acceptable boundaries of marriage, and their children function as corporeal reminders of their transgressions. In spite of their sexual activity, however, they are still mothers who complicate easy categorization. Also, Cleage provides the reasoning behind their actions, sexual or otherwise, so that they become humanized women for the reader. Bernadette Adams Davis states, "Unlike some images depicted in mainstream media, Cleage is careful to provide balance to the image of Imani's biological mother [a delinquent teenage mother] by showing younger moms who are trying to make a difference in their own lives and the lives of their children" (2). These women step outside the stereotype of the capricious teenage mother who is sexually irresponsible to illustrate multi-dimensional women in the process of development.

A more familiar image of the mother is evident in Joyce's character. She is the suffering martyr who fights selflessly for her children. In her article, "Remembering Mama" Davis says that "Joyce ... creates a safe haven for the baby and becomes an ideal ... mother" (2). Cleage problematizes this image by making it clear that Joyce is not a biological mother. She adopts her daughter and serves as a mother figure for the young women in the Sewing Circus, but she does not have her own children. She further complicates a simple assessment of Joyce as a Madonna figure by sexualizing her. In *What Looks Like Crazy*, Ava remembers as a young girl listening to Joyce and her husband have sex. In *Red Dress*, the novel begins with Joyce experiencing orgasmic pleasure. Also, throughout the book she is involved in a romantic relationship that has strong sexual undertones. Through these examples, Cleage demonstrates that the black mother can be loving and giving, but she can still have a healthy sexuality. By creating Joyce as a complex and imperfect woman, "Cleage shows duality in motherhood: Joyce is able to raise her adopted daughter, but she is also a free woman, one who does not conform to the rules and regulations society has made for her" (Nordmark).

Shifting Our Views of Womanhood and Manhood

The shift in the way society, African Americans in particular, must consider sexuality and spirituality are not limited to only those concepts for

Cleage. These paradigm shifts must necessarily engender a shift in the way femininity and masculinity are considered as well. In order for us to change the way we think about our relationships to God and our relationships to our bodies, both encompassed in our relationships with others, it is imperative to abandon the antiquated ideals of what it means to be a woman and what it means to be a man. The expectations of womanhood and manhood are currently chained to a past of hierarchy, power and dominance, but this is no longer productive for black people, if it ever was. In her *Obsidian III* interview with Shelia Smith McKoy, Cleage explains how and why this shift is vital: "We're both making revolution so you got to cook too. It's not like we're both going to make revolution then we're going to go home to the traditional roles that you're thinking about, we're going to make revolution in here just like we're making revolution out there" (17). For Cleage, the fight for black freedom is important, but equally as important is the fight for free womanhood and to bring that about there must be a revolution in the way we view the roles for men and women. According to Tikenya Foster-Singletary, women and men must participate in this revolution in order to ensure the "collective wellness of African Americans" (50).

Cleage encourages the reshaping of womanhood by revealing the expectations that are currently in place within society and then offering a new idea (l) that she terms "Free Womanhood." While the expectations for women in general have included sexual purity and submissiveness to male authority, black women have had to walk a fine line between these expectations and those that have grown out of being a member of a racially oppressed group. They have existed in somewhat schizophrenic states of having to be strong and aggressive to fight for themselves and their families, while at the same time being submissive and silent to be deemed appropriately womanly. They have had to exercise sexual restraint in the face of unrelenting characterizations of looseness and promiscuity for the good of the race and to the detriment of their true selves. But because what was often given primacy in the community as a whole was the freedom of the black race (many scholars, including Cleage, would argue this often meant black men), black women accepted this tight wire walk of expectations and lived according to it. This existence in which others were placed before the black woman, however, led to an experience of neglect, pain and unproductive silence. In "the Other Facts of Life," Cleage asserts that women "are under siege, incredibly vulnerable, totally unprepared and too busy denying the truth to collectively figure out what to do about it" (1).

Nikki Solomon and Shelia Lattimore, both members of the Sewing Circus in *Red Dress*, further illustrate the dangers of neglect and silence. At 19 years old, Nikki feels her only viable career option is to be a stripper, despite the objectifying nature of the work and its threat of danger. However, her job is the least of her troubles. Since the age of 14, she has been sexually involved with Junior Lattimore, who is described as four years her senior and the craziest of a family of volatile brothers. Throughout the novel, Nikki is in an on-again/off-again relationship with Junior in which he threatens her, harasses her, physically assaults her, and ultimately violently attacks the people in her inner circle. In addition to the pass Nikki's consistent re-admittance of Junior into her life provides, when Joyce confronts Nikki's mother with his abuse of her daughter she dismisses the claim, saying, "They might have a little tussle every now and then like everybody else, but he ain't never *ripped her up* or nothin' like that" (Cleage 116). In fact, when Junior comes to Nikki's mother's home and hits Nikki, her mother leaves the room and turns up the sound on the television. Nikki explains, "She wadn't gonna help me or call anybody to help me, so she didn't want to know what he was doin' to me" (Cleage 303). Nikki's situation illustrates the denial that exists surrounding women's pain. It is telling that her own mother refuses to stop it or even acknowledge that it is happening. She is representative of the women in society who should be fighting for the freedom and peaceful existence of all women, everyone's daughters, but who are instead too much in denial about the truth that the people they are "struggling against are the people that [they are] sleeping with" (Smith McKoy14).

While Nikki's situation illustrates the silence from other women that tacitly permits male violence to characterize female existence, Shelia's situation reveals how such violence silences the women themselves. Shelia is Junior's sister and therefore much closer to his and his brothers' volatility. The Lattimores (including the mother) regard her as their personal servant; they expect docility from her and physically assault her when they are angry. Although she adamantly denies it, it is even rumored that her youngest son has been fathered by her eldest brother. This continued abuse causes Shelia to become so frightened and miserable that she is incapable of taking action to move out of the house with them or even speaking up for herself. Her silence imprisons her. However, she maintains this silence about her brothers' abuse toward her in general, and specifically Junior's abuse toward Nikki and her friends, out of loyalty to her family. Like many black women, Shelia is guided by the notion that one must remain loyal to family against perceived attacks by the outside world, even if family is the one attacking the woman. Living within a white male-dominated society, black women have often felt it their responsibility to the race to defend black men against attacks by mainstream society. Unfortunately, sometimes this defense includes maintaining silence about situations that are destructive to black women's psyche and person. In "What's in a Name? Womanism, Black Feminism and Beyond," Patricia Hill Collins explains that family rhetoric is often used to describe the black race and it encompasses the expectations and rules attendant with the family unit. She asserts that "[w]ithin African-American communities, one such rule is that black women will support black men, no matter what" (Collins 132). Cleage is calling for an end to women's silence and the perspective that it is disloyal to family to speak out against male violence. As Joyce tells Shelia when she finally speaks out, "You did the right thing.... He's your brother, but Tee's your sister, remember?" (Cleage 271). Sheila has a responsibility to the whole family and allowing the oppression of one member, even herself, in favor of another offending member abdicates the responsibility to the whole.

In finding her voice, the black woman is working toward what Cleage calls Free Womanhood. According to Aisha Francis, Free Womanhood will bring about "communal redemption and individual transformation" (32). By establishing specific goals aimed toward living a liberated life, the concept of Free Womanhood creates a new way of viewing womanhood that will benefit women as well as the community. Because it is so central to Cleage's call for a paradigm shift, she includes the idea of Free Womanhood in both *What Looks Like Crazy* and *Red Dress*. Joyce's statement of purpose in the mission statement for The Sewing Circus articulates this concept (Cleage, *Crazy*, 157). It declares that, in order to be a free woman, one must be able to think for herself, be honest with herself and others, and be willing to chart her own course in life. In the list of specific goals Cleage (through Joyce) writes that a woman should have basic literacy, math and computer skills; she should know how to take care of herself and her child through self-defense, first aid skills, prenatal and childhood development care, and preparing nutritious food; and she should be physically, economically and spiritually fit. While these goals seem basic, they are the building blocks for establishing an independence that will allow a woman to depend on herself for her livelihood and survival. According to Francis, these goals will also help "free women ... find a way out of anger into action" (40). Because she is not beholden to a man or misguided dogma, the free woman is able to fight injustice, when it wears the mantle of racism *and* when it wears the mantle of sexism.

Cleage is not only calling for women to fight sexism, but she is also demanding it of men. The old standard of allowing "boys to be boys" which condones violence, sexual abuse, and dominance is no longer acceptable. Although Cleage is much more of a black feminist than she is an Africana womanist, her discussion of black men's roles in the struggle for a better community overlaps with Clenora Hudson-Weems' agenda of the Africana womanist. Like Cleage's characters, the Africana womanist is a self-namer, a self-definer, and she is family centered. She believes in the genuine sisterhood of women and recognizes a higher spiritual power in her life. She also understands that the struggle for liberation, both racial and gender, must be in concert with males and not exclusive of them. It is this last point of overlap that is most significant in this discussion. Hudson-Weems contends that the white feminist sees her struggle as "independent of and oftentimes adverse to male participation, [but] the Africana womanist invites her male counterpart into her struggle for liberation and parity in society...." (61). Cleage invites positive male participation into the struggle, insisting upon it, in fact. She is unwilling to dismiss men because she sees them as the enemy. Certainly, there are men whose behavior is hostile toward women, but she also acknowledges that there are men who are good and men who can be instrumental in the fight for liberation. However, before any real progress can be made, there must be a paradigm shift. She argues through her positive male characters that this new paradigm for masculinity must be established, one that includes strength of character, courage and a love for black women.

The expectations of black men, like those for black women, have been shaped by living in an oppressed society. Definitions of masculinity have included domination and oppression; for the black man the assertion of such traits has meant defining one's self as a man in the face of a racist system that seeks to emasculate and dehumanize him. Within historical images and contemporary media, black men have been portrayed as hyper masculine at best and criminal, at worst. In *What Looks Like Crazy*, Ava's love interest, Eddie, is both. In high school he had been "Wild Eddie"—fighting, drinking, smoking marijuana, making babies. After high school he was a soldier in the Vietnam war, sold drugs, killed someone and went to prison for ten years. As a black man, many in the mainstream society (and even some in the black community) would not expect anything different from Eddie. They would expect him to be like Gerry Anderson's grandson Tyrone and his friend Frank who are vicious black thugs. They would expect him to be like Junior Lattimore and his brothers. Each of these men is violent and performs sexual violence toward women.

While Eddie may seem to be illustrative of the stereotype, he is actually an example of new manhood. During his stay in prison, Eddie experiences a transformation. He becomes more in tuned with the spiritual which allows for him to gain a stronger sense of security (not arrogance) about himself. This self-confidence makes room for recognizing the humanity and equality of women. He understands that "a progressive vision of manhood and masculinity transgresses the boundaries of patriarchy" (Lemons 81). As a man entrenched in patriarchal control, Eddie would not be able to engage in a loving relationship with a financially and sexually independent woman. Certainly, he would be unable to wholly love a woman with HIV — a relationship that necessarily requires patience, nurturing, sacrifice and reciprocity.

Cleage further demonstrates that the old ideas of masculinity can be changed in *Red Dress*. Her two most positive characters, Nate Anderson and Bill, are not without their sexist thoughts. However, through constant discussions and debates on the topic of women's liberation, they struggle to come to a more enlightened space. Although "male supremacy and white supremacy function interconnectedly to devalue Black womanhood," many black men fail to recognize the connection, choosing instead to see only the ways in which racism affects the black community (Lemons 86). Through Nate and Bill, Cleage is speaking to black men, challenging them to recognize the damaging effects of racism and sexism and their role in the latter, especially when they deny it or use the former "as an excuse for the subjugation, exploitation or sexual and/or physical abuse of women" (Lemons 84). By the end of the novel, Nate, who mentors a small group of teenage boys, has come to terms with the sexist behavior of black men. He tells Joyce he gave his mentees, "a ten-minute educational diatribe on the crushing burden of sexist oppression ... [and] the role of all men in that shameful patriarchy" (Cleage, *Red Dress* 260). Bill, a poet, has even created with his all-male poetry class a list of ten goals for Free Manhood. Among those goals are: no hitting women and kids, no raping, be a father to the baby you make, and bring the love. This list and Nate's "diatribe" both point to the understanding that these men have of their role in the struggle for women's liberation and ultimately, the liberation of the community. They seem to understand, as Gary Lemons understands, that "We are sorely in need of an emancipatory vision of liberation that honors our past struggles — struggles in which black women and men fought together against race and gender oppression" (72). Without a transformative vision of masculinity, however, this understanding would not be possible and the black community would experience "racial genocide" (Lemons 87).

It is never easy to confront our own shortcomings and certainly not easy to confront them in the public eye. But that is just what Pearl Cleage is calling on her readers and the Black community to do. We can no longer accept life as it has always been; we can no longer remain silent about our individual and collective pains. We must change our perception of the problems so that we can have newer, fresher images that will allow us to envision newer, more effective solutions. In this way, "We build our temples for tomorrow, strong as we know how, and we stand on top of the mountain, free within ourselves" (Hughes 1271).

Works Cited

Butler, Lee. "The Spirit Is Willing and the Flesh is Too: Living Whole and Holy Lives Through Integrating Spirituality and Sexuality." *Loving the Body: Black Religious Studies and the Erotic*. Eds. Anthony B. Pinn and Dwight N. Hopkins. New York: Palgrave Macmillan, 2004. Print.

Cannon, Katie G. "Sexing Black Women: Liberation from the Prisonhouse of Anatomical Authority." *Loving the Body: Black Religious Studies and the Erotic.* Eds. Anthony B. Pinn and Dwight N. Hopkins. New York: Palgrave Macmillan, 2004. Print.
Carroll, Rebecca. *I Know What the Red Clay Looks Like.* New York: Carol Southern, 1994. Print.
Cleage, Pearl. *I Wish I Had a Red Dress.* New York: HarperCollins, 2001. Print.
_____. "The Other Facts of Life." *Deals with the Devil and Other Reasons to Riot.* New York: Ballantine, 1987. Print.
_____. *What Looks Like Crazy on an Ordinary Day.* New York: Avon, 1997. Print.
Collins, Patricia Hill. "What's in a Name? Womanism, Black Feminism and Beyond." *Race, Identity, and Citizenship.* Eds. Rodolfo D. Torres, Louis F. Miron, and Jonathan Xavier Inda. Malden, MA: Wiley-Blackwell, 1999. Print.
Davis, Bernadette Adams. "Remembering Mama: Images of Mothers, Good, Bad, Real or Fictive Abound in Our Literary Tradition." *Black Issues Book Review* 7.3 (May/June 2005): 1–3. Print.
Dyson, Marcia L. "When Preachers Prey." Essence 29.1 (May 1998): 120ff. Web.
Foster-Singletary, Tikenya. "A Contemporary Vision of Female/Male Romantic Love: Pearl Cleage's *What Looks Like Crazy on an Ordinary Day.*" *Obsidian* 10.1 (2009): 50–67. Print.
Francis, Aisha. "In Search of Free Womanhood: Black Conduct Literature, Contemporary Cultural Production, and Pearl Cleage." *Obsidian* 10.1 (2009): 32–49. Print.
Higginbotham, Evelyn Brooks. *Righteous Discontent: The women's movement in the Black Baptist Church, 1880–1920.* Cambridge: Harvard University Press, 1993. Print.
Hudson-Weems, Clenora. *Africana Womanism: Reclaiming Ourselves.* Troy, MI: Bedford, 1993. Print.
Hughes, Langston. "The Negro Artist and the Racial Mountain." *The Norton Anthology of African American Literature.* Eds. Henry Louis Gates and Nellie Y. McKay. New York: W.W. Norton, 1997. Print.
Lemons, Gary L. "When and Where [We] Enter: In Search of a Feminist Forefather — Reclaiming the Womanist Legacy of W.E.B. DuBois." *Traps: African American Men on Gender and Sexuality.* Eds. Rudolph P. Byrd and Beverly Guy-Sheftall. Bloomington: Indiana University Press, 2001. Print.
McKoy, Sheila Smith. "A Conversation with Pearl Cleage." *Obsidian* 10.1 (2009): 9–31. Print.
Nordmark, Chris, Renata Pardo, Mai Yia Her, Jessi Miller, and Jenny Falor. "Pearl Cleage." *Voices from the Gap. University of Minnesota.* Web. September 27, 2011.
Turner, Beth. "The Feminist/Womanist Vision of Pearl Cleage." *Contemporary African American Women Playwrights: A Casebook.* Ed. Philip C. Kolin. London: Routledge, 2007. Print.
Weekly, Ayana. "Why Can't We Flip the Script: The Politics of Respectability in Pearl Cleage's *What Looks Like Crazy on an Ordinary Day.*" *Michigan Feminist Studies* 21.1 (Fall 2007–Spring 2008): n. p. September 19, 2011. Web.

Critical Thinking Is for Everyone: Social Work as the Praxis of Communal Love in *I Wish I Had a Red Dress*

AISHA FRANCIS

This title of this essay recalls bell hooks' now canonical text, *Feminism is for Everybody* (2000), which maintains that any empowering idea must be translated and translatable to the masses in order for it to be truly transformational. As is her practice with every novel, in her second published fictional manuscript in *I Wish I Had a Red Dress* (2001), Pearl Cleage interrogates a broader theme related to a significant contemporary social or political problem with the intent of broadcasting the issue and potential avenues of resolution to the masses. Among the weighty topics considered in Cleage's novels are: the HIV/AIDS epidemic among young black women, modern day human trafficking, the impact of gentrification on inner city neighborhoods, and brothers on the "down-low."[1] The central issue of *Red Dress* is how to mend the fraying social fabric that African American communities are facing under pressure from a confluence of ills including teen pregnancy, misogyny and domestic violence, drug and alcohol abuse, and chronic poverty, all of which are contributing to a dismal outlook for the youth of Idlewild, Michigan, the small town in which the novel takes place.

Cleage adroitly presents *Red Dress* as a collective teaching moment for her audience at large. Cleage shifted from playwriting and essays to crafting novels because there was a story that she longed to read that hadn't yet been told. Similarly, bell hooks wrote *Feminism is for Everybody* because she "spent more than 20 year longing for" it though she "kept waiting for it to appear, and it did not" (ix). In so doing, her motivation echoes that of Toni Morrison who also proclaimed the need to fill a perceived void as the reason she took pen to paper to craft *The Bluest Eye*. Drawing a connection between hooks and Cleage, calls attention to the intense demand there was and still is for understandable writings that consider the intersection of gender, race and class. And so hooks laments that her long held desire for such a book on feminism, "not a long book; not a thick book with hard to understand jargon and academic language, but a straightforward and clear book — easy to read without being simplistic" (viii). Cleage places a similar premium on transparency and translation. This essay's purpose is to interrogate the practical value of applying a litmus test of accessibility to society's most complex ideas.

Critical Thinking on the Homefront

The setting of Idlewild, Michigan, is an analog for Anywhere, USA. Idlewild is an all-black, rural town with big city problems common in many urban and rural areas of the country. By locating the story here, Cleage aligns her tale with working poor black America. There's no denying that profoundly challenging social outcomes are plaguing the black community such as the high rates of single motherhood, which deeply impacts the economic status of black families. In fact, households headed by single mothers regardless of race make up the majority of the poor in the United States. In one bright spot, the rate of teen pregnancy among African Americans actually declined by 45 percent between 1990 and 2005.[2] Yet, African American girls still have higher rates of teen pregnancy than any other demographic group in this country. Cleage's early novels peel back the layers behind statistics such as these and can help audiences consider how the complexities of being young, black, and poor in America play out against the backdrop of contemporaneity. The pressures and depression the young women of Idlewild face by not having the resources or resilience to support themselves and raise their children in what amounts to an under resourced and isolated community is a phenomenon that is occurring all too frequently throughout the United States.

First appearing in Cleage's debut novel, *What Looks Like Crazy on an Ordinary Day*, Idlewild is a historically significant town. The fact that Idlewild was once hailed as a premier resort town for the black elite, with the likes of W.E.B. DuBois owning land there in the first half of the twentieth century, demonstrates just how much the culture and social fabric of the town have devolved in the post–civil rights era.[3] The city is reimagined in Cleage novels as a small place that retains an all-black demography and idyllic possibilities though it is now reeling from big city problems, mainly extreme poverty along with the societal desperation that accompanies it and hapless, misdirected youth who are retreating into lives of violence, abuse and illicit activities.

As someone who grew up in Detroit and spent occasional time in Idlewild, the familiar town setting appealed to Cleage as the ideal locale for her early novels primarily because it was small enough to wrap her mind around.[4] Initially, the bustling and ever popular Atlanta backdrop of Cleage's subsequent West End novel series was too overwhelming for the burgeoning novelist to consider. Cleage is fiercely invested in the possibility and promise of healthy — but not perfect — black communities, which serve as the setting for every fictional work and play in Cleage's corpus. Places like Idlewild, Michigan; Nicodemus, Kansas; and the West End neighborhood of Atlanta, Georgia, are important statements of solidarity and community building for this child of the 1960s who grew up and has always lived in majority black towns.

By locating her first two novels in a small town, Cleage also leaves room for the social problems that plague Idlewild to be tackled and overcome plausibly without the reader succumbing to the fatalist conclusion that nothing can be done to improve the social fabric of black communities. With Cleage, redemption seems manageable and possible, which saves Idlewild from seeming too much like a fantastic utopian vision to inspire the optimism that the author seeks to encourage. Even when Cleage later tackles Atlanta, she does so from the perspective of an all-black neighborhood that is similar to Idlewild, which again allows Cleage to focus on forces at work to undermine black communities within a post-modern, urban landscape.[5]

However, Idlewild doesn't figure into *I Wish I Had a Red Dress* as a character so much as it is a canvas upon which Cleage paints a picture centered on a community of progressive, well-educated and rooted African-American adults who are bound and determined to save the youth of their town. At the center of this town are two black couples, Sister Judith and Bill, who are married, and Joyce and Nate, who are introduced early on in the plot and function more and more like a pair as the story progresses. All of the primary adult characters have professions connected to youth development. And collectively, they are piecing together a patchwork of resources and alternative images of life for their young charges to draw from and be inspired by. Though the only one among this quartet who is actually a person of the cloth is Sister Judith, they each have a ministry or "calling" to reach out to younger generations through community work. Sister Judith is a full-time pastor in one of Idlewild's churches; Bill is a poet who runs a young men's group using his own poetry and that of others as a starting point for intervention with the goal of helping the participants carve more meaning out of their lives. Joyce is a former teacher turned social worker and her theory of implementation, described later, forms the backbone of this essay. Joyce's partner, Nate, is a recent divorcée and a transplant to Idlewild, whose new job is as the principal of Idlewild's public high school.

Red Dress opens with a manifesto from protagonist, Joyce Mitchell, who offers her personal and professional mission statement as her first gift to the reader. In so doing, the reader learns that Joyce's motivation for leaving the teaching profession to become a social worker stems from the discord she had long observed among the teen mothers in Idlewild, Michigan. While these young women comprised a large number of the high school students when she was teaching, for years Joyce glossed over the details of their lives. When she actually began to "see" their inept efforts at mothering, lack of self-respect, and inability to articulate anything beyond the most basic and self-centered thoughts, Joyce pursues a mid-career change to social work in search of "a better way to communicate with these girls" (Cleage 5). Her mission is to impart the girls in her small town with practical life skills and clearer pathways to options for the future, which they lack and sorely need. Since she is a womanist in vision and application, Cleage's deeming of these teen moms as "girls" instead of young women calls attention to their underdevelopment and immaturity despite the fact that they are engaged in the extremely adult task of parenting.

In a tradition that is so familiar in African American communities that it is replicated in African American cultural production, these girls and their children make up a non-traditional extended family for Joyce.[6] In addition, Joyce is a widow whose husband died in a tragic fishing accident years before the novel opens. She and her sister, Ava, who moved to Idlewild from Atlanta, effectively share custody of a toddler, Imani, who Ava and her husband, Eddie, adopted. Suffice it to say that Joyce's caring heart and the immense need that exists in her community take up tremendous room in her life. The women she works with comprise a wide circle of surrogate daughters. And between co-raising Imani and founding the Albert B. Mitchell Sewing Circus and Community Truth Center, a non-profit social service group that assists the teen moms she once taught, Joyce's life is overflowing with responsibility.

The Community as a Classroom

Considering the environment in which the typical teenager lived in the early to mid–1990s, a time frame similar to that in which *Red Dress* is set, it is not surprising that Joyce finds the student/teacher binary an impotent and ineffective modality for transforming the lives of her students. Furthermore, she is not even equipping them with the literacy, numeracy and comprehension skills they need to function in life as educated young adults. In her series foreword to the Greenwood Press "Using Literature to Help Troubled Teenagers Series," Joan Kaywell presents a plethora of nationally compiled data points and statistics overlaid onto a typical twelfth grade classroom of 30 students, and makes the following conclusions of these average students:

> eight to 15 are being raised by a single parent, six are in poverty, eight to ten are being raised in a families with an alcoholic, four have experienced some form of family violence, eight of the female and five of the male students have been sexually violated ... 27 have used alcohol, 18 have used marijuana and 12 have used other dangerous drugs. Twenty-two have had sexual intercourse and 12 used no protection. Three students are gay, 8 will drop out of school and 6 of that 8 will become criminals.[7]

Against this dismal backdrop, Joyce finds herself standing in front of a classroom of black public high school students in Idlewild trying to teach an E. E. Cummings poem, which she realizes is an absolutely useless exercise. Dismayed and frustrated, yet also self-reflexive and empowered, Joyce changes careers expressly to have greater impact on the teen moms in her midst, whose messy lives and inability to navigate parenthood while also trying to raise themselves distressed Joyce. Her choice and her intentions are clear: "I used to be a teacher. Then one day I looked around and realized that what I was teaching and the way I was teaching it was completely irrelevant to my students' real lives" (4). Joyce harnesses her own agency so as not to stay mired in the futility of her work. She adjusts her life's calling to find a way to reach and connect with the girls from her community who had captured her attention.

Confronted with a classroom of unprepared students who are resistant to traditional teaching methods to which the vast majority of American public schools subscribe, Joyce is rendered ineffective and the students remain disengaged. Ultimately, Joyce is faced with the reality that teaching E. E. Cummings poems won't prevent teen pregnancy. Among others, education reform activist Jonathan Kozol has spent his career bringing the disparities of public school education into clearer focus. Most recently, he has outlined the negative repercussions of what he calls "the restoration of apartheid" in American education. As noted in Kozol's *The Shame of the Nation*, Michigan public schools are among the most segregated in the country (18).[8] One can imagine that in response to the challenges of an inflexible pedagogy and the re-segregation of public schools, Joyce turns to social work as an opportunity to become a community educator. In the tradition of both Paulo Freire and bell hooks, Joyce positions informal or popular education as a tool for empowerment within her community and believes that meeting people where they are leads to transformation.⁹ A transformative practice of teaching is what Joyce is missing from the classroom and what she strikes out to implement through social work.

In heeding the call to do something more influential with her life, Joyce recalls the tradition of African American club women who dedicated their lives to "lifting as they climb."[10] Just as the teen moms adrift in Idlewild draw Joyce's attention, some of the earliest work of the formidable black women's club movement involved opening homes for single black women and unwed mothers. A proliferation of boarding homes, day cares, and YWCAs commonly named after Phyllis Wheatley sprung up across the nation at the turn of the twentieth century to offer a safe haven for some of the most vulnerable members of black communities. They provided room and board, child care, parenting skills, and other services at a time when adherence to the politics of respectability often made it particularly difficult for a woman to retain familial ties after bringing a child to term outside of the confines of marriage.[11] What's striking is that a century later, the need for these social services has not diminished in black communities. In fact, some might argue that the demand has only grown stronger. So much so that, in *Red Dress*, the aforementioned direct services are casually referred to as "the usual assistance—jobs counseling, GED classes, day care" (11). If the need for external programs to offer these basics is pedestrian, there are two elements of The Sewing Circus that are not: (1) the Theory of Change is based on the concept of Free Womanhood and (2) the process of eliciting conversation and fostering critical thinking through which Free Womanhood is achieved.

Free Womanhood is the theory that underlies The Sewing Circus, but what are the methods applied to bring it to life in a way that moves and transforms teen moms who are at-risk of repeating cycles that led to their own early pregnancies? The ideology of Free Womanhood has been explored fully in a previous article, and this paper builds on that explication of this theory to uncover the practical tenets Cleage applies to teach critical thinking.[12] Certainly, Cleage employs didactic methods to instruct a group of people who truly need to start with the basics. While theoretical notions of pedagogy underlie Joyce's methods, ultimately, she is moved by her connection to humanity and not by strict adherence to one particular theology or conceptual approach. The fluidity of her methods mirrors the complexity of her program participants' lives. Still, it is useful to trace the pedagogical approaches presented in the novel in order to gauge the success and transformative power of these tenets. Joyce is inspired by the change in these girls' lives and that their inch-by-inch progress bolsters her level of commitment to the cause. Cleage's task is to engender these troubled young women with enough promise that the readers also want to believe in their redemptive possibility.

Whether they know it or not, these women are desperate for some semblance of how to deconstruct the triple threat of racism/classism/sexism that they face every day. In Joyce's words, "They need a way of decoding the world at least as much as they need basic computer skills" (12). Joyce holds herself accountable for demonstrating and teaching the Sewing Circus members empowering life skills and strategies that lie behind Free Womanhood. While in some danger in over reliance on prescriptive didacticism, these particular young women suffer more from lack of guidance about their options in life. A lack of information can be just as damaging as the confining pressure of an environment that is overly protective. But if reaching them in a traditional classroom setting won't work, what will?

Entire non-profit and for-profit industries have arisen to offer solutions to this conundrum and to a closely related one in *Red Dress*, which is "solve" the problem of the troubled teen girl. The collective failure for girls of color to thrive has become a canary in the coalmine of American culture. In terms of the non-profit world, there are organizations like the Sewing Circus that attempt to bridge the gap between what African American girls are missing in their home lives and the structure they need to successfully navigate the world and become self-supporting. In the for-profit sense, the prison industrial complex has expanded and placed commercial value on the process of detaining teens so much so that African American girls are now the fastest growing population of new inmates in both the juvenile detention and adult prison system (Harris-Perry 46).

Cleage presents several different approaches for building young women's critical thinking skills so that they can see options other than those that are right in front of them and thereby begin to make (or at least consider) different choices for themselves. The first is to focus on the future. The social work that Joyce practices is grounded in using popular culture to catapult The Sewing Circus members into conversations about the future, long-term outcomes, and the consequences of their decisions. By getting these young women to believe in their future and have a modicum of self-respect, Joyce hopes this will translate into a focus on the future even as they are piecing together their lives in the here and now. While the reader is unclear what the final outcome is of the life choices that the women of the Sewing Circus made, there is evidence that some of them are shifting to approaches that demonstrate some concern for future consequences.

Secondly, Cleage employs popular culture as primary texts. Accordingly, the curriculum for Free Womanhood is comprised of popular and classic films, poetry, and the *New York Times*. The premise is that E. E. Cummings won't work, but explicating the *New York Times* and digesting Bill's poems will because they are accessible and relevant in a way that Cummings' work is not. Bill is there in the classroom to help translate his poems. He works with his young men's writing group — an analog to The Sewing Circus — trying to get young men to focus on positive expressions of their emotions, using his own creative writing as Exhibit A for what's possible. Assigning literature that doesn't reflect the experiences of students is reminiscent of the British imperialist practices of the 1900s through early 1960s in which school children in conquered Caribbean were required to memorize poems from traditional English authors extolling the virtues of daffodils and winter snow — cultural references that had little to no resonance for inhabitants of tropical islands.

In encouraging The Sewing Circus members to read the national paper of record, Joyce is equipping them to recognize broader interpretations of the world around them. In her own words, Joyce relies on a curriculum of everyday use in which she "guides" discussions in ways that help young women "draw useful conclusions" while also "giving them the pleasure that comes with a free exchange of ideas" (141). Since storytelling conveys important national values, reading the Sunday *New York Times* is posited as a key stepping stone towards media literacy. Joyce asserts the importance of being able to interpret and anticipate how others may view young black women, like Sewing Circus members, Tee and Nik — undereducated teen moms who are struggling to build a secure future for themselves and their families. By paying attention to the types of stories reported, they can begin to pinpoint what is valued most in U.S. culture. Teaching approaches to critical interpretation of mainstream media is one part of the equation.

The second half of the equation is exposing the Sewing Circus to the art of meaningful casual conversation and civil discussion with those of the opposite sex, their peers, and their elders. Straying from gossip and tacking toward substance can be a challenge for young women who have never been taught to recognize that their ideas have merit and weight. These skills can only be borne out with practice, so the Sewing Circus initiates substantive discussions through movie marathons that later become small fund-raisers and offer a testing ground for oral idea exchange, which the members sorely need. While Joyce has a heavy hand in the Sewing Circus' encouraged reading assignments, the films are chosen by the girls with the exception of some Dorothy Dandridge features that Joyce suggests for the sake of exposure. The dozen or more films named in the novel have one commonality — they feature African American casts. They include classics starring Dorothy Dandridge, or films like *Eve's Bayou*, *The Best Man*, and *Set it Off*, which have become modern day favorites destined to become new classics. Through regular film screenings and post-discussions, the women not only learn the art of conversation, but they learn identify and compare positive African American role models who counter the images of the community in which they live and love.

Of all of the reels that Sewing Circus takes in as part of their informal film studies course, movies starring Denzel Washington consistently take center stage. Denzel is placed on a pedestal for his behavior and for the discipline with which he chooses his characters. Tee and others have come to expect and relish that in each role, "he act [sic] like a man *'spose* to act. He take care of his family. He look out for his friends. He always got a job and he ain't never hit no woman or abused no kid" (105). Yet, there is a certain sadness in this representation. It is troubling that the only way for the Sewing Circus to gain perspective and a lasting illumination about the markers of a respectful man is through film. Ultimately the underlying question "What does a good man look like?" is partially answered through images of Denzel. For Cleage this instructive use of cultural production is reflexive since it is written into the plot of *Red Dress*, which in and of itself is loaded with viable life lessons.

The idea of employing cultural production as a tool of advancement is controversial in and of itself and recalls the familiar debate concerning the value of practicing "Art for Art's Sake." Within the context of African American literature, Alain Locke, Langston Hughes, and W.E.B. DuBois, all weighed in significantly on this issue. DuBois' now well known opinion in support of art as propaganda, first presented in the October 1926 issue of *The Crisis*, is a fitting segue into Cleage's use of art throughout her career: "Thus all Art is propaganda and ever must be, despite the wailing of the purists. I stand in utter shamelessness and say that whatever art I have for writing has been used always for propaganda for gaining the right of black folk to love and enjoy" (DuBois 1000). Cleage cares tremendously about the relationship between the fiction she writes and the real world blackness that she and her readers experience. The Sewing Circus members are learning to find meaning in cultural production whether or not there was an intended practical application of the creative work.

By paying attention to the types of stories reported, they can begin to appreciate what behaviors and assumptions are valued in U.S. culture. Though most of them don't heed Joyce's suggestion, those who do find that reading the *Times* exposes them to a world outside of Idlewild. Joyce's encouragement is grounded in the hope that they develop some facility with thinking through what's possible instead of focusing solely on what is. This shift from here and now thinking to focus on the future is a mainstay of the social worker aesthetic. The underprivileged teen moms who participate in the Sewing Circus have learned to survive by carefully calibrating the best response to the hot-headed and harsh nature of the men, boys, and embattled mothers. Living in the moment and walking on egg shells are some of the most critical life-skills that hold value in the abusive environments in which they live. According to the National Council on Crime and Delinquency, black girls in low-income communities often lack a sense of safety and attachment in their own homes and neighborhoods (Wordes and Nunez 2002). In shedding light on the stress and fragility entailed in living life in this type of environment, Cleage bridges the gap between the real and the imagined dangers that young black women face in their own communities, where one would hope and expect that they should experience the most security. And Cleage does it in such a way that the audience is inclined to see in Tee, not a stereotype, but a specific rendering of one young single mom's difficult circumstances rearing her child and seeking love from people who don't have it to give because they have not yet learned to love themselves.

Chief among Joyce's approaches is modeling the practices she asks the Sewing Circus to implement. In service to walking in truth and fully embodying Free Womanhood, (and against the conventional wisdom of her grant writing course instructor) Joyce boldly includes an outline of "The 10 Things Every Free Woman Should Know" in a major grant proposal being presented to the state legislature. The components of Free Womanhood prove far too radical for the Michigan senators in charge of the public funding for which The Circus has applied. In retrospect, Joyce admits that she shared the code with her stodgy white male audience while "secure in [her] delusion" that privileging truth and transparency would shield her and the young women of the Sewing Circus from the trappings of stereotypical misrecognition (17). Forging ahead, she presents the mission and intent of the Sewing Circus to a panel of state legislators who have the power to decide whether or not to grant state funding to the social service program to which Joyce has dedicated her life. These government officials who hold the purse strings of funding for community service programs repay Joyce's honesty with denigration.

Not only does the Sewing Circle grant proposal fall prey to negative stereotypes of black women who are also teen moms, but the lawmakers are also subsumed with stereotypes of the women's liberation movement in general. As one senator sneers to another, "I have it on good authority that Mrs. Mitchell here is something of a *women's libber*," as if women's lib were a four-letter word. But, unlike many who might have been wary of showing their anger and indignation of being disrespected by lawmakers who conclude, "I can't see much point in spending people's hard-earned money giving sex education to unwed mothers" (Cleage 19). This condescending statement, and a few others, illicit snickers and smirks from the committee working to determine the grant recipients. This painful scene demonstrates that operating within a context of Free Womanhood can prove difficult, when the construct is deemed irrelevant by powers that be. Joyce briefly endures this atmosphere of condescension, degradation and blatant bias, but in so doing she experiences something all too familiar in the political sphere.

In the political context, it has traditionally proven very difficult to persuade lawmakers and opinion leaders to see beyond the stereotypical whore/mammy/Sapphire as possible options for the young women who are benefiting from Joyce's work. Despite knowing this, Joyce fiercely rejects the notion that there is too much to lose by challenging men with political power. She not only challenges their line of questioning, much to the chagrin of the men in charge, but she ultimately withdraws the funding application after confronting the senator whose comments were the most egregious. In *Sister Citizen*, Melissa Harris-Perry offers a historical reading of the myth of the Sapphire that provides a helpful interpretation of the politics and history at play in the state house scene that Cleage constructs. Harris-Perry concludes, "The angry black woman stereotype hamstrings sisters who find that they cannot forcefully and convincingly advocate their own interests in the public sphere" (95–96). Yet, anger can also be used effectively to protest affronts. This righteous indignation is precisely what Joyce demonstrates when she realizes that her life's work has been sacrificed to potentially gain a few votes in an election year.[13] The power struggle is draining, and at least in the short-run, the Sewing Circus will be underfunded. However, justice as a virtue holds little meaning until it is put in practice. In some ways, pulling the plug on the proposal is brave; in other ways, it's a move that represents the lesser of two evils, since the grassroots organization is dependent on philanthropy.

Joyce fully understands the stereotypes at play during the state capital presentation. She realizes that the senators believe that the Sewing Circus members "are a bunch of wild women" who do not deserve Michigan taxpayers support. However, Joyce carries on with the knowledge that she's "seen the changes these girls can make once they have a working definition of what it means to be a *free woman*" (7). With the knowledge of these transformations in mind, Joyce steels herself for the question and answer session with lawmakers, which is a required part of the state funding proposal process. She offers her best possible performance, keeping the truth in mind at all times. However, Joyce later learns that the virulent opposition to the proposal is all part of orchestrated political gamesmanship from lawmakers who are seeking to improve their reelection chances at her expense. Being tough on Joyce and the women of the Sewing Circus is akin to a performance of being tough on crime and government spending as represented by freeloading welfare queens.

When Joyce withdraws her proposal and walks out of the state house, Cleage signals that there is no room for her in the political process and that the Sewing Circus will "stand or fall on [its] own reality" (22). Generations of largely reactive tactics and strategies devised to combat and defend against the dominating stereotypes that hegemonic culture have heaped upon black women (primarily the hypersexual whore, the angry and emasculating Sapphire, and the doting asexual Mammy) have been draining and on the whole ineffective. Literary scholar Candice Jenkins asserts that this hedging against literal and psychic abuse from white culture via what she calls the salvific wish, is problematic, though the inclination itself emanates from a healthy desire for self preservation.[14] Still, while the insecurity of the Sewing Circle's funding stream might be troubling to this reader, it is not the primary concern for Joyce, or for Tee, who is the most mature member of the girls group. Rather, their de-briefing of Joyce's Michigan Capital Hill visit ends on a high note with Joyce and Tee agreeing on the fact that money or no money, the most important consideration was whether or not that Joyce's response was indicative of what a free woman would do.

Cleage's text, then, presupposes the ineffectiveness of various outmoded defense mechanisms that hold majority culture's perception of African Americans at the center. *Red Dress* explores the impotence of the salvific wish, the culture of dissemblance, the politics of respectability and other defense mechanisms that took hold over the past century all out of the collective desire to rescue and protect the black community from racist accusations of inescapable social pathology. The common thread running through all of these tactics is that each rests on the thorough embrace of bourgeois propriety and values that are supposedly solely in the purview of the white middle class. Years of adherence to these notions based on socially constructed subject positions have further empowered the oppressor by elevating a narrow version of normativity (i.e., nuclear families, heterosexuality) over all others. These approaches, while well meaning, and certainly understandable given the historical context, place too much emphasis on constraining behaviors of the traditionally underserved. The onus is on them to perform blackness in such a manner that others are somehow able to see beyond the typical degrading stereotypes of African-American women. The futility of this approach, along with the psychic energy it takes for those invested in the process, makes it even more crucial that we have something to offer the current generation, some other way of intervening with dominant images of themselves that they find counterintuitive. Constantly mapping one's life to the gaze of another is a particularly inefficient way to live a full life.

In addition, it makes for stressful living especially for the black middle class, who end up being the ones who have the most to prove. In reflecting on the heavy burden of managing public behavior verses private realities, Cleage writes that Joyce and her close friends happened to find their genuine professional passion in "jobs that require a certain amount of public decorum ... .we're expected to assume as part of our public responsibilities, a quiet dignity, an unshakable reserve, and a constant seriousness that can sometimes become oppressive. Left unchecked, they can lead to a certain self-righteousness that is counterproductive to the work that we do" (30). It is precisely this persistence of this conundrum that led 19th century black men and women of the middle class to purse and invest in the salvific wish. Without others to keep one's own sense of entitlement at bay, the persistence of classism can be hard to overcome. To their credit, Joyce and her friends hold each other accountable for not becoming the kind of condescending people who can't see beyond personal shortcomings of the people who comprise the communities they serve. They decompress together at regular Friday night dinners sharing the joys and pain of their small successes and colossal failures they encountered in the previous weeks. They share a certain set of common core beliefs — namely in the equality of men, women and children, and that informed agency and grassroots activism are essential elements of reifying healthy black communities.

Cleage's mantra throughout *Red Dress* is that anyone invested in modern day social work must also possess an abiding faith in the possibility of reinvigorating communities from the inside out. That is, by centering on teaching an individual to value their own well-being, a saner community can begin to emerge. Still, certain important and practical elements regarding implementation hang in the balance. Now that Joyce has stood her ground and withdrawn her funding application, how will The Sewing Circus model carry on? Surely, charging $5 per person for movie marathons will not close the program's funding gap. Still, while her close friends and mentees support her choice, Joyce still doesn't present a clear alternate plan for funding the work of The Sewing Circus. While empowering for the women who are demonstrating their leadership skills by organizing them, this element is not a solution and no alternative is offered. In practical terms, the long-term tenability of The Sewing Circus hangs in the balance and movie nights are not going to fill a gap left by the missing government funding from the state of Michigan. Instead of tying up this loose end, Cleage offers her readers a happy ending of Joyce's new love life with Nate, the tall, handsome, ex-police officer turned principal, who arrived in town just in time to help defuse community violence involving members of The Sewing Circle and their abusive male partners.

Perhaps Cleage is gesturing to the fact that the path to Free Womanhood can be achieved with or without significant financial resources. The reader suspends disbelief long enough to rest assured that the Sewing Circus will carry on. Despite all they lack in monetary assistance, the women have gained a fortune in terms of social capital now that Nate, the Smitherman Twins, and others are invested in their collective success. One supposes that when Joyce's sister Ava, who is the primary fundraiser for the group, returns from her summer sojourn to California, revisiting the organization's funding model will be priority number one. But the literalists in the reading audience, especially those who have become invested in the practicality of Cleage's own approach, can only assume that a plausible outcome is on the horizon. While uncomfortable, this ambiguity further illuminates the depth of Cleage's primary allegiance is to freedom. The reality is that living in alignment with this ideology of Free Womanhood is not without its own set of negative consequences and difficulties; yet, the rewards make the journey worth the risk. In the end, this assertion underlies *Red Dress* from beginning to end. The practicality of implementation can only become germane if collective social action follows from it. Cleage and hooks have done their part. They saw and felt a void and wrote furiously to fill it. As with so much else in life, the rest is up to us.

An Addendum on Praxis

One of the key tenants of Cleage's writing is that community connectedness is elemental. And one of the key tenants of bell hooks' writing is that praxis is the most fruitful point of engagement for feminist work — that is, one should aim to walk in the space created by the nexus of theory and practice. Cleage's early novels live this intersection and therefore lend themselves to use in service-learning courses on college campuses, on the reading list of non-profit youth groups with a focus on building self-esteem, and should be passed from mother to daughter to generate discussion about important topics as a starting place for critical life-skills conversations. Surely there are other venues where Cleage's writing could be of use, as they are applicable in any environment that seeks to bridge the gap between the imaginary and the real in terms of the implications of social problems and attempts at remediation.

Among many kernels of truth in Cleage's work is the existence of non-profits whose missions and models are similar to that of the Sewing Circus. Their populations have needs that mirror those of the young black women featured in Cleage's *Red Dress*. As a proponent of service-learning, by highlighting a few of these organizations here I hope to encourage readers to consider aligning with organizations in their community that may be akin to the Sewing Circus. What follows is a short list of organizations with a mission to help at-risk young women and girls of color find their way in the world using literature and popular culture as primary tools to encourage critical thinking and self-awareness. The point of calling attention to these few programs among the many that undoubtedly exist is to continue in the tradition of Cleage and hooks by infusing this essay writing with a call to action among my own readers. I thank you for the indulgence and I challenge you to find and make room to share consciousness raising and Free Womanhood among your own community.

TeenVoices, Boston, Massachusetts. *http://www.teenvoices.com/.* Program Goals: To develop core language arts, communication and media skills in Boston area, low-income teen girls of color. To educate participating teen girls and their audiences on critical issues of concern to teen girls in a manner that promotes social justice. To publish and disseminate the voices of teen girls through self-generated media and other communication vehicles. To develop a growing cadre of feminist leaders. To accomplish our mission, we run an out-of-school time program, a leadership program, publish a magazine and web site, and host public forums.

Do the Write Thing, Boston, Massachusetts. Program Goals: Founded by the Rev. Dr. Gloria White-Hammond, a minister and pediatrician with a long history of involvement in community service, this church-based creative writing/mentoring ministry focuses on high-risk black adolescent females. The project, which began in 1994 with four girls, now serves over 200 young women through small groups in two Boston public schools, two juvenile detention facilities in Boston and on site at Bethel African Methodist Episcopal Church.

PEARLS for Teen Girls, Inc. Milwaukee, Wisconsin *http://pearlsforteengirls.com/About.* Program Goals: PEARLS for Teen Girls, Inc. is a dynamic and innovative non-profit leadership development organization serving at-risk, primarily African American and Latina girls, ages 10 to 19 in Milwaukee, Wisconsin. PEARLS helps girls achieve in school, avoid teen pregnancy, and use their personal power to achieve their goals and dreams. In 2010 PEARLS served 791 girls citywide.

NOTES

1. The "down low" phenomenon refers to the prevalence of Black men who have sexual relationships with both men and women, but whom self-identify as heterosexual.
2. Kost K, Henshaw S and Carlin L, "U.S. Teenage Pregnancies, Births and Abortions: National and State Trends and Trends by Race and Ethnicity," 2010, *http://www.guttmacher.org/pubs/USTPtrends.pdf.*
3. For more on the importance of Idlewild, Michigan in terms of African American history, see Ben Wilson's article, The Early Development and Growth of America's Oldest Black Resort — Idlewild, Michigan, 1912–1930.
4. As explained by Cleage during an NPR interview about another of her novels, *Babylon Sisters.*
5. One can argue that Cleage transforms the metropolis of Atlanta into a small town, by focusing almost all of the action in the West End, a geographic space that is similar in scope to Idlewild. She creates a town within a town, such that the social dynamics are manageable and focused.
6. Patricia Hill-Collins and others write extensively about the tradition and concept of "other mothering" within African American communities.
7. Kaywell, Joan series foreword. "Using Literature to Help Troubled Teenagers Series." Greenwood Pressxiii. This series is extremely useful to those interested in learning more

about bibliotherapy. Each volume in the series explores social problems and issues of teenagers through contemporary young adult literature and is focused on a general area of problems for teenagers: family issues, identity issues, societal issues, abuse issues, health issues, and end-of-life issues. The volumes provide information for teenagers, parents, teachers and others working with young adults by exploring particular issues through fictional characters. The unique format pairs experts in young adult literature with a psychologist who provides analyses of fictional characters in the featured books. The coping techniques exhibited by each main character are explained in lay person's terms with the goal of being accessible to both trouble youth and adults with or without clinical training (i.e. teachers, mentors, coaches, clergy, etc.) who are trying to help them process with their problems.

8. According to Harvard's Civil rights Project, the four most segregated states for public school education during the 1990s were New York, Michigan, Illinois and California (Kozol,18).

9. Freire's most well known text continues to be the *Pedagogy of the Oppressed*, which takes as its thesis the idea that dialogue and exchange based on a relationship of equality open up the broadest possibilities for encouraging literacy among those who represent what amounts to a permanent underclass.

10. See Dorothy Salem's *To Better Our World* for more on the Black women's Club movement.

11. Jones, Adrienne Lash. "Phyllis (Phillis) Wheatley Clubs and Homes" in *Black Women in America, A Historic Encyclopedia*. Ed. Darlene Clark Hine. Brooklyn, New York. Carson Publishing. 1993.

12. See Francis, Aisha. " In Search of Free Womanhood" in *Obsidian* for a full explication of Free Womanhood as a theoretical concept underlying the totality of Cleage's body of writing for the past two decades or more.

13. For more information on this subject, readers should refer to *Righteous Discontent: The women's movement in the Black Baptist Church* by Evelyn Higginbotham and to *The Artistry of Anger* by Linda Grasso.

14. See Jenkins, *Private Lives, Proper Relations*.

WORKS CITED

Cleage, Pearl. *I Wish I Had a Red Dress*. New York: Morrow, 2001. Print.
_____. Interview. "Pearl Cleage: 'Babylon Sisters.'" NPR.org. 26 April 2005. Web. 31. Aug. 2011. Web.
DuBois, W. E. B. *Writings: The Suppression of the African Slave-Trade The Souls of Black Folk Dusk of Dawn Essays*. The Library of America Series. New York: Penguin, 1986. Print.
Francis, Aisha. "In Search of Free Womanhood: Black Conduct Literature, Contemporary Cultural Production and Pearl Cleage." *Obsidian*, Vol. 10, no. 1 (Spring–Summer 2010): 32–49. Print.
Freire, Paulo. *The Pedagogy of the Oppressed*. New York: Penguin, 1972. Print.
Grasso, Linda M. *The Artistry of Anger: Black and White Women's Literature in America, 1820–1860*. Chapel Hill: University of North Carolina Press, 2002. Print.
Harris-Perry, Melissa V. *Sister Citizen: Shame, Stereotypes and Black Women in America: For Colored Girls Who've Considered Politics When Being Strong Isn't Enough*. New Haven, CT: Yale University Press, 2011. Print.
Higginbotham, Evelyn Brooks. *Righteous Discontent: The women's movement in the Black Baptist Church, 1880–1920*. Cambridge, MA: Harvard University Press, 1993. Print.
hooks, bell. *Feminism is for Everybody: Passionate Politics*. Cambridge, MA: South End, 2000. Print.

Jenkins, Candice. *Private Lives, Proper Relations: Regulating Black Intimacy*. Minneapolis: University of Minnesota Press, 2007. Print.

Jones, Adrienne Lash. "Phyllis (Phillis) Wheatley Clubs and Homes" in *Black Women in America: A Historic Encyclopedia*. Ed. Darlene Clark Hine. Brooklyn, NY: Carson, 1993. Print.

Kozol, Johnathan. *The Shame of the Nation: The Restoration of Apartheid Schooling in America*. New York: Three Rivers, 2005. Print.

Kaywell, Joan. Series Foreword. *Using Literature to Help Troubled Teenagers Series*. Westport, CT: Greenwood, 1999, xi-xvi. Print.

Salem, Dorothy. *To Better Our World: Black Women in Organized Reform, 1890–1920*. Brooklyn, NY: Carlson, 1990. Print.

Wilson, Ben C. "The Early Development and Growth of America's Oldest Black Resort — Idlewild Michigan, 1912–1930." In *Perspectives on Black Popular Culture*. Ed. Harry B. Shaw. Bowling Green, Ohio; Bowling Green State University Press, 1990. Print.

Wordes, Madeline, and Michell Nunez. "Our Vulnerable Teenagers: Their Victimization, Its Consequences, and Directions for Prevention and Intervention." Oakland, CA: National Council on Crime and Delinquency. 2002. Print.

An Ode to Black Feminism: Reciprocal Empowerment and Anti-Sexism in *I Wish I Had a Red Dress* and *Some Things I Never Thought I'd Do*

MONICA L. MELTON

I Wish I Had a Red Dress (2001) and *Some Things I Never Thought I'd Do* (2003) are arguably Pearl Cleage's tribute to black women. At first glance they appear to be love stories, but upon deeper reflection, the story lines capture Cleage speaking truth to power about love, about loving oneself more fully, about black women loving, teaching, supporting, empowering, and caring for themselves and one another. Although understudied, Cleage is a prolific writer and skilled in several genres. Scholars locate her body of work in a unique place because it bridges literature, contemporary culture and the principals and beliefs surrounding black women's empowerment (Henderson 83). Similarly, Francis argues that Cleage's literary renderings are a "workbook" with "solutions to the tangible socio-political and economic trials of being black in an unjust society that is nonetheless full of possibility and hope" (33). Her works name the problem and offer creative solutions. Foster-Singletary asserts, "while Cleage's novels might be categorized as 'popular' culture, they retain the substance of engaging, artful literature" (50). Cleage's publications are part and parcel of popular culture as well as substantive literature. Recently, Cleage's work was the subject of a special edition of *Obsidian* (2009). A richly deserved celebration of Cleage's sagacity and long overdue, Smith-McCoy, editor of *Obsidian* was insightful in being the first to pay tribute to Pearl Cleage with a critical examination of her "prolific" literary texts (7–8).

Cleage's *Red Dress* and *Some Things* are grounded in tenets of black feminism and demonstrate reciprocal empowerment and anti-sexism in the lives of its characters. Both novels challenge sexism while simultaneously struggling to create anti-sexist relationships with black men and safe spaces free from violence against women. Cleage challenges her reader to think about the circumstances of her characters because they may be similar to their real life experiences. She also introduces an alternative black masculinity where black men consciously and actively work to reform their sexist thoughts and deeds. Being anti-sexist, argues Rose, in a culture that rewards sexism "doesn't come naturally" (322). Therefore, mindfulness is imperative in anti-sexist work. Characters Bill, Nate, and Blue in both novels, illustrate the struggle of rethinking sexist notions and the benefits of doing so. I define a black feminist man, similar to Mark Anthony Neal, as one who is aware that he has been raised in a patriarchal culture which has led him to believe in the false notion of male supremacy and superiority (29). Additionally, a black feminist man actively works to decenter himself from a patriarchal sexist philosophy, recognizing that this involves constructing alternate masculinities based upon respect for all women, gender equity, and compassion. Cleage brings black feminist theory to life by using the mundane, the everyday, ordinary occurrences of black folks' lives, and she inserts them into a feminist framework, thereby allowing her reader to think critically about that which is, for many, habitual and routine.

Joyce and Regina, the main protagonists in *Red Dress* and *Some Things* are empowered women, and they adhere to the philosophy of reciprocal empowerment. The technique of combining the processes of self and community, often simultaneously, of first self-defining and then working for the common good of a group or community, has been successful for some women and is preferred by African American women in particular (Darlington and Mulvaney 1–3). This format nurtures egalitarian relations, shared respect and responsibility, partnership and collaboration (2–3). Agency is being self-defined, self-determined, and having the ability to live life on one's own terms (Collins "Thought" 98–100). Classic power is "dominance, authority, pecking order, control-over and [the ability] to conquer" someone or something (Darlington and Mulvaney 10–11). The singular use of these power models have yet to meet the needs of most women (12). The unequal distribution of power is central to feminist analysis of gendered relations, social structures, and political forces because traditional power structures have worked in tangent with other systems of oppression to subordinate individuals or groups, especially women. Reciprocal empowerment has the potential not only to transform social identities but to change social structures (Darlington and Mulvaney 1–24). Herein Cleage aligns her politics on power with

Darlington and Mulvaney, who argue that reciprocal empowerment encourages reciprocity, which can assist in eliminating power hierarchies that are part and parcel of traditional power exchanges (1). Like Mulvaney and Darlington, Cleage understands the politics of power and its gendered dimensions and creates characters who use reciprocal empowerment as a mode of transformation.

Inspiring people can be a helpful strategy when using the reciprocal empowerment model and can be an important component of grassroots activism. Black women's activism often emerges out of their lived experiences where community sustainability or survival is at stake (Grayson 131–134). Gender specific activism is often overlooked in social movement literature, yet, women's tactics circumvent injustice (Kuumba 50–53). For example, beauty salons, churches, and grassroots organizations are some of the foremost sites for women's health activism (Grayson 132). Historically, African American women's involvement (in activism) has not been separate from men's (activist) organizations. Yet, in mixed sex groups, women end up doing most of the organizing and grunt work, while men take public leadership positions and receive most of the recognition (Smooth and Tucker 241–258). Moreover, it is black women's social, informal, and formal networks that have been the catalyst for movement mobilization in the past (244). A sense of that type of post–Civil War activism precipitated upon reciprocal empowerment is a central theme in many of Cleage's texts and illustrate her adeptness at relating contemporary culture to reciprocal empowerment and grassroots activism — all tenets of black feminism.

Activism in both novels is evident in the anti-sexist creed followed by the main characters. Cleage is so dedicated to anti-sexism that she uses characters of both genders to wage a war on sexist thoughts and acts. In fact, she has developed what I call the black feminist man. Let it be noted that these are not the only novels of Cleage's with feminist men characters. In fact, this phenomenon may warrant an exploration of its own, specifically, Pearl Cleage and the black feminist man — encompassing an examination of all of her written work and her use of the feminist man as a character. hooks argues that, "Collectively Black men have never critiqued the dominant cultures norms of masculine identity, even though they have reworked those norms to suit their social situation" ("Looks" 96). Normative constructions of masculinity are problematic at best, and race complicates it even more. But here hooks suggests that instead of merely tweaking normative masculinity, the opportunity should be used to create alternative masculinities. The problem for progressives engaged in the fight for liberation is that freedom cannot come at the expense of subordinating another (Collins, "Politics" 200). Violence, for instance, is a problem globally and within the African American community. Allen calls for black men to challenge sexism in ways similar to the manner in which they challenge racism within the wider community in "Stopping Sexual Harassment" (129–141). Yet, while black organizations will oppose neighborhood violence, they rarely speak out against violence against women and children (Collins, "Politics" 212). Herein, Cleage's ideology is aligned with some feminists who argue that black folks can not adequately face the challenge of racism without dealing with sexism, and the influence of socially prescribed notions of masculinity on Black men and in their relationships with black women and children (Cole and Guy-Sheftall 217–222).

Main characters Joyce Mitchell and Regina Burns are committed to social justice and challenging sexism on both macro and micro levels. These protagonists' relationships go against the status quo of representations of black relationships in popular culture, of the controlling imagery of the past, and of presenting the challenges faced by African Americans as irredeemable. Instead *Red Dress* and *Some Things* draw on and create black feminist epistemologies. Their challenge to sexism gives the reader different strategies for creating anti-sexist relationships. They open up a transformational space for black women with empowering images of black women and representations of how life can be for black folks who embrace principles that can help them bring about change for themselves and their society.

In *Red Dress*, widow and the protagonist Joyce, her protégé Tomika (Tee) and Joyce's best friend Sister live in a small town called Idlewild, Michigan that used to be a booming African American resort. Joyce is a frustrated educator turned social worker who left the public school system to open her own business, the Albert B. Mitchell Sewing Circus and Community Center. Better known as "The Circus," her center is a place where Joyce educates, mentors, and empowers young black women and their kids for improved life skills and better living. Joyce sees critical thinking as key for "The Circus." Honing critical thinking skills is on the path toward empowerment, and Joyce is a beacon of reciprocal empowerment and is passionate about her own agency and the agency of the young women at the center and in her community.

In *Some Things* Regina has just come out of a substance abuse rehabilitation program and is beginning her life anew. When she returns home she finds her post-menopausal aunt, Abby taking care of her home while she was away. Aunt Abby encourages Regina, who is vulnerable upon her return from rehab to be bold and courageous in her pursuit of personal renewal and transformation. Aunt Abby is a crone, a wise woman, and a visionary. Like The Crone Goddess,[1] she celebrates old age, and she uses her wisdom to guide and help others when they are in transition (Caputi 11,14). Abby states, "Estrogen is fine, but it definitely blocks a lot of female magic" (11). Regina concurs. Cleage subverts contemporary notions about women of a certain age with her character Aunt Abby; the woman is bold, courageous, and celebrates the postmenopausal stage of life as a gift. Her presence is contrary to mainstream culture that worships a woman's youth and beauty.

Abby's vision is that her niece would go on a journey she did not want to take and that that she would finish an assignment for a "fallen friend." Regina rescues a woman in distress, and meets a man with blue eyes in Atlanta who has been searching for Regina across time, according to her Aunt. Abby uses reciprocal empowerment with Regina to help her complete her self-actualization into an empowered woman. The characterization of Abby as a seer, a guide to women on their life journeys, a supportive, affirming, empowered personality who encourages women to be fully free is a subversive act. Cleage's ability to finesse controversial concepts as she subverts popular ideologies without alienating the reader is superb, a talent next to none. Cleage uplifts women's empowerment, black feminism, and violence-free living for women and children.

This Is What a Black Feminist Woman Looks Like

Cleage creates complex characters who are relevant to women today. She covers topics in areas that challenge young black women such as motherhood, relationships with black men, employment, education, and substance abuse. Joyce, Regina, Sister, Tomika, and the crew comprise some of the black woman's multiplicity, in contrast to the way in which popular culture in general has not been kind to black women. In fact, bell hooks asserts that the black women she spoke to armed themselves before going to the movies by not expecting to see "compelling representations of black femaleness" ("Looks" 119). Popular portrayals of African American women are controlled images because they are generally based upon stereotypes versus the nuanced complexities that make up the experiences of black women living in a xenophobic world (Collins, "Thought" 69–72). These stereotypes are gendered and racialized and often fall back on bigoted world-views of days gone by that still linger in the national psyche and for the most part these are the only available images of African American women in the media.

In *Some Things,* Cleage's main character interrupts controlling images of black women in the popular sphere. Prominent controlling images of black women visible in popular media include the hyper-sexed woman, the bad mother, the unwarranted angry and overly aggressive woman, and the welfare queen, to name a few (Collins, "Thought" 78–84; hooks, "Looks" 67; Rose

323, Neal 50–51). Since these are the primary images presented to African American women, it is difficult to contest them with representations that are more nuanced, complex, and reflective of the lived experiences of black women. Yet, Cleage's skill and proficiency in bringing forth the plurality of black women's lived experience is commendable. Just as Cleage disrupted images of elderly black women in popular culture with the character Aunt Abby, so too does Cleage destabilize contemporary stereotypic notions of black womanhood.

In this passage, Cleage openly takes issue with the portrayal of black women in popular culture. Regina and her new housemate discuss Aretha's photography project that involves women who strip for a living. There is about a ten-year age difference between the two women and Regina analyzes some of the changes that have occurred in the imagery of black women over those years:

> In that one little decade, thanks to music videos, the character of the fantasy stripper, and her fantasy sister, the sexually rapacious, unapologetically materialistic ghetto goddess, with all the latest clothes and cars and no visible means of support, have emerged and become the dominant symbols of black women in the popular culture [77].

Regina acknowledges that music videos in the last decade have controlled the imagery of African American women in contemporary culture. Popular portrayals include fictitious strippers and consumerist women who worship material goods and possessions over a vocation or profession. Negative representations of the hyper-sexed black body are not new, but these displays are different because today black women can "work that body" in ways previously unseen. The author clearly illuminates the fine distinctions in black images in the popular sphere as a result of the prevalence of domineering negative representations of women in music videos. Regina problematizes the influence of controlling images on black relationships when she reflects that this is not helpful to women's liberation even though "it clearly impacts everything from clothing styles to the sexual expectations of adolescent boys who think there is actually a place where women are always perfectly coiffed, scantily clad, and ready for sex" (Cleage, *Some Things* 77). Cleage understands, like scholar Tricia Rose, that black folks have a somewhat symbiotic relationship with popular culture because African Americans use the popular sphere to express themselves as well as depend on contemporary culture for "reflection, support, and affirmation" (324). Consequently, the issue of the misrepresentation of black women only heightens gender conflict in black America.

Realizing that self-actualization can counteract the impact of prevailing portrayals of popular culture, Cleage's protagonists in both novels are agents of reciprocal empowerment. Joyce's entrepreneurial spirit, for instance, is based upon the principle of reciprocal empowerment. Under the tutelage of

Joyce (Miz J), Tee handles the day-to-day operations of "The Circus," and she begins to also read the Sunday *New York Times* weekly. However, Tomika (Tee) is the only one who does, even though it was Miz J's recommendation to read frequently. Reading, according to Miz J, heightens a person's capacity to think critically. Tee, in fact, is developing a critical feminist consciousness which she uses at every opportunity for work and in her personal affairs. As a result of Tee's receptivity to Miz J's mentorship, Tee's abilities to resolve life's problems in a healthy manner improved. She also developed the skill to think of innovative ways to inspire other members of the center.

When Tee was in an unhealthy relationship with Jimmy, for example, the critical thinking skills that she learned from Miz J helped her to end that relationship. Tee states: "Miz J, you only need to see one do *right* to see all the others are *wrong*" (106). Once Tomika accepts this realization, she goes home and puts out her ex-boyfriend. Jimmy is Tee's ex-live-in lover who holds no job, pushes Tee around, threatens to hit her baby, and steals her money. Tee doesn't have any models for a "good guy" in her inner-circle. So Tee uses the "good guy" characters played by actor Denzel Washington as a prototype for what type of behavior to expect from men. Joyce thought Tee's idea was a wonderful way to employ critical thinking skills given the absence of anything better and a clever way to overcome the paucity of positive images of men in their community.

This passage illuminates the process of change. Tee knew that her situation with Jimmy was not beneficial to her, and through her interaction at "The Circus," a strong support network, reading more, and honing her critical thinking skills, she came to the realization that she had the power to end her destructive relationship. Cleage's genius is not in creating a black woman who was abused by her man or in having the woman kick the man out. Cleage's brilliance is in creating a method that met Tee right where she was at that moment in her life. Tee was in the initial stages of change; she was not educated, well read, financially stable, or necessarily empowered — a situation similar to that of some young black women today. Tee was a single woman with a child, the head of her household, and was more familiar with movies than with feminist theory. Here Cleage crafts a way for women who have more access to movies than the halls of academia to use what they have and create what they need. Cleage is a master at creating scenes where her flawed characters meet women who do not condemn or point fingers even though chagrined by their behavior. Rather, her empowered characters are beckoning lights that captivate other women with the idea of living in a way that enhances who they are or who they want to be. Joyce, Sister, and Aunt Abby are experts at reciprocal empowerment and wonderful sages that inspire the desire for liberation in others.

The Evolution of the Black Feminist Man

Challenging sexism is rarely seen in popular culture, and it is even more rare when it comes to relationships between black women and men. Yet, the author confronts misogyny and sexist behavior in both novels and proscribes a solution — the feminist black man. Cleage, like other feminists, believes that black men can transform sexist and patriarchal perspectives regarding dominant black gender norms and behaviors (hooks, "Cool" 14, Neal 28–30). Characters Bill and Nate from *Red Dress* and Blue from *Some Things* exemplify the standpoint that African Americans and men in particular can heal from patriarchy and sexism. Healing and transformation are imperative to mend the divide among black folks in order to constructively love one another and work towards their joint liberation (Collins, "Politics" 2004; hooks, "Cool" 138–139; Byrd and Guy-Sheftall 20–22, 347). Bill, Nate, and Blue started their anti-sexist pilgrimage by developing a consciousness that sexism does not benefit men. Similarly, Kevin Powell, in real life, describes his own personal journey to heal himself from the wounds of patriarchy in "Confessions of a Recovering Misogynist":

> Just as I feel it is whites who need to be more vociferous about racism in their communities, I feel it is men who need to speak long and loud about sexism among each other.... The fact is there was a blueprint handed to me in childhood telling me this is the way a man should behave, and I unwittingly followed the script verbatim. There was no blueprint handed to me about how to begin to wind myself out of sexism as an adult.... Everyday I struggle with myself [52–58].

Struggle, according to Powell, the process of awareness of flawed thinking and actions transformed into thoughtful actions and behaviors, can create friction.

Likewise, Nate, Bill, and Blue struggle with themselves, the women in their inner-circles and other black men over anti-sexist behavior. Friction is often indicative of a conflict between intellectual consciousness with everyday habits; it is an idea also expressed by Neal (29), a black man and feminist scholar. These three men are at different stages of their evolution into feminist men. Nate is in the initial stages; he knows that there is a problem, and he is not quite sure how to solve it, but he is open and willing to listen and learn. Nate states a desire not to be like his father during a conversation with Joyce where he reveals that his primary relationships did not equip him with the necessary skill set for sound gender relations, much less anti-sexist relations (299). In this statement, he admits that he is ill-equipped, but he also declares that he is willing to learn and reconstruct his prior training. Nate's path to becoming a feminist man is in its infancy. Bill, on the other hand, has been married to feminist Sister for some time and is further along on his anti-sexist journey than Nate. Sister and Joyce are best friends and over the years Joyce has also developed a close relationship with Bill. Bill and Joyce are tender with one another, and they have a profound respect for one another that is grounded in a keen sense of the other's value and worth. It is because of the sincere regard that they have for one another that they are able to test the boundaries of their friendship by challenging one another to de-colonize their minds from patriarchal and sexist thinking.

One night while having dinner at Sister's and Bill's house Joyce challenges Bill's sexist thought process. Joyce tells them about Tee's plans to purchase a pistol after being threatened by Junior, her friend Nikki's "baby daddy." When Junior finds out that Nikki's new place of employment is at a strip club he aggressively confronts Nikki, who lives with Tee. Tee pulls out a toy gun on Junior and advises him to get off her property and leave them alone. Later, when Junior discovers the gun was fake, he becomes aggressive with Tee. Gun violence is a sensitive subject for Bill who has lost several loved ones to man-on-man violence. Bill becomes incensed when he finds out Tee wants to buy a gun and informs Joyce:

> "You're supposed to say no!" he said, his face grim and tight. "You're supposed to say 'Guns don't solve anything!' 'Practice peace!' 'Thou shalt not kill!' You're supposed to say *something!*".... "It's a terrible idea" [244–245].

Bill is so upset over the possibility of another person that he loves being murdered that he cannot be reasoned with until later. In the meantime, Sister sides with Joyce and advises Joyce to go with Tee to the firing range because she asserts that everyone has the right to feel safe.

Later, Sister pulls Bill aside and talks to him about his disagreement with Joyce. Although there is no dialog of their conversation, the result is that Bill clears the air with Joyce before she leaves their home. Aside from Bill's commitment to non-violence, male privilege may have also allowed him to discount the magnitude of a woman's need to feel safe. Culturally, male strength is valorized and extolled at every turn, therefore some men may not fully comprehend how it feels to be physically vulnerable all the time. This is a good illustration of the struggle Powell writes about. Even though Bill promotes women's empowerment, there is a conflict between his attachment to his belief system (non-violence) and the reality of Tee's need to feel protected in the face of being overpowered by male physical strength.

On the other hand, Blue is fully aware of the ways in which men physically abuse women and girls. He is dedicated to anti-sexism as a way of life. Blue has evolved, although it took him several lifetimes to get it right. In his first life he was a black emperor who led and helped create a black progressive civilization. However, after years of prosperity, his empire was overtaken by another nation. Blue states that the only way his civilization was defeated was because the women of his great nation helped the enemy. His empress (Regina) left when Blue disregarded her warning that she refused to live in a place where women were abused, beaten, and raped. She took many women with her and never returned, allowing the men to fight each other. As a result, Blue spent several lifetimes looking for the love he lost because he was oblivious to sexism in his first life. Since then Blue's self-appointed task has been to correct his previous mistakes (186). Gender relations suffer when women live in fear of being abused, an experience that Blue now fully understands. Unlike his first life, Blue is now dedicated to eliminating violence against women and children. He has cultivated himself into a feminist man so that when he finds his lost love she will take him back and they can spend eternity together. Finally, after spending eons looking for his lost love, Blue is reunited with her (Regina) in this life. In short, Nate, Bill, and Blue are Cleage's prototypes for black gender politics because she believes in the necessity for alternative black masculinities. Guy-Sheftall states:

> At the beginning of a new century, black men and women must struggle for "revolutionary selves, revolutionary lives, revolutionary relationships," which Toni Cade Bambara asserted three decades ago. Rejecting the traps of patriarchy, sexism, and homophobia, African Americans might continue our journey toward freedom in racist America and offer new visions and possibilities for this nation, the world, and generations yet unborn [Byrd and Guy-Sheftall 347].

These feminist scholars argue the importance of transforming the self and society, to envision and disrupt the status quo for a just and equitable society.

Cleage models revolutionary agents of change with many of her characters, particularly, Bill, Nate, and Blue and their evolutionary trajectory of becoming a black feminist man. A reconstruction of black gender ideology could mean that black folks could come together in ways that benefit the whole in order to combat the social, political, and institutional ails that still plague them in the twenty-first century (Cole and Guy-Sheftall 217–219; Collins, "Politics" 182; Rudolph and Guy-Sheftall 22, 347). The healing work done by Blue, Nate, and Bill is reminiscent of the work that is critical for black men. Cleage's sensitivity to the fine nuances of black gender relations and her flair for creating characters in various stages of becoming black feminist men is a talent that sets her apart from her contemporaries.

The Personal Is Political

In the '60s and '70s the slogan, "The personal is political" was synonymous to a war cry for the women's movement. Liberal feminists took up this mantra and used it to blaze trails for women. Pearl Cleage, in the tradition of the second wave feminist movement, uses what is personal to her as a theme in her novels to make political statements *for* black folks *by* black folks on violence against women (in the vein of *For Us By Us*). Cleage experienced intimate partner violence as a student at Howard University and uses her lived experience as a platform to advocate for her political views on violence against women. Both her work and her life testify that "[d]omestic violence is often triggered when a man with a false sense of power feels threatened or challenged and moves to regain a sense of control through beating, raping, or berating his partner and/or children" (Cole and Guy-Sheftall 218).

Intimate partner violence is very prevalent in black America, however, these reports are rarely publicized in the media, and they never receive the kind of coverage given to Lacy Peterson, Natalee Holloway, or Chandra Levy.[2] Moreover, black women may be perceived as traitors to their race if they publicly speak out about their issues with black men (Cole and Guy-Sheftall xxix). Rose argues that "for black women — who are already marginalized in larger society — taking a stand in a way that might alienate them from their local community is painful and difficult and often not worth it" (323). The threat of being further marginalized from one's position in the margins may be a difficult situation for some black women who look to their *sista* circles as a means of support to help overcome oppression (Melton 297). Like other media personalities who have also experienced domestic violence, Cleage presents the problem: black men's violence against black women and children. But unlike others, she empowers her characters with creative tactics and solutions to the problem of intimate partner violence. Reciprocal empowerment, for instance, is one method that Cleage's characters use to help build violence free zones.

In *Red Dress*, Joyce and her inner-circle come up with various ways to create violence-free zones. Tee is reading *The Times* one day and notes a curious study. There was a reported increase in violence against women on Super Bowl Sunday. Tee and Miz J discuss the incidence of this occurrence in Idlewild, and confirmed the existence in their neighborhood. Tee declares that women only watch the Super Bowl in hopes of being close to the men in their lives. She proposes a female "anti–Super Bowl party" that would leave men to themselves on that day. Consequently, if "they want to beat on somebody, at least it'll be a fair fight" (37). Miz J agrees that this kind of party would pose as a viable alternative for a safe place for women on game day. Miz J likes to use popular culture to teach critical thinking because it is easier to analyze and discuss the mistakes of others. So they eat and watch movies and have lively discussions around women's empowerment. Sister drops off a bag of goodies, her contribution to their violence-free zone. Sister creates a special Anti-Super Bowl ritual in light of her belief that women used to engage in rituals in pro-women cultures of the past. With the rise of patriarchy, goddesses were destroyed and other women friendly rites were abandoned due to fear. Sister's Anti-Super Bowl ritual is a symbolic coup de grâce on violence against women and children. In short, Cleage adheres to the philosophy asserted by Collins that "any progressive black gender ideology can not be based on someone else's subordination" (Collins, "Politics" 200) and anything else should be rejected.

Another message in advocating for spaces free of violence that is central to both novels is the theme that "good men" are also responsible for violence against women and children. Joyce, upon hearing of Tomika's run in with Junior (who tried to kill her by running her off the road) is angry, upset, and enraged over the entire incident. She feels increasing anger "[n]ot at Junior, but at all the ones Nate calls "the good guys." What good are they if they can't protect us any better than this?" (289). Cleage tackles head-on the notion that violence against women is not a social problem; she draws focus to the women and children being abused, as well as "the good guy" whose silence makes him unwittingly complicit in continued violence against women.

Sister and Bill invite Joyce and Nate for dinner. Upon hearing that Tee was in good condition after her surgery, Bill requests that they talk about something other than the violent incident. Bill complains that his poetry students (a group of ten young black men) do not read the paper and have no knowledge of the meaning of current events. After careful consideration, Joyce brings up the topic again and suggests that Bill could teach them about current events by discussing Junior's attack on Tee. Bill was upset during the exchange because he felt that as one of the "good guys" why should Joyce beat up on him? Joyce proceeds to inform him why "good men" are also responsible for violent events. Bill, an ever-evolving feminist man, rethinks their conversation and comes up with an assignment for his students. They have to define a "good man" and come up with the traits of a "good man." Although somewhat simplistic, the "For Men Only" concept was a good way for Bill to advocate non-violence with his students as well as give them a venue to begin to think and discuss with other men ideas about alternative manhood — a conversation that is desperately needed given the connection between violence and manhood in contemporary culture.

Cleage's character in *Some Things* knows the difference between manhood and the socially constructed hegemonic norm of masculinity that incorporates violence as part of its definition. In this story too, Cleage's characters are a means for her to advocate "the personal is political" in her fight against intimate partner violence. Her character Blue embarks upon a project to turn the West End in Atlanta, Georgia, once known for its high levels of crime, violence, and sexual assault into a virtual oasis — free of violence against women and children. Blue's West End is "a place where [Regina] could go to the twenty-four hour salon and walk home safely at whatever hour." It is a safe place for women to walk the streets, day or night, without any qualms. Regina thinks to herself: "I can walk home alone in the twilight and allow myself to fall so deeply into the beauty of the moment that I don't even notice a man coming up behind me, and *it's okay*" (263). As a result of violence against women, in public women are guarded and often look over their shoulders and peruse their surroundings to ensure their safety. Many of Cleage's novels are centered in the re-created West End, a thriving communal space that is flourishing in black culture, with no crime or violence. The author provides a tantalizing vision of the infinite potential of the West End neighborhood, one that could possibly be the impetus for change.

Blue the character that created the change in *Some Things* is described as part "Don Corleone, part Darth Vader, and part Johnny Appleseed" (64). His presence is so strong in the West End that people are scared to be anything other than respectful to women and girls, and to themselves. After his best friend's sister was brutally raped and murdered in Atlanta's West End, Blue takes matters into his own hands and acts similar to a vigilante. Collins suggests that, "It may be difficult to uncouple ideas about Black male strength from notions of aggression and violence, but placing Black male strength in service to community might catalyze much-needed changes" ("Politics" 212). It is a radical idea to use the strength of black men to serve the community (like Blue does) but it is a strategy that is alluring when considering its benefits. Some might argue that this concept is fanciful and that *Some Things* is more utopian feminist fiction than a formula upon which everyday black folks can use to transform their neighborhoods. Yet, the promise of thriving, safe, neighborhoods where women and children walk and play, and where communities are sanctuaries for black folks and black culture — are visions worthy of implementing or at least trying to implement: "When confronting a social problem of this magnitude, rethinking black gender ideology, especially the ways in which ideas about masculinity and femininity shape black politics becomes essential" (Collins, "Politics" 245). Violence on all levels is a major problem and hurts African Americans because overlooking gender politics hinders the liberation of the entire community (Collins, "Politics" 200–212; Cole and Guy-Sheftall 217–219; hooks, "Cool" 62, 65; Rose 324).

Conclusion

Pearl Cleage's works of fiction *I Wish I had A Red Dress* (2001) and *Some Things I Never Thought I'd Do* (2003) challenge sexism while simultaneously struggling to create anti-sexist relationships with black men and safe spaces free from violence against women. Her protagonists create black feminist epistemologies and live by feminist creeds that challenge themselves and others to eradicate sexist thoughts and deeds. Regina, Joyce, Sister, Tomika and Aunt Abby are representations of black feminism in action — a space for black folks to see images of a life where women and men embrace black feminist thought. Cleage's protagonists epitomize substantive and transformational images of African American womanhood and illustrate the veracity of depictions of black folks committed to anti-sexist beliefs and gender equity. Bill, Blue, and Nate are prototypes for evolving black feminist men, a vision that is almost non-existent in the popular sphere. Cole and Guy-Sheftall suggests that "the only cure for fractured families and hostile relations is a new model of partnerships in which we work together rather than against one another" (218). Cleage's novels give us a model of how to struggle with and against black men to create partnerships and a better community. All in all, Cleage's genius is in writing popular culture fiction novels that express the belief that crucial to the liberation of a people is the ability to engage in the struggle to end sexism, reconstruct normative gender roles, and eradicate intimate partner violence and other forms of domination through a reciprocally empowering process for black men and women.

Notes

1. The Crone Goddess is wise, a seer, and a supernaturally powerful old woman: "If we want to make it through, we might take as our guide the Grandmother, or Crone — the enduring one" (Caputi 246). She has resisted patriarchy for eons and survived the war against women. She celebrates women's post-menopausal years as the best and most powerful time of a woman's life, and inspires women to be wild and free.

2. These three White women were missing persons and/or violently murdered whose cases received extensive media coverage within the past ten years. To date no Black woman in similar circumstances has received equal coverage.

Works Cited

Allen, Robert L. "Stopping Sexual Harassment: A Challenge for Community Education." *Race, Gender, and Power in America: The Legacy of the Hill-Thomas Hearings*. Eds. Anita Faye Hill and Emma Colman Jordan. New York: Oxford University Press, 1995. 129–41. Print.

Byrd, Rudolph P., and Beverly Guy-Sheftall. *Traps: African American Men on Gender and Sexuality*. Bloomington: Indiana University Press, 2001. Print.

Caputi, Jane. *Gossips, Gorgons and Crones: The Fates of the Earth*. Sante Fe, NM: Bear, 1993. Print.

Cleage, Pearl. *I Wish I Had a Red Dress*. New York: Perennial, 2001. Print.

_____. *Some Things I Never Thought I'd Do*. New York: One World/Ballantine, 2003. Print.

Cole, Johnnetta B., and Beverly Guy-Sheftall. *Gender Talk: The Struggle for Women's Equality in African American Communities.* New York: One World/Ballantine, 2003. Print.

Collins, Patricia Hill. *Black Feminist Thought: Knowledge, Consciousness, and the Politics of Empowerment*, 2d ed. New York: Routledge, 2000. Print.

_____. *Black Sexual Politics: African Americans, Gender, and the New Racism.* New York: Routledge, 2004. Print.

Darlington, Patricia S.E., and Becky M. Mulvaney. *Women, Power, and Ethnicity: Working Toward Reciprocal Empowerment.* New York: Haworth, 2003. Print.

Davis, Angela Y. *Blues Legacies and Black Feminism: Gertrude "Ma" Rainey, Bessie Smith, and Billie Holiday.* New York: Vintage, 1999. Print.

Foster-Singletary, Tikenya. "A Contemporary Vision of Female/Male Romantic Love: Pearl Cleage's *What Looks Like Crazy on an Ordinary Day*." *Obsidian: Literature in the African Diaspora* 10.1 (2009): 50–67. Print.

Francis, Aisha. "In Search of Free Womanhood: Black Conduct Literature, Contemporary Cultural Production, and Pearl Cleage." *Obsidian Literature in the African Diaspora* 10.1 (2009): 32–49. Print.

Grayson, Deborah R. ""Necessity Was the Midwife of Our Politics: Black Women's Health Activism in The 'Post'-Civil Rights Era (1980–1996)." *Still Lifting Still Climbing.* Ed. Kimberly Springer. New York: New York University Press, 1999. 131–48. Print.

Henderson, Frances D. "Coming Full Circle: Reverse Migration in Pearl Cleage's *What Looks Like Crazy on an Ordinary Day*." *Obsidian Literature in the African Diaspora* 10.1 (2009): 83–97. Print.

hooks, bell. *Black Looks: Race and Representation.* Boston: South End, 1992. Print.

_____. *We Real Cool: Black Men and Masculinity.* New York: Routledge, 2003. Print.

Kuumba, Bahati M. "'You've Struck a Rock' Comparing Gender, Social Movements, and Transformation in the United States and South Africa." *Gender and Society* 16.4 (2002): 504–523. Print.

Melton, Monica L. "Sex, Lies, and Stereotypes: HIV Positive Women's Perspectives on HIV Stigma and the Need for Public Policy as HIV/Aids Prevention Intervention." *Race Gender and Class* 18.1–2 Part B (2011): 295–313. Print.

Neal, Mark Anthony. *New Black Man* New York: Routledge, 2006. Print.

Powell, Kevin. *Who's Gonna Take the Weight?: Manhood, Race, and Power in America.* New York: Three Rivers, 2003. Print.

Rose, Tricia. *Black Noise: Rap Music and Black Culture in Contemporary America.* Hanover, NH: Wesleyan University Press, 1994. Print.

_____. "There Are Bitches and Hoes." *Gender, Race and Class in Media: A Critical Reader*, 3d ed. Eds. Gail Dines and Jean M. Humez. Los Angeles: Sage, 2011. Print.

Smith-McCoy, Sheila. "Notes from the Editor." *Obsidian Literature in the African Diaspora* 10.1 (2009): 7–8. Print.

Smooth, Wendy G., and Tamelyn Tucker. "Behind but Not Forgotten: Women and the Behind-the-Scenes Organizing of the Million Man March." *Still Lifting Still Climbing.* Ed. Kimberly Springer. New York: New York University Press, 1999. 241–58. Print.

Shattering Silence: Pearl Cleage and Black Female Sexual Empowerment

SANDRA C. DUVIVIER

> To be sure, maintaining the silence on issues of Black sexuality is exacting too high a price from the Black community.
>
> [...]
>
> Indeed, the conditions are right for Black genocide if something does not happen to break the hold that [racial stereotyping] has had over Black people's bodies, psyches, and spiritualities. A modern and transformative discourse [on sexuality] must begin. — Kelly Brown Douglas[1]
>
> [O]ne of the most enduring and problematic aspects of the "politics of silence" is that in choosing silence black women also lost the ability to articulate any conception of their sexuality. — Evelynn Hammonds[2]
>
> More than ever before it is essential that we advance a discourse on sexuality that is liberating for those who engage in it [...] — Paula Giddings[3]

Silence and respectability politics surrounding black female sexualities have allowed black communities to challenge pervasive stereotypes of black female bodies as lascivious and hypersexual, thus creating a counternarrative that places blackness within the realm of morality and equality.[4] Nevertheless, silence has failed not only to eradicate these misrepresentations of black female sexuality, but also to provide a discourse on black female sexual agency and empowerment. More specifically, and as many scholars and activists have noted, the ramifications of this lack of discourse, especially within the last two decades, have proven deleterious and, at points, life-threatening: black women have been infected with HIV/AIDS in disproportionately large numbers, especially in areas with large black populations such as Harlem, Atlanta, and Washington, D.C.; black girls and women are at risk for other STIs, which make the body more susceptible to HIV infection; black teenage pregnancy rates, while decreasing, still remain much higher than white teenage pregnancy rates; and black girls and women continue to engage in risky sexual behavior and often do not insist on protective measures, thus becoming vulnerable to infections and unwanted pregnancies. All of these ramifications attest to a need for (further) serious dialogues concerning black female sexual empowerment and sexual health.

Acknowledging the necessities of such a discourse, Pearl Cleage envisions empowering black female sexualities in her understudied novel *What Looks Like Crazy on an Ordinary Day* (1997). While Cleage's novel is a fictional treatment of black female sexualities, it serves metonymically for more progressive African American communities' efforts to combat potentially dangerous sexual practices. It also implicitly admonishes black families, religious institutions, and communities who continue to enforce silence that their actions are exacerbating, rather than assisting, sexual issues plaguing black communities. This essay explores Cleage's shattering of silence in providing an empowering narrative of black female sexualities. In so doing, it also analyzes her exposing the problematics of silence, thus illuminating the need for a discourse of black sexualities, particularly black female sexualities.

Silence: Roots and Repercussions

Cleage's *What Looks Like Crazy*, which is set over a span of six months, foregrounds the black female community in 1990s Idlewild, Michigan, while centering specifically on Ava Johnson's readjustment to life and dating after an HIV-positive diagnosis. It also delineates the efforts of Ava's sister Joyce — alarmed by the ramifications of risky sexual practices, including her sister's diagnosis, as well as widespread pregnancies and dependence on the welfare system in the community — to combat silence and educate young Idlewild women and teenage girls about healthy sexual practices. It is important, then, to expand on the effects of silence in Cleage's novel, especially considering that, well over a decade after its publication, they continue to threaten black communities.

Ava's becoming infected and diagnosed in Atlanta, where she spent years as a very successful beautician before returning to Idlewild, helps illuminate the city's disproportionately high rate of HIV infections among African Americans. In fact, even as of now (roughly fourteen years after the novel's publication), according to Project Q Atlanta's "CDC: Blacks face higher HIV infection rates," Atlanta is the eighth highest ranked metro area in its HIV-infection/per-population ratio. This evidences continued high-risk sexual behavior in the area. In Ava's case, her failure to use protection with various sex partners over the course of several years leaves her clueless about the actual source and date of her HIV transmission. Not only is she unaware of her HIV transmitter, but her risky sexual practices before learning of her infection very likely exposed other sexual partners to HIV. An angry woman's confronting Ava and demanding her to retract the warning in Ava's notification letter to her husband suggests Ava's spreading the virus to this woman's husband, and, by extension, the angry woman.

As Ava's narrative fails to elucidate any engaging in discourse of sexuality and sexual empowerment pre–HIV diagnosis, it could be extrapolated that her upbringing was one enforced by the politics of silence surrounding sexuality. While the 1960s-born Ava would have to contend with STIs possibly resulting from unprotected sex — thus rendering protection/preventative measures for her multiple sexual encounters an imperative — her upbringing largely predates the first official cases of HIV/AIDS, which surfaced in 1981; and former President Ronald Reagan's refusal to acknowledge AIDS until 1987, six years after taking office as well as after the disease was officially named, evidences a collective national silence about the disease that has heavily contributed to a lack of public knowledge of HIV/AIDS and proper preventative measures. Moreover, heterosexist, homophobic ideologies designating AIDS as retribution for an ungodly sanctioned lifestyle shaped early U.S. perceptions of it as well as Reagan's silence and failure to take measures to eradicate the disease.

Homophobia has also continued to shape many ideologies concerning transmission of HIV/AIDS, even as society has adopted a more progressive stance toward the disease over time. In *What Looks Like Crazy*, which is set after Magic Johnson's well-publicized 1991 HIV diagnosis resulting from heterosexual sex, Ava's wondering about which man actually infected her includes "[t]he lying, bisexual one" (205) — though acknowledging her culpability for her risky sexual behavior. When Joyce introduces HIV prevention to the young girls and women during a meeting of the Sewing Circus, the name of her meeting group with Idlewild's black female youth, one member responds with the problematic "'Ain't nobody in here fucking no faggots'" (91). The vast majority of the girls and young women in the Sewing Circus, up to this point, had yet to use condoms, despite the fact the heterosexuality that supposedly renders them immune to HIV does not grant them immunity from other widespread STIs.

Silence, coupled with and informed by biblical interpretations of sex outside of a married, heterosexual, and procreative context as sinful, has largely shaped perceptions of HIV as a "gay disease" within black communities. Scholar-activists, including Johnnetta Cole, Beverly Guy-Sheftall, and Kelly Brown-Douglas, have noted that this misperception is inherently linked to a lack of discourse on black sexuality in general.[5] A sexual expression of same-sex desire unequivocally evidences a breach of the sexual script; nevertheless, a display of sexual desire outside of "biblically" informed respectability (i.e. heterosexual marriage and child-rearing within the institution) also diverges from respectability politics. When these sexual engagements are addressed in private/family and religious discourse, they are often castigated and condemned. These conservative ideologies prevent proper education about healthy sexual practices, while concomitantly enforcing a dangerous culture of silence or even concealment among large numbers of blacks who continue to express their sexual desire outside of the confines of these restrictive (and, for them, self-denying) confines. In fact, some conservative religious figures who endorse these ideologies publicly are often accused of engaging in clandestine "immoral," adulterous sexual affairs with parishioners—and some are even alleged to have *same-sex* encounters.[6] Such a conservatism, then, has proven dangerous and, at points, futile.

Additionally, and what merits further consideration, Ava's and the young Sewing Circus member's comments also implicate a supposed "down-low" culture, a racialized phenomenon placing culpability for HIV infections in African American women with closeted gay and bisexual black men. Rather than place culpability with, as Ava later concludes, questionable sexual practices, same-sex encounters are assigned blame. The 2000s saw a noticeable increase in main-stream media's reporting on the down-low phenomenon and the rising popularity of "down-low brotha" J.L. King, whose *On the Down Low: A Journey into the Lives of 'Straight' Black Men Who Sleep with Men* (2004)—and subsequent appearance on the Oprah Winfrey Show about these surreptitious same-sex encounters (that he also associates with high infection rates)—also exacerbated homophobic ideologies about HIV and contributed to a culture of terror amongst black women. While some black men engaging in sexual intercourse with men infect their black women partners and/or wives—which also evinces the need for women who suspect their partner or husband of any type of infidelity to use protection—associating the virus largely with down-low men would be inaccurate at best. Beyond a lack of condom use being the real culprit for HIV transmission through sexual activity, other issues plaguing African Americans, including poverty and lack of access to resources, contribute to higher infection rates. Nevertheless, these issues are downplayed, while a "phenomenon" with racialized and homophobic undertones is emphasized.

In *Beyond the Down Low: Sex, Lies, and Denial in Black America*, which challenges the scapegoating of gay and bisexual black men with HIV/AIDS transmission, as well as debunks certain myths concerning it, activist and former Clinton White House aide Keith Boykin notes these undertones informing the down-low phenomenon:

> The down low fit perfectly into larger cultural dynamics because it confirmed stereotypical values that many of us already believed. For some whites, it confirmed their hypersexualized perception of black people, and for some blacks it confirmed their hypersexualized perception of gay men. Given society's stereotypical view of black men combined with societal beliefs about homosexuality, the story became more believable because it vilified a group of people we did not understand and many of us did not want to know. And for those of us who had been victimized by black men, it gave us a way to express our grief and rage [151].

Larger Euro-American perceptions of black hypersexuality and deviance have informed many blacks' perceptions of sexuality and HIV transmission, which accounts for the failure to constructively address HIV/AIDS in many black communities. While black communities have gotten more progressive in their approach to HIV/AIDS, more remains to be done to subvert the damaging silence surrounding and castigation of homosexuality and black sexuality in general.[7] Until then, many black communities will remain complicit in the enforcement of a racially hegemonic, heterosexist narrative that renders black sexuality "the other."

Joyce, with Ava's assistance, attempts to extricate Idlewild's teenage girls and young women from the trappings of collective silence with the Sewing Circus. The group's discussion topics and activities include, among other things, demonstrations of proper condom usage and the importance of the young members' respect for their bodies and, therefore, insistence on their partners using protection. Nevertheless, Joyce and Ava face resistance from the newly arrived Reverend and Gerry Anderson at New Light Baptist Church, where their meetings are held, because of the church's concomitant espousals of silence and castigation of sexuality. Gerry Anderson, the reverend's wife, vehemently disproves of the Sewing Circus, and wishes to return the church to more "traditional" practices. Echoing many conservative churches' stances on sexuality, particularly during the novel's setting but also very prevalent today, Gerry's philosophy concerning the Sewing Circus members and sex is that the girls should simple suppress their (and their partners') sexual desires. Some of Reverend Anderson's Sunday sermons also link sex with Satan. Additionally, and very importantly, within a racialized context, many black churches' conservative ideologies lie in their responses to societal stereotyping of black sexualities as hypersexual, animalistic, and, therefore, inferior.

When Gerry discovers the proper condom-use demonstration upon making an uninvited and intrusive visit to the SC meeting, she attempts to silence their efforts under the guise of Christian doctrine. In particular, she forces her husband to send an "eviction" letter to Joyce, ejecting her and her group from the church. Rather than merely ignore sexuality in their church, the Andersons further evidence the pervasiveness of silence in their attempts to squelch any dialogues of healthy sexual practices on church grounds. Couched in respectability and biblical rhetoric, the Andersons' letter posits that the Sewing Circus' activities are antithetical to the church's principles as well as proper conduct for a respectable woman. Therefore, in accordance with their letter, Joyce's actions are not empowering but sinful in their acknowledging sexuality before marriage and contesting abstinence-only advocacy.

Gerry's efforts to dismantle the Sewing Circus gatherings extend even beyond church grounds, especially as an undeterred Joyce temporarily holds meetings at her house before moving to a permanent location. Ava and Joyce later learn that the actual impetus behind her actions is not to preserve the sanctity of the church and its members in the face of the supposed dangers of living a sinfully lustful life. Instead, her efforts are meant to protect her husband — who is associated with the Sewing Circus because of its church meetings as well as photographs of him and the members — from legal action for violating a condition of a settlement resulting from discoveries of his pedophilia prior to his tenure at New Light: he molested young male church members in Chicago, where he previously worked. Besides having to leave town, the Reverend pledged to refrain from associating with any youth ministries for five years. Another part of the settlement requires public silence from the families of the molested young boys in exchange for financial retribution. (A mother of one of the young boys, fearing that and consumed with guilt over the Reverend possibly molesting other children, breaches this silence after seeing a photograph of him with the young Sewing Circus members.)

In rendering the church's failure to publicly address the sexual abuse of its young members, Cleage alludes to a culture of silence surrounding these abuses existing among various churches of all races and ethnicities. Some of these churches may privately acknowledge these indiscretions, even ensuring the future financial and material comfort of the victims, but their silence fails to protect the abused or prevent further sexual abuse, especially of young vulnerable church members or youth generally. For instance, it is very much implied that Reverend Anderson, who does not face legal repercussions for his pedophilic sexual exploitation, sexually abuses his 16-year-old grandson Tyrone — whom Ava sees without pants upon her impromptu visit to the reverend's house. The reverend, the only other person in the house with Tyrone prior to Ava's visit, instructs Tyrone to wear pants, causing the teenager to incredulously reply, "'now it's time to put the pants *on*, huh'" (199). Ava also notices in Tyrone a strangely unidentifiable expression connoting his adverse reaction to abuse and the culture of silence perpetuating it. I would add that Tyrone's delinquency, including breaking into some Idlewild residents' homes and raping his equally delinquent best friend's girlfriend, stems partially from the trauma of his molestation and (very likely) rape.

Furthermore, church payouts for these sexual offenses suggest a financial-sexual molestation exchange in alignment with the commercial sexual exploitation of children, which is defined by the World Congress against the Commercial Sexual Exploitation of Children defines as "sexual abuse by the adult and remuneration in cash or kind to the child or to a third person or persons [...] [I]t constitutes a form of coercion and violence against children and amounts to forced labor [...]."[8] These transactions signify that underage sexually abused parishioners are commodities paid for their services, though they are not yet at the age of legal consent and, as the boys in the reverend's previous church elucidate, are unwilling participants. In these instances, the church, the very institution that castigates expressions of sexuality beyond heterosexual marriage, sanctions these practices in their concealment of abuse. All of these render the silence of such churches culpable for perpetuating a cycle of abuse and molestation, especially of its most vulnerable members, as well as creating a prostitution-like environment of financial transactions for sex-related activities.

Anderson's indiscretions with males exacerbates the nature of his sin, as the castigation of supposedly ungodly same-sex sexual encounters would render male-male sexual acts a gross violation of putative religious tenets. It is important to note that conservative biblical doctrine cannot force Anderson to eradicate his sexual attraction toward males or resist his temptation to act upon it. His inability to successfully ward off his sexual urges toward males while attempting to have a "sanctified" existence speaks to the inner conflicts of many religious individuals who cannot control or regulate their attraction toward the same sex. Their experiences and tenuous relationship to conservative interpretations of biblical doctrine beg for a more progressive discourse on sexuality, religious institutions, biblical/religious-doctrine interpretation, and, in the case of *What Looks Like Crazy*, race. While many clergy challenge unprogressive sexual politics of the church — especially noting the ways in which religious works such as the bible have been manipulated to enforce and preserve racial, ethnic, religious, and/or gender hegemony — others, such as Reverend Anderson, continue to internalize biblical interpretations of the sinfulness of same-sex sexual encounters. Anderson responds in the most destructive of ways, including medicating himself with alcohol.

Thus, the Andersons' actions, as well as their previous church's declining to seek legal action against him, help to foster a culture of silence at New Light. As Reverend Anderson is not permitted to have any affiliation with the youth, his association with the Sewing Circus must not be publicized — which means, to Gerry, that the Circus' attention-grabbing dialogues of black female sexual empowerment must be squelched. As a result, Gerry "sacrifices" the sexual and personal health of the Sewing Circus members to protect her husband, who may easily sexually violate other young church and Idlewild community members.

Silence in *What Looks Like Crazy*, then, has not proven beneficial to the sexualities and overall empowerment of the Idlewild community, particularly its female members. Instead, it has been destructive, as it has contributed to the cycle of pregnancies, STIs and other ailments plaguing them. Ironically enough, the outcome of silence surrounding sexuality has been contradictory of its motives of squelching sexual activity outside of conjugal heterosexual union: the prevalence of unmarried teenage mothers unequivocally elucidates its ineffectiveness. Thus, the failures of silence attest to the imperativeness of a discourse on black female sexual empowerment that would, as Joyce and Ava's work with the Sewing Circus intends, help increase sexual self-esteem and lessen participation in risky sexual behaviors.

Sexual Empowerment: Advancing the Discourse

In "The Transformation of Silence into Language and Action," scholar-writer-activist Audre Lorde asserts that in transforming silence into language, it is imperative that women acknowledge their role and also recognize it as essential in the transformation process (43). Joyce and Ava, in their work with the subversive Sewing Circus, knowingly play an integral role in shattering silence surrounding sexuality and, therefore, advancing an empowering discourse on sexual and personal esteem. Moreover, Ava further becomes sexually empowered as she cultivates a healthy sexual and romantic relationship with Eddie Jefferson — widowed Joyce's "brother-figure"/husband's best friend — whom she informs of her HIV status before engaging in a sexual relationship.

Ava's observation about "discomfort [being] a necessary part of the process of enlightenment" (5), in relation to her discomfort with "integrating" a first-class flight, very much applies to her existence post–HIV diagnosis. Rather than react in self-destructive ways, or deteriorate spiritually and emotionally, Ava lives a more aware and healthy lifestyle that enables her to evaluate her prior unhealthy sexual choices. In recounting her past behavior, Ava comes to an unfortunate conclusion: she was not even having an abundance of great sex, which was mostly obligatory and boring. Her unfulfilling sex life, which appears lacking in desire, stems from her mother's suicide because of chagrin over her father's death when she was a very young girl. Consequently, Ava decides not to become emotionally or romantically attached to men, as she may lose a sense of herself just as her mother had done. However, the lack of an erotic sensuality or connection that would enhance sexual experiences has accompanied her romantic detachment.

The erotic, as Audre Lorde posits in "Uses of the Erotic: The Erotic as Power," is a "measure between the beginnings of our sense of self and the chaos of our strongest feelings. It is an internal sense of satisfaction to which, once we have experienced it, we know we can aspire. For having experienced the fullness of this depth of feeling and recognizing its power, in honor and self-respect we can require no less of ourselves" (54). With that stated, it could be argued that Ava's unfulfilling sex life does not render her sensually empowered, though it grants her sexual experience. As an erotic sensuality enhances sexual experiences, Ava's previous sex life was not fully *sexually* empowering, even as she exhibited agency and control over her body. Additionally, I argue, there is an implied silence in Ava's lack of sexual fulfillment, as it emblematizes her failure to vocalize to her partners what pleasures her sexually and/or part ways with the men she met before engaging in disappointing sex. Her negative assessments of love resulting from her mother's suicide also silence or squelch her desire for a romantic partner that would enhance her sexual experience.

Ava's transformation from silence to sexual empowerment is not devoid of an erotic sensual connection, which she finds as she cultivates a romantic relationship with Eddie—who, in turn, helps her locate the erotic within herself. From Cleage's introduction of Eddie, who picks Ava up from the airport upon her arrival in Michigan and invites her to wait at his house before meeting up with Joyce, it is apparent that there is a budding attraction between the two, which intensifies as *What Looks Like Crazy* progresses. Ava and Eddie initially develop a deep friendship that, because of their mutual attraction, allows for an intimate connection. However, once Ava acknowledges her desire, she fears Eddie's response to her HIV status, which will forever change her sex life. Ava's fears are not unfounded and based on the experiential, especially as she recalls that men who would have previously been very much attracted to her would now respond in fear.

It is important to note here that Ava faces a very difficult task of navigating her way around relationships as an HIV-positive woman. As emblematized by men with whom Ava has interacted post-diagnosis, the dating habits of many HIV-negative persons are often very discriminatory in relation to HIV, regardless of the efficacy of proper condom use in its prevention. Ava's HIV status seriously limits her selection of potential partners post-diagnosis, although she begins to yearn for a sexual relationship while still in Atlanta.

Her yearnings and newfound limitations bring her to HIV dating groups, where she fails to find a partner because of its largely dispirited atmosphere and her lack of connection with any of the members. In fact, Ava leaves her meet-up group and, later, Atlanta with the realization that while she has had quite a bit of sex, she has yet to have the experience of making love.

Ava's fears surrounding rejection based on her status and not engaging in a romantic relationship surface with Eddie, to whom she has a sexual and sensual attraction. Her fears of possible undesirability prove untrue when she finally informs Eddie, who asserts that her status renders condom use an imperative and, therefore, does not nullify his attraction to her. Their first sexual encounter is fulfilling sexually, as well as spiritually and emotionally, even consisting of sensuous dialogue such as *"Can I touch your heart? Your soul? Your spirit?"* (141). As a result, and diverging from her previous sexual experiences, Ava finally makes love. Her first sexual experience with Eddie, which includes a connection to the powerful erotic, is an empowering one that is healthy emotionally and spiritually.

With her delineation of Ada and Eddie's lovemaking, Cleage responds to the lack of discourse on empowering sexualities. Silence has altered Ava's existence, but it fails to control it. Her candidness about her HIV status does not hinder her opportunities for a more fulfilled relationship. Instead, Ava gradually becomes more sexually and spiritually aware with Eddie, whose own transformation from drug addict/person who has killed to peaceful and upstanding citizen in ways parallels Ava's transformation from dangerously sexually care-free to responsible. Their connections to each other span beyond the sexual/sensual, as they have encountered trying processes that, rather than debilitate them spiritually, helped mold them into more aware and enhanced individuals. These processes strengthen their personal and sensual connection, thereby also bettering their sexual relationship.

Sensuality and the erotic are salient for Ava's loving relationship with Eddie. They are also important components for Ava's loving relationship with herself. In "Textual Healing: Claiming Black Women's Bodies, the Erotic, and Resistance in Contemporary Novels of Slavery," scholar Farah Jasmine Griffin notes the importance of touch in black women's healing and empowerment. Sensual touch — self-produced, female-female, and/or male-female — "embraces a greater range of physical contact" (522) than merely sexual touch. Consequently, it serves as a healing presence for black female bodies suffering from larger Western discourse's devaluation of black female bodies. Ava and Eddie's lovemaking provides a space for Ava's healing from her devaluation of her own body, which is epitomized by her risky yet unfulfilling sexual behavior pre-diagnosis. (Her prior actions were undoubtedly informed by the politics of silence surrounding black sexuality, which surfaced in response to

Euro-American stereotypes of black female sexuality.) Now, as a result of Ava and Eddie's intimate encounter Ava discovers a level of sensual fulfillment that facilitates her "[whispering] a thank-you to whatever spirits were hovering in the darkness" (146).

Eddie's professed attraction and love for Ava assuages her fears about the ways HIV's ramifications on her body would plague both her and Eddie, who would be her caregiver and have to watch her possibly deteriorate should their relationship progress. Perceiving their first sexual experience as the "initiation," Eddie continues to nurture their relationship, despite Ava's expressed fears; and, at the novel's end, which is roughly five months after Ava's return to Idlewild, Ava and Eddie are married. Ava's description of her wedding further elucidates a love-filled, sensual, and spiritual union with Eddie: "Eddie leaned over and kissed me like we were alone in that room, and right then, right there, I didn't care what came next ... it would be part of the same unbroken line we were all walking in, which is, of course, the *real* lesson" (244).

Ava's loving and sensuous connection with Eddie, as previously asserted, will enhance her sex life, which will extend beyond the physical. Her assertion of her ability to boldly confront any (health-related) obstacles she may face, in spite of whatever fear or discomfort it causes, is grounded in faith and spirituality. Ava is empowered not just sexually but spiritually and sensually as well.

While Eddie plays an imperative role in Ava's journey from silence to empowerment, as does Ava play a role in his own transformation, Ava's own epiphanies concerning life and love dictate her life choices. Her HIV diagnosis forces her to acknowledge her own mortality and, therefore, evaluate her experiences constructively. Ava's assessments and actions post-diagnosis facilitate her body's transformation from a site of silence and its repercussions to one of healing, sensuality, and empowerment. Additionally, as Ava serves metonymically for black female bodies, her bodily transformation allegorizes the liberating possibilities for black female bodies. Through Ava, Cleage's delineation of the vitality of black female sexualities attests to these possibilities of reclaiming black bodies from degradation and devaluation to empowerment. Nevertheless, it also serves a caveat for the futility and dangers of silence.

Ava and Eddie's decision to have their wedding coincide with the Sewing Circus' official opening at its new location signifies their cognizance of the parallels between Ava's and the SC members' journeys from silence to greater awareness. Ava's wedding and the Circus' official opening day concretize the possibilities for further enlightenment and sexual empowerment as well as the shattering of silence. The Sewing Circus' inception also attests to the salience of contesting silence. It initially begins as Wednesday meetings with young female church members, the majority no older than (the very young age of) eighteen, about starting a Sunday nursery for their children; however, the meeting discussions soon evolve from nursery-room responsibilities to men, sex, and childrearing. As the teenagers' single-mother status evidences, and as Ava observes, the "words *safe-sex* were not a part of their erotic vocabularies any more than birth control entered into their family planning options" (90). Some of the teenagers also have more than one child, and rely on the welfare system, which often fosters a sense of dependence rather than self-actualization.

In addition to many of the teenagers' unfounded attestations of discarding protection because of HIV being a "gay disease," many SC members fail to use protection not because of their personal tastes but to comply with their partner's demands. When Joyce stresses to them the importance of condom use, after convincing them that HIV is very non-discriminatory, she is met with responses that reflect their partners' preferences rather than their own. Their explanations are devoid of concerns over their own sexual and personal health. Another telling omission is any sexual or sensual pleasure they have experienced from their risky sexual activities. Observing this, Ava notes that their sex lives are lacking in "making love" or "creative, mutually pleasurable foreplay" (92). Instead, their responses regarding condom use suggest that their sexual exchanges with their male partners are obligatory and sexually unfulfilling. Though they consent to sex, their sexual activities are not performed on their own terms and are mainly for their partners' pleasure. Missing, then, is *their* sexual empowerment.

Despite the girls' protests, Joyce informs them that condom use could be incorporated into their sexual activities while not compromising the intimacy of the moment for either party. To demonstrate, she asks the girls to touch, smell, and look at the condoms in their hands before inserting them on hot dogs, which, while making them uncomfortable, also intrigues them. The girls and young women delightedly take turns practicing condom use, and ask Joyce relevant questions concerning situations that would seemingly render putting on condoms more difficult. Joyce's condom-use demonstration fascinates the young Sewing Circus members because it provides them autonomy regarding their sexual activity and, by extension, their own bodies. Additionally, they are intrigued by the *act* of putting on the condom, which epitomizes a possible level of sexual excitement that has not been the most apparent in their sexual encounters. After an interloping Gerry dismisses the group, the girls and young women, who were previously disinterested in condom use, eagerly take condoms with them as they disperse. Member Tomika even mentions that Joyce's demonstration was timely, despite Gerry Anderson's objections (95).

Rather than merely emphasize the necessity of safe sex, Joyce delves into the reticence of the members' male partners regarding condom use, debunking their ideologies concerning it interfering with intimacy and desire. In so doing, Cleage delegitimizes well-known "justifications" for failing to use protection. It is also implied that partners who refuse protection even upon the members' insistence are the not worthy of pursuing sexually.

According to writer-activist Diana Scholl's "Condom Use Higher Among Blacks, But Still Not Enough," a recent survey conducted by the Indiana National University Sex Study reports that 100 percent of black female teenagers surveyed used condoms during their last sexual encounter, illustrating their responsible sexual behavior and agency over their sex practices. Nevertheless, the condom-use rates drop at an alarmingly significant rate after age eighteen, as many use other contraceptive measures. While helping to prevent pregnancy, these other contraceptive measures do not eradicate risks for STIs; and, therefore, even as of now, many black women face the same risks and ramifications as the Sewing Circus members prior to Joyce's intervention. Additionally Boykin's *Beyond the Down Low* challenges the notion that all black girls and women prefer to use protection in his citing a survey conducted on the sex practices of black women. Many used condoms at the beginning of their relationship but ceased to use it throughout because, like some of the Sewing Circus' male partners, they also felt that the feeling of condoms was an unfavorable one (182) — that most likely "invalidated" the experience to a degree. Others engaged in high-risk sexual behavior also refused to use protection for these reasons. All of these evidence that salient discussions like Joyce's instructions on making condom use part of an erotic, sensual encounter, rather than a necessary precaution that compromises sexual desire, are as necessary today as they were during the time of Cleage's novel's publication.

Gerry's "evicting" of Joyce's Sewing Circus does not deter Joyce, who holds the meetings temporarily at her house until moving into a new location purchased by financially secure Ava. The move from the church leads to a vast increase of SC members, which speaks to both the inability of the Anderson-led church to attract young members and the necessity of black female organizations divorced from marginalizing conservative doctrine often espoused by (black) churches and/or respectability politics. No longer confined to the ideologies of New Light, Joyce and Ava construct a statement of purpose of the "new and improved" Circus, which is "*to nurture free, independent women who can take care of themselves, choose their lovers wisely, and raise their children right*" (157). As the statement evidences, there is a correlation between nurturing oneself, sexual empowerment, and, often, childrearing. Girls and women who are "free" from having internalized marginalizing forces often take care of themselves and their responsibilities — including their sexual health and, products of their sex lives, children, respectively.

Ava also assists Joyce in drafting a list of things "every free woman should know" to include tenets on sexual responsibility and empowerment. Ava's list notes that sexual responsibility should include sexual desire and satisfaction as well as protection and birth control. It also stresses the imperativeness of the members asserting their sexual needs to their partners if necessary in order to be sexually fulfilled, which also evidences the importance of voice and potential repercussions of silence if these needs are not vocalized. As her previous experiences attest, sexual encounters without sexual fulfillment are not fully empowering. Consequently, female sexual satisfaction is also integral to empowerment.

After debating with Ava over tenet 1, which prohibits women from having sex with men they don't like, Joyce believes "like" should be substituted with "love." Joyce accepts Ava's important observation that, as the Sewing Circus members' feelings towards their mates appear to corroborate, love is too exceptional to require it for sex (160). Additionally, Joyce protests the list's failure to include the range of black female sexual orientations, and an agreeing Ava changes "men" in tenet 1 to "people." Joyce and Ava do not marginalize and isolate lesbians and/or others who are sexually attracted to women as well as many of the members who do not love or are not in love with their partners. They realize that an exclusionary list would make the Circus objectives complicit with the religious and social dogma (responsible for the need to create the Circus) they seek to challenge. It would also undermine the Sewing Circus' efficacy, as it would advocate sexual empowerment for girls and women whose sex lives fit only within the confines of love and heterosexuality.

The Sewing Circus' inclusiveness and contestation of dogma place it squarely against the Anderson-led church, and provide Gerry with ammunition to attempt to permanently quiet the organization. In addition to evincing the unprogressive politics of conservative churches, as well as serving as a pretense to keep her husband out of legal trouble, Gerry's response to the Sewing Circus illuminates the difficulties of those who contest silence surrounding sexuality.[9] Gerry, epitomizing an unprogressive status quo, attempts to stop the Sewing Circus from meeting at Joyce's house and moving to a different venue. She even resorts to contacting Joyce's funding agency that, at her request, denies the Sewing Circus a change-of-venue as well as necessary funding.

Yet, none of Gerry's attempts deter Joyce, who continues to fight for her organization, which is made easier once the Reverend's history of molestation is made public and, subsequently, her grant is returned and change-of-venue is approved. By the novel's end, Joyce and Ava are writing grants for additional funding that will help the SC function properly. While the Sewing Circus meetings are barely mentioned from before Ava and Joyce draft the mission statement to the planning of Ava and Eddie's wedding toward the end of the novel, it is more than implied that they continue to uphold the Circus' statement and informative sexual principles. The novel ends, then, with the Circus gaining momentum, members, and, therefore, narratives of transition from silence to empowerment among its black female members.

The novel also ends with a more progressive New Light Baptist Church, as the discovery of the Reverend's molestation leads to the Andersons' exodus and arrival of Sister Judith, who, by virtue of her gender, challenges sexism regarding church leadership. Also, unlike Reverend Anderson, her sermons do not include a castigation of sexuality as the work of Satan. Instead, immediately after her arrival, Sister Judith approaches Joyce about relocating the Sewing Circus back to the church (though, at this point, the renovations for the new place where the meetings would be held are almost done, leading Joyce to decline the invitation). Sister Judith typifies newer directions for previously conservative black churches that will — in alignment with the history of black churches in black communities — provide a space for a discourse on liberation. Yet, this newer discourse will include challenging silence and the lack of black (female) sexual empowerment that it entails. No longer seeing sexuality as antithetical to biblical writings, many radical newer leaders also see a connection between the body, soul, and spirit. They encourage dialogues on healthy sexual behavior, particularly in the face of sexual issues plaguing black communities because of silence. Thus, they foster empowering female and male sexualities, realizing, as womanist theologian Kelly Brown Douglas asserts, that "[o]nly when the taboo of sexuality is discarded will Black women and men be free to experience what it means to wholly love and be loved by the God that became flesh in Jesus" (Douglas 143).

Like a few of her literary foremothers' works — such as Nella Larsen's *Quicksand* (1928) and Toni Morrison's *Sula* (1973) — Cleage's novel contests silence surrounding black female sexualities. However, *What Looks Like Crazy* was published during an era when HIV/AIDS was quickly transitioning into a "black disease" because of disproportionately high newer infection rates among blacks. Also diverging from Cleage, these literary foremothers' works often feature characters that challenge the respectability politics that accompany silence, providing a space for a *public* discourse on the limitations of silence, but often present isolated characters rather than those engaging in dialogues on sex and sexual responsibility in the texts. Cleage's novel was also published during a time of increasing unplanned pregnancies and STI rates among African Americans that most likely occurred because of a challenging of respectability politics (including having premarital sex) without a discourse on sex and sexual responsibility. *What Looks Like Crazy*, then, addresses very timely issues plaguing black communities, especially female members, and illumines the *need* for an effective discourse on black female sexual empowerment that contests the confines of respectability politics as well as the limitations of silence.

What Looks Like Crazy ends with the possibilities for even furthering discourses on black female sexual empowerment on a few levels: in romantic relationships, communal forums/organizations, and, to a degree, more progressive churches. As the novel implies, these various outlets are needed in the fight against silence and for black (female) sexual empowerment. I would add that families are also essential in fostering a dialogue on sexuality that would eliminate or reduce the possibilities of risky sexual behavior. As many scholars and activists have noted, a sexual revolution among black communities will help combat silence, restrictive respectability politics, and their debilitating effects on black communities. This change in perceptions of sexuality would continue to shatter silence, thus lessening the number of blacks engaging in risky practices and, therefore, fostering empowering black female and male sexualities.

Notes

1. Kelly Brown Douglas, *Sexuality and the Black Church: A Womanist Perspective*, 142.
2. Evelynn Hammonds, "Black (W)holes and the Geometry of Black Female Sexuality," 488.
3. Paula Giddings, "The Last Taboo," 425.
4. Often accompanying silence, respectability politics advocate black female "purity" and engaging in sexual activity only during heterosexual marriage.
5. See Douglas' *Sexuality and the Black Church* and Johnnetta Betsch Cole and Beverly Guy-Sheftall's *Gender Talk: The Struggle for Women's Equality in African American Communities*.
6. One of the most recent alleged cases of such sexual misconduct is a pastor Bishop Eddie Long of New Birth Missionary Baptist Church in Lithonia (Georgia), who was accused by four young men of manipulating his position and exploiting their vulnerabilities by having sexual relationships with them during their mid-teenage years.
7. For instance, black churches in Harlem, many of which had been notoriously silent on HIV, have begun HIV ministries in large numbers. See Ingrid Rojas' "Black Churches in Harlem Tackle HIV prevention."
8. Jayne Hoose, Stephen Clift, and Simon Carter, "Combating Tourist Sexual Exploitation of Children," 75.
9. For instance, in 1994, Dr. Joycelyn Elders was fired from her post as surgeon general of the Clinton administration because of her remarks about masturbation as an important component in sexual self awareness that should be taught to students. Her remarks linked sexual self-awareness to the lessening of risky sexual practices that lead to AIDS.

Works Cited

Boykin, Keith. *Beyond the Down Low: Sex, Lies, and Denial in Black America*. New York: Avalon, 2005. Print.

Cleage, Pearl. *What Looks Like Crazy on an Ordinary Day*. New York: Avon, 1997. Print.
Cole, Johnnetta Betsch, and Beverly Guy-Sheftall. *Gender Talk: The Struggle for Women's Equality in African American Communities*. 2003. New York: One World, 2004. Print.
Douglas, Kelly Brown. *Sexuality and the Black Church: A Womanist Perspective*. Maryknoll, NY: Orbis, 1999. Print.
Giddings, Paula. "The Last Taboo." *Words of Fire: An Anthology of African-American Feminist Thought*. New York: New, 1995, 414–428. Print.
Griffin, Farah Jasmine. "Textual Healing: Claiming Black Women's Bodies, the Erotic, and Resistance in Contemporary Novels of Slavery." *Callaloo* 19.2 (1996): 519–536. Print.
Hammonds, Evelynn. "Black (W)holes and the Geometry of Black Female Sexuality." *African American Literary Theory: A Reader*. Ed. Winston Napier. Washington Square: New York University Press, 2000. 482–495. Print.
Hoose, Jayne, Stephen Clift, and Simon Carter. "Combating Tourist Sexual Exploitation of Children." *Tourism and Sex: Culture, Commerce and Coercion*. Eds. Stephen Clift and Simon Carter. London: Pinter, 2000. 74–90. Print.
Lorde, Audre. "The Transformation of Silence into Language and Action." *Sister Outsider: Essays and Speeches by Audre Lorde*. 1984. Freedom: Crossing, 2001. 40–44. Print.
_____. "Uses of the Erotic: The Erotic as Power." *Sister Outsider: Essays and Speeches by Audre Lorde*. 1984. Freedom: Crossing, 2001. 53–59. Print.
Project Q Atlanta. "CDC: Blacks Face Higher HIV Infection Rates." *Project Q Atlanta*. 3 February 2011. Web. 9 April 2011.
Rojas, Ingrid. "Black Churches in Harlem Tackle HIV Prevention." *Northattan*. 19 December 2010. Web. 9 April 2011.
Scholl, Diana. "Condom Use Higher Among Blacks, But Still Not Enough." *BlackDoctor.org*. 2 December 2010. Web. 16 April 2011.

PART II:
MULTIMEDIA CLEAGE: PLAYS, ESSAYS AND THE DIGITAL DIVIDE

Teaching Feminist Lessons in *Late Bus to Mecca*

AMA S. WATTLEY

It is often stated that black women are doubly oppressed, suffering the burdens of both racism and sexism. Together, these two burdens often lead to another, economic oppression, from which many black women also suffer. Pearl Cleage's *Late Bus to Mecca* (1992), takes up the theme of female oppression, with the subject being the sexual exploitation of a black woman in prostitution. As with so many of Cleage's plays, which tend to "feature black women who, either by choice or circumstance, take their lives into their own hands" (Peterson and Bennett 91), so the female protagonist in *Late Bus to Mecca* not only voices her displeasure at her situation, but takes steps to remedy it by escaping her oppressive conditions. What the play suggests as a requirement is that women join forces to help, affirm, and support one another in their self-development and in fighting their common oppression. *Late Bus to Mecca* exposes issues of male supremacy and sexual oppression, issues that began to receive much artistic and critical attention within the black community in the 1970s with the influence of the women's movement and the experiences of black women in the black power movement. Hence, through its five concluding morals, the play seeks to empower black women with some of the necessary lessons and advice for survival in a racist and sexist society.

As a self-described feminist and black nationalist who came of age in the late 1960s, it is clear that Cleage's work has been influenced by both the women's liberation movement, with its emphasis on economic, social, and political equality for women, and the black power movement, with its oftentimes sexist rhetoric and practices, but emphasis on racial equality. Black women were often caught in the middle of these two movements, and they usually decided to continue the fight for racial equality, both because of the racism they discovered in the women's movement and because of the criticism they received from black men within the black power movement if they showed an interest in feminism.[1]

Early on, black women did not wish to jeopardize solidarity with black men or to undermine the Black Liberation Movement with charges of sexism, with many black women adhering to the notion that black liberation should take precedence over sexual liberation. Nevertheless, the high visibility of the feminist movement and the legitimate concerns feminists raised about sexist oppression eventually began to influence black women who had already experienced sexism within civil rights and black power organizations. So, as the women's movement gained momentum, more black women began to speak out against the sexism which they experienced within the civil rights and black power movements. As Deborah K. King writes:

> Even among those black women who expressed grave reservations about participating in the women's movement, most recognized sexism as a factor of their subordination in the larger society and acknowledged sexual politics among blacks. They could identify the sexual inequalities that resulted in the images of black women as emasculating matriarchs; in the rates of sexual abuse and physical violence; and in black men assuming the visible leadership positions in many black social institutions, such as the church, the intelligentsia, and political organizations [301].

As a result of their frustration and discomfort with the racism and sexism embedded in these movements, many black women formed black women's groups whereby they could seek support and solidarity with other African American women who shared, and therefore, could relate to the double oppression of racism and sexism.

In a 1993 *Washington Post* article, Cleage's recollection of the black power movement reiterates the charge of sexism that marred the call for racial equality. Of the movement, Cleage says: "When I was coming of age in the '60s, a lot of black nationalists were the most rampant chauvinists around ... I mean, [insisting that black women] walk five steps behind, and all that" (French C1). She also asserts the significance of feminism for black women while acknowledging the ambivalence many of them continue to feel toward it when she states: "I think black women have the right to claim feminism, although many of us don't, because we think of it as a white woman's thing, and we're certainly encouraged in thinking that by black men" (French C1).

One reason Cleage believes black women have a right to claim feminism is addressed in her 1987 book *Deals With The Devil* where she addresses the need to take issues of sexual oppression seriously in the black community.

Cleage notes that sexism is "still not a word that gets used much in the black community, even though it describes a form of oppression that affects the majority population in the community — women!— and is no less virulent and deadly than racism" (*Deals with the Devil* 24). She further states that "black men routinely and cavalierly deny" sexism's existence as a "critical element in our African American female identity" (25), and because of their denial, black women are "rob[bed] ... of the possibility of working cooperatively with our brothers on defining the problem and trying to solve it" (25). Hence, Cleage's plays often focus on the oppressions black women face due to the interlocking forces of racism and sexism, and her solutions often include acts of female assertion that are strengthened through alliances with other black women.

In dramatic structure, *Late Bus to Mecca* is unconventional, employing the Brechtian[2] technique of projecting titles of scenes onto screens. The play consists of thirteen short scenes which are accompanied by thirteen slides, each one containing a quotation from the monologue of the upcoming scene. Like Brecht's epic theater, *Late Bus to Mecca* is meant to be didactic — to teach the spectator a "certain quite practical attitude; ... to make it possible for him to take a critical attitude while he is in the theatre (as opposed to a subjective attitude of becoming completely 'entangled' in what is going on). Catharsis is not the main object of this dramaturgy" (Brecht 78). Part of getting the spectator to think critically is to achieve an "alienation effect," which involves the use of film projections "to help bring the social complex of the events taking place to the forefront" (Brecht 79).

In addition to utilizing a Brechtian technique in her play, Cleage shares with Brecht certain philosophical beliefs about the theatre as well. Both feel that a play should incite its spectators to action and that part of their task as playwrights is to offer solutions to the problems they confront in their drama. For example, Brecht asserts that "the object of inquiry in epic theatre, whether it be hunger, cold, oppression, etc. is not just to arouse moral objection to such circumstances but to discover means for their elimination" (Brecht 75). Similarly, Cleage notes that "my response to the oppression I face is to name it, describe it, analyze it, protest it, and propose solutions to it as loud as I possibly can every time I get a chance" (Perkins and Uno 46). Furthermore, both Cleage and Brecht suggest that these solutions can be found by making efforts to unite and struggle together. Brecht says: "Man can improve his condition only by banding together and joining forces. It is only then that he stands a chance" (Brecht 68). And Cleage, speaking to black women, declares: "Let's bond together as a group with our own specific interests as black women that cross arbitrary lines of economic and social class and join us at the womb" (*Deals with the Devi*, 35). In *Late Bus to Mecca* Cleage proclaims this message of black female solidarity. In an author's note to the play, Cleage states that *Late Bus to Mecca* is the first in a series of morality plays, the intention of which will be to "identify and highlight the values and actions that will be necessary if black women — and by extension black people — are to survive into the twenty-first century" (297). To this end, Cleage concludes her play with five maxims, projected onto the screen, that offer practical advice to her audience.

Late Bus to Mecca was co-produced by the Women's Project and The New Federal Theatre, and opened at the Judith Anderson Theatre in New York City on February 28, 1992.[3] The play dramatizes the encounter at a bus station between a black prostitute named Ava and a nameless black woman (referred to as A Black Woman) who never speaks a word during the course of the entire play. Ava has plans to meet a friend, and then take the bus to Atlanta in order to capitalize on the large number of black people who will be flocking there to view Muhammad Ali's first boxing match after a three-year exile, resulting from his refusal to fight in the Vietnam War on the grounds of his religious beliefs. Her plan to leave Detroit results from having reached the limit of how much sexual exploitation she will endure.

The first scene, "Did they just call the bus to Atlanta?" provides the audience with a quick visual of the play's two female characters. It opens with a view of A Black Woman sitting huddled and shivering on a bench, looking dirty, disheveled, tired, and fearful. Cleage makes it clear that while A Black Woman is supposed to represent "every physically battered, spirit-bruised black woman whose words have been ignored or used against her" (300), there is no monolithic black female experience that she is supposed to represent. Rather, her experiences are specific to her particular circumstances. Upon first impression, her presence in the bus station, coupled with her disheveled appearance, might suggest homelessness. However, because of her silence, neither Ava nor the audience discovers the specifics of A Black Woman's circumstances during the course of the play, and therefore, can only speculate about them. Early in the play, for example, when Ava asks if she is traveling to Atlanta, A Black Woman's panicked expression conveys that she does not want her whereabouts or her travel plans known. Her reaction suggests, as Ava surmises, that she is fleeing from someone or something, or that someone is pursuing her. Hence, it is apparent that she has experienced some kind of traumatic, exploitative, or abusive situation.

In contrast to A Black Woman, Ava is talkative and direct. She enters in flashy, tight clothing and high heels, a visual clue to her profession as a prostitute. In the stage notes, Cleage informs that Ava is not a caricature, and should appear attractive and confident. Spotting A Black Woman, Ava asks about the bus departure time and if she has seen another woman pass through. Ava continues talking even though A Black Woman gives no response. Finally realizing this, Ava dashes out, only to re-enter in the next scene and again try to engage A Black Woman in conversation. When A Black Woman continues to be unresponsive, Ava is not offended but begins talking about herself.

In keeping with Cleage's feminist ideal of bonding between and among black women, the first lesson or moral of *Late Bus to Mecca* is the directive to "take care of your sisters." The notion of female bonding has roots in the women's liberation movement, in the concept of "consciousness-raising" sessions whereby women came together to share personal experiences, problems, and feelings. These "consciousness-raising" sessions that began to spring up all over the country during the early 1970s was the first step to creating a safe space and a climate for women to speak about the oppression they faced. As Winifred D. Wandersee notes: "The emergence of feminist consciousness with respect to male violence was a natural consequence of the women's liberation movement, its emphasis on women's right to control their bodies and lives, and on the connection between the personal and the political" (91). Women began to speak out about such issues as rape, spousal abuse, incest, and sexual harassment which prior to this period, had been cloaked behind a veil of privacy. By finally recognizing the social causes of these personal issues and placing them into a political perspective, women were empowered to take collective action to find solutions.

The character of Ava heeds this advice to "take care of her sisters" in her actions and monologues throughout the play. From the beginning, Ava takes on a nurturing, protective role toward A Black Woman as she lectures her about the dangers women face from men. She believes A Black Woman is not familiar with bus travel because she is sitting alone in a dim area where men can easily prey upon her. A woman alone, she asserts, is vulnerable to harassment from any male predator, one of whom she spots across the station, looking her over: "You see that guy over there? I saw him looking at me when I first came in.... Don't worry. He ain't coming over here. They don't mess with you unless you're all by yourself.... They get real brave then. Can't tell them shit then! (304–305; sc. 2).

Moreover, despite A Black Woman's early withdrawal and unresponsiveness to Ava's questions and comments, Ava does not give up, but instead, attempts to establish a pattern of non-verbal communication between herself and A Black Woman by having her blink if she is able to hear what Ava is saying. When A Black Woman closes her eyes in response to this request, Ava chooses to perceive it as a sign that A Black Woman does indeed hear her, and so, Ava continues to talk to her. Gradually, Ava's friendly persistence yields some positive results and A Black Woman begins to show trust in Ava.

For example, at one point, Ava draws attention to A Black Woman's dirty face, and while A Black Woman shows concern, she does not take the handi-wipes Ava extends to her with which to clean her face. Therefore, Ava gently cleans it for her and A Black Woman allows her to do so. During the course of the play, Ava's nurturance will also include encouraging A Black Woman to eat a sandwich Ava purchases for her, and grooming A Black Woman to make her more presentable.

Ava's attempts to nurture, however, are not without frustration. She often finds herself annoyed when the women she seeks to help rebuff her. Before attempting to befriend A Black Woman, Ava has shown a propensity to help and rescue another downtrodden black woman, namely her friend Sherri, another prostitute. Ava has endured a lot with Sherri and has stuck by her when others did not think she would make it. It is Sherri for whom Ava is now anxiously waiting at the bus station. However, irritated by Sherri's lateness and A Black Woman's silence, Ava remarks sarcastically at one point, "Great! I got one on the way who can't tell time and one sittin' here who can't talk. This must be my lucky night" (311; sc. 6).

Moreover, Ava almost loses the trust she had begun to establish with A Black Woman, when, in scene 8, A Black Woman returns from the bathroom to find Ava rummaging through her backpack in an effort to learn her identity or discover some clues that will provide information about her. There is no identification in the backpack, though, only some money in a wallet and an empty, cap-less pill bottle, an object that fuels Ava's speculation. As a result of Ava's betrayal, A Black Woman again withdraws, now suspicious of Ava, while Ava feels guilty at having been caught and chagrined at having lost the confidence A Black Woman was beginning to show in her. All of this is depicted wordlessly in a short tableau scene entitled "What Can I Say?" in which both women stare straight ahead, A Black Woman clutching her backpack to her and Ava smoking a cigarette and jiggling her foot nervously.

In the end, the two women re-establish a connection. Ava's silence does not continue for very long, and in the next scene, "Not after I got to know you," she admits that she probably would have stolen A Black Woman's money before she got to know her, but hopes A Black Woman knows that she was not going to rob her, and in the last scene of the play, entitled "You could have told me," Ava's bus is called and she gets ready to leave. She gives A Black Woman ten dollars and goes to hand in Sherri's ticket. While she is gone, A Black Woman pulls the scarf that Ava gave her from her head and lets it drop to the floor, suggesting that she feels abandoned by Ava. A Black Woman does not know that Ava is watching her, and having seen this action, she returns with Sherri's ticket, and offers it to A Black Woman, who accepts it and smiles for the first time. They leave together with Ava having a plan for A Black Woman to communicate her name non-verbally. Hence, Ava fulfills Cleage's mandate to take care of her sisters in her treatment of A Black Woman. The nurturance that she has shown ultimately creates a sense of safety in A Black Woman that allows her to accept Ava's invitation to join her in her travels.

The three moral lessons sandwiched between the first and last ones are related. They include: be resourceful; have a plan; and make a move — all of which involve an assertion of agency and an attempt at self-actualization — important strategies for women's survival and autonomy. Feminism itself is committed to action and change. As Patricia Hill Collins notes: "The existence of Black feminist thought suggests that there is always choice, and power to act, no matter how bleak the situation may appear to be. Viewing the world as one in the making raises the issue of individual responsibility for bringing about change" (237). In "Late Bus to Mecca," Ava is committed to changing her life for the better through her own resourcefulness, planning, and action.

Ava's attempts to find solutions to her problems, make plans to eradicate them, and act upon the plans she has established are crucial notions she exhibits throughout the play, first, when she reveals the reason she is going to Atlanta during the weeklong celebration of Muhammad Ali's victory over the American government and his return to the boxing ring. She hopes to sell her body for the last time by catering to the large crowds in attendance in order to make enough money to enroll in beauty school, noting that the only two options open to women as a means for independent living are to become a prostitute or a beautician, and in doing so, she speaks to the basic sex inequality in our economic structure. As Jennifer James notes, the limited economic options open to women help us to understand prostitution as an "occupational choice for some women, rather than as a symptom of the immorality or deviance of individuals ... [S]ome women, in choosing the occupation of prostitution, are reacting to their victimization by this sex based economic inequality" (183). Ava desires to work at a legitimate profession, and believes this week in Atlanta will be the first step toward making her dream come true. She devised her plan after her pimp, Tony, loses his money gambling and is unable to accompany her and Sherri on the trip. Believing this is the perfect time to break away from Tony, leave Detroit permanently, and work independently — without having to surrender any of her earnings to Tony, and thus, save for beauty school — Ava makes a move. Later on in the play, Ava will lecture A Black Woman about the need to always have a plan of survival. She surmises that A Black Woman has no such plan because she is at the bus station but does not seem to have a destination in mind. Ava announces that she always has a plan of action, which is what her trip to Atlanta is all about.

Not surprisingly, then, it is passivity and a lack of purpose that irritates Ava, and she sees these qualities in both A Black Woman and Sherri. So, when once again realizing the probability that Sherri is not going to show up to meet the bus, Ava lashes out at A Black Woman, inferring that she has been institutionalized in a mental hospital due to her earlier discovery of the empty pill bottle in A Black Woman's backpack:

> AVA: ... You not gonna make it! You hear what I'm telling you? They ought to lock you up now and save you and them some trouble. I don't know how they let you out in the first place. I'm tired of being around crazy bitches who don't know how to make a move! Why don't you fix yourself up! [316; sc. 10].

Ultimately, Ava softens and returns to showing sympathy for A Black Woman's plight. At the beginning of scene 11, for example, she is shown giving A Black Woman a make-over in response to her question, "Can't you fix yourself up?" She combs A Black Woman's hair and gives her a new blouse to wear. Moreover, Ava speaks about her understanding of mental institutions as oppressive places that are complicit with the patriarchal society and exploitative toward women. She reveals that Sherri was in a mental hospital once and says of it:

> AVA: I think they scared her real bad in there. Made her think she might be crazy for real.... They didn't make you think that did they? (*Ava looks directly at ABW who returns her gaze and then turns away.*)
>
> AVA: Why do you bitches believe that shit? Of course that's what they're gonna say. What else are they gonna tell you? "It's niggas driving you crazy. Cut them loose. Close your legs and open your eyes and make a move!" They not gonna tell you no helpful shit like that. They'd be out of a job in a minute! (*Ava catches her gently by the chin and turns her face back around.*) I'm sorry, honey. You don't need for me to be fussing at you. You're doing real good. At least you got nerve enough to be out here trying, right? The only time it's really over is when you stop trying, right? (*Softly.*) Isn't that right? (*Ava looks at ABW, leans over and kisses her very gently on the mouth.*)[4] [320; sc. 12].

Ava perceives the mental hospital and society in general as working to keep women subordinate and dependent upon men. She believes they have no desire to aid women in becoming self-sufficient and independent or in recognizing the role men play in women's oppression. Rather, they make the woman believe she is inherently unstable. Her condition is seen as internally rather than externally caused. Ava believes that like Sherri, A Black Woman has been brainwashed to believe this. Thus, unlike in her moment of anger when Ava denounced A Black Woman as being unable to take care of herself, now she gives A Black Woman encouragement for the efforts she has made to change her situation. Ava realizes that while A Black Woman may not have a well-conceived plan of action, she has already taken a courageous first step of removing herself from whatever dangerous, traumatic, or exploitative environment she has been enduring.

The last of Cleage's moral lessons — "Don't do animals" — helps to explain Ava's own exploitative circumstances and what has led her to the bus station on this day. The warning speaks to the sexual degradation in which Ava is embroiled as a prostitute. In her decision to make Ava a black female prostitute, Cleage breaks boundaries. Black women's relationship to prostitution has always been fraught with extra baggage because, historically, black women have been stereotyped as sexually wanton and objects of uncontrolled sexual feeling. As a result, many black playwrights have avoided representations of black female prostitutes for fear of perpetuating existing stereotypes about black women. This is also true in critical and scholarly writing as well. Patricia Hill Collins notes, for example, that there has been a "virtual silence of the black feminist community concerning the participation of far too many black women in prostitution. Ironically, while the image of the African American woman as prostitute has been aggressively challenged, the reality of African American women who work as prostitutes remains unexplored" (164). In the creation of Ava, however, Cleage has begun a fictional exploration of the black female prostitute that other black women playwrights have shied away from because black women have so long been stereotyped as sexually loose and promiscuous. As Lisa Anderson points out, Cleage is among a younger generation of black women playwrights who "do not feel restricted to representing only 'positive' images ... and some of [their] plays use black female sexuality that might seem stereotypical. Their use here is not to titillate or to reinforce stereotype; rather, their use, makes a larger point about U. S. culture and the lives of real black women" (123).

The larger point Cleage is making by casting Ava in the role of a prostitute, an image that would seem to reinforce a negative stereotype of black women, is one of solidarity and inclusiveness. The playscript of *Late Bus to Mecca* provides a note to the director in which Cleage not only gives directions on how Ava should be portrayed, but explains why she gave Ava this occupation as well. Cleage notes that "Ava represents the possibility of consciously extending the circle of sisterhood to include every black woman specifically, in all her complexity and terribleness. Ava has to be a prostitute because we have to see the potential for our salvation in every segment of our group. We cannot allow class distinctions, superficial moral judgments, and personal prejudices to divide and conquer us" (300).

Nevertheless, despite having greater freedom to represent a wider range of black female images, Cleage is careful in her depiction of Ava, due both to her knowledge of how black women have been perceived historically and to her didactic purpose for the play. As a result, Cleage instructs that Ava not be "painted in broad comedic strokes"; she must be an "admirable and likeable character so that the audience's identification with her can help them confront and release their own class prejudices" (300). Acutely aware of society's attempt to stigmatize the prostitute as "immoral," Cleage wants to make sure she is a figure with whom women share a commonality and thus cannot automatically dismiss as deviant. In essence, Cleage takes a stance similar to Susan Brownmiller, who notes that "the male sex has always tried to ... separate the woman engaged in prostitution from the rest of women in the culture. It calls her 'the other,' it makes her the bad woman, it sends her to jail, and it tells the rest of us that we are very good and virtuous and we have nothing in common with her" (73). She goes on to point out that "the feminist movement identifies with the female victim of the male-created institution known as prostitution" (74). This kind of understanding and insight is what Cleage wants from an audience as well, in order to build bridges among black women. Therefore, Cleage infuses Ava with strength and fortitude to survive and a compassion for other struggling women that make her an appealing character, one who not only imparts, but carries out, the lessons Cleage wants her audience to learn.

Although not written in the 1960s or 1970s, the play is set in 1970, and throughout the 1970s, feminists took up the issue of physical and sexual violence against women — domestic violence, child abuse, incest, rape, as well as the more public forms of exploitation, such as sexual harassment and pornography. While prostitution did not get as much attention as pornography from feminists, it was perceived as another form of violence against women, another institution of male supremacy. The prostitute was perceived as a victim, and her lot encapsulated some of the issues of the feminist movement, such as gender-based economic inequality and sexist laws. As noted before, prostitutes were often believed to be motivated by a desire to make money and obtain material possessions that could not be fulfilled in other professions because of limited career opportunities open to women. Susan Brownmiller wrote in a paper entitled "Speaking Out On Prostitution," that "There is a serious problem in our society, when women with ambition must sell their bodies because there is no other way that they can earn fifteen thousand a year" (76). Also, prostitution exposed the double standard against women established in law enforcement that made the female prostitute subject to arrest, prosecution, and jail time, while her male customers were protected from involvement in the criminal justice system. Hence, prostitution was believed to be another example of male power and female powerlessness, and its end was demanded. However, Brownmiller acknowledged that, "Prostitution will not end in this country until men see women as equals. And men will never see women as equals until there's an end to prostitution, so it seems that we will have to work for the full equality of women and the end of prostitution side by side" (76).

The warning "Don't do animals" serves as the title of scene 6 of the play, and it is in this scene that Ava reveals she works as a prostitute. She tells A Black Woman about Tony, her pimp, who lured Ava into prostitution when she was contemplating quitting her job as a dancer in a disreputable club. But the protection he provided was from everyone but himself. She hopes to go to Atlanta to make enough money so that she won't have to return to Detroit and to Tony's exploitation of her, which most recently has included pressure to engage in deviant practices like sex with animals. Having lost his ticket to the boxing match by gambling, Tony had hoped to save face with his cronies and impress them by putting on a show where Ava and a dog are the main attraction. Thus, Ava becomes the solution to a problem he created. As Brock and Thistlewaite assert, "Using women sexually is one way men bond together for entertainment ... However women are used sexually, their purpose is to show male dominance, power, and prowess" (172). By pressuring Ava to participate in this sexual practice, Tony oversteps the bounds of tolerance, even for Ava who declares that "I can do about anything a regular human being can think up to ask me if they paying cash money, but animals is different" (311–12; sc. 6).

While Ava has enough self-respect not to engage in a degrading sexual practice, Sherri neither assented nor refused. So although she and Ava had planned to leave Detroit together, as time goes by, Ava begins to realize that Sherri has probably decided to stay and oblige the manipulative Tony because he has cajoled and complimented her into complying. Sherri, a drug addict, can be more easily controlled by Tony because, as Ava says, "[S]he zig zags all over the damn map, depending on who's holding the most dope" (317; sc. 11). Thus, for Sherri, drugs and money outweigh her self-respect. This is also true of Sherri's sexual encounters with Ava, which Sherri regards as freakish and which she will only perform for pay, not merely for Tony's voyeuristic enjoyment. Ava, on the other hand, regards these encounters with Sherri with greater emotional attachment.

Needless to say, Ava's work as a prostitute has caused her to harbor a great deal of hostility toward men and she distrusts them all. As she told A Black Woman earlier when she was caught rummaging through her backpack, Ava would rather steal from a man than another woman. Moreover, speaking of the male sex, she claims that "ain't none of them shit" (308; sc. 4) and that she "don't believe one word that comes out of a man's mouth" (310; sc. 5). Ava is suspicious of men because she feels that so many of them are only interested in sex and are ready to exploit women. Ava's work as a prostitute and her experiences with Tony have made her increasingly aware of men's expectation that "women will and ought to serve their sexual needs and that sexual access to women is their right" (Brock and Thistlewaite, 15). Hence, because of what appears to be a developed contempt for men and the ready identification of them with clients, Ava turns to other women for loving human relationships. Sherri provided Ava with her first same-sex sexual experience, and she perceives it as a part of sisterhood — two women together, helping each other out (319; sc. 12).

At the end of "Late Bus to Mecca," in addition to being placed on the slides, the play's five morals are distributed on fliers to the audience by the two actresses who have played Ava and A Black Woman. As shown, the lessons have all been incorporated into Ava's monologues and actions. Once Ava reached the limit of how much exploitation she would endure, she devised a strategy for extricating herself from that situation, and found the courage to act on that idea. Her strategy was not a selfish one, but involved attempts to first help Sherri and then A Black Woman to free themselves from their oppressive conditions and environments and gain a sense of independence and self-worth. While Ava failed in her attempt to aid Sherri, she succeeds with A Black Woman because, like Ava, A Black Woman has already taken steps to help herself, and thus shows a desire to move forward with her life.

Through her two female characters, Cleage calls attention to the oppression black women face as a result of gender, race, and class. Although A Black Woman never speaks during the play, Cleage demonstrates in writing *Late Bus to Mecca* that to remain silent about the physical and emotional abuse, exploitation, and manipulation black women suffer would be to deny the existence of this sexist oppression and to sacrifice issues and concerns important to black women. Had she decided to conform and adhere to the boundaries that had been set in regard to speaking about sexist oppression within the black community, the very real experiences of black women would have once again been placed on the periphery and not given voice. Instead, Cleage uses her voice to suggest that black women's survival rests in their ability to expose sexism, impart practical wisdom, and build bonds of solidarity with other black women. Together they can provide support, affirmation, and the strength to empower one another to overcome shared hardships and oppressions.

Notes

1. For further information on black women and the Women's Liberation movement of the 1960s and 1970s, see Paula Giddings's *When and Where I Enter: The Impact of Black Women on Race and Sex in America*, 1984; bell hooks' *Ain't I a Woman?: Black Women and Feminism*, 1981; and Toni Cade's *The Black Woman: An Anthology*, 1970.

2. For an introduction to Brecht and his theories, see Peter Brooker's essay "Key Words in Brecht's Theory and Practice of Theatre" in *The Cambridge Companion to Brecht*, 1994.

3. Mel Gussow reviewed *Late Bus to Mecca* for *The New York Times* and found it to be "shorter and pithier" than Cleage's other one act play "Chain," which were on a double bill. He writes that: "The play is not without its clichés, and [Ava's] monologue ... is repetitive," but "the relationship has its tender side, and the two actresses are keenly attuned to their characters" (C19).

4. The scene ends with this kiss by Ava, so A Black Woman's reaction to it is not shown. By this time in the play, Ava has already revealed that she has engaged in and enjoyed homosexual encounters with Sherri. Although she never specifically identifies herself as a lesbian, by voicing her homoerotic feelings and kissing A Black Woman, Ava presents another rare image within black women's drama, in addition to that of a prostitute.

Works Cited

Anderson, Lisa M. *Black Feminism in Contemporary Drama*. Urbana: University of Illinois Press, 2008. Print.

Brecht, Bertolt. *Brecht on Theatre*. Trans. John Willett. New York: Hill and Wong, 1964. Print.

Brock, Rita Nakashima, and Susan Brooks Thistlewaite. *Casting Stones: Prostitution and Liberation in Asia and the United States*. Minneapolis: Fortress, 1996. Print.

Brooker, Peter. "Key Words in Brecht's Theory and Practice of Theatre." *The Cambridge Companion to Brecht*. Cambridge: Cambridge University Press, 1994. 185–200.

Brownmiller, Susan. "Speaking Out On Prostitution." 1971. *Radical Feminism*. Eds. Anne Koedt, Ellen Levine, and Anita Rapone. New York: Quadrangle, 1973. 72–77. Print.

Cade, Toni, ed. *The Black Woman: An Anthology*. New York: Mentor, 1970.

Cleage, Pearl. *Deals With The Devil and Other Reasons to Riot*. New York: Ballantine, 1987. Print.

_____. *Late Bus to Mecca*. 1992. *Playwriting Women: 7 Plays From the Women's Project*. Ed. Julia Miles. Portsmouth, NH: Heinemann, 1993. 299–322. Print.

Collins, Patricia. *Black Feminist Thought*. New York: Routledge, 1990. Print.

French, Mary Ann. "In the Chasm of Racism and Sexism: Pearl Cleage Fighting Back With Nationalism and Feminism." *Washington Post*. 29 July 1993: C1, 4. Print.

Giddings, Paula. *When and Where I Enter: The Impact of Black Women on Race and Sex in America*. New York: Bantam, 1984. Print.

Gussow, Mel. "'Chain' and 'Late Bus to Mecca.'" *The New York Times*. 4 March 1992: C19. Print.

hooks, bell. *Ain't I a Woman? Black Women and Feminism*. Boston: South End, 1981.

James, Jennifer. "The Prostitute as Victim." *The Victimization of Women*. Eds. Jane Roberts Chapman and Margaret Gates. Beverly Hills, CA: Sage, 1978. Print.

King, Deborah K. "Multiple Jeopardy, Multiple Consciousness: The Context of Black Feminist Ideology." 1988. *Words of Fire: An Anthology of African American Feminist Thought*. Ed. Beverly Guy-Sheftall. New York: New, 1995. 164–173. Print.

Peterson, Jane T., and Suzanne Bennett. *Women Playwrights of Diversity: A Bio-Bibliographical Sourcebook*. Westport, CT: Greenwood, 1997. Print.

Wandersee, Winifred D. *On the Move: American Women in the 1970s*. Boston: Twayne, 1988. Print.

Pearl Cleage as a Dirty Realist

Kelly DeLong

In 1983 the British literary magazine *Granta* dedicated an issue to American writers the magazine dubbed "Dirty Realists." The magazine said that these American writers wrote about "the belly-side of contemporary life — a deserted husband, an unwed mother, a car thief, a pick pocket, a drug addict — but they write about it with disturbing detachment [... , u]nderstated, ironic, sometimes savage, but insistently compassionate" (*Granta* 1). In America these writers were given many different labels: "new realists," "neo-domestic realists," "pop realists," and, lastly, "minimalists," which was the label that finally stuck (Herzinger 8). Kim A. Herzinger, writing in the *Mississippi Review* in 1985, described these writers as writing fiction that focused on "ordinary subjects," with "recalcitrant narrators," and "deadpan narratives." He said that their work featured a slightness of story and characters "who don't think out loud" (8). Thomas McGuanne, in the same essay, says that the Dirty Realists/minimalists wrote "'about the bitter, grim, domestic aspects of living'" (qtd. in Herzinger 9). Critics agreed that this new type of writing could be found mostly in short fiction. However, when pressed for a conclusive list of these writers, critics rarely agreed. Found on most of the lists were the writers Tobias Wolff and Richard Ford. The only name on all the lists was Raymond Carver. Carver, as most of the writers on the list of Dirty Realists/Minimalists, was male. While some female writers were included on some of the lists, by and large, this new style of writing was seen as the realm of male short story writers. On no one's list could there be found a black writer. Now, with nearly thirty years since *Granta* identified Dirty Realism/Minimalism as a style of writing, the time has come to make an adjustment to the list of Dirty Realists/Minimalists. The scope and breadth of this literary movement begun in the 1980s merits fresh reflection. This list now may be expanded to include Pearl Cleage.

Cleage's 1991 work *The Brass Bed and Other Stories* is as realistic and as minimal in presentation as any of the writers identified and celebrated in the 1980s. Classified as "fiction/African American Studies," Cleage's brief book is a collection of monologues, short fiction and poetry. Nearly all of the pieces are told from the first person point of view, and, when the narrator is identified by name, that name is Pearl Cleage, reminiscent of Tim O'Brien's celebrated collection of Vietnam stories *The Things They Carried*, published the year before *The Brass Bed and Other Stories*. As in O'Brien's collection, Cleage lends the main character in the pieces her own name, in this way giving each tale a heightened sense of credibility, as well as showing that these aren't so much stories imagined as they are stories lived. At no time in *The Things They Carried* does the reader question the authenticity of the narrator. The same holds true for *The Brass Bed and Other Stories*. The reader is never asked to suspend disbelief, and the character Pearl Cleage comes across as an honest to goodness, flesh and blood person.

Also lending credibility to the pieces in Cleage's collection is the style in which they are presented. In the tradition of Dirty Realism/Minimalism, Cleage's stories are written in a clipped, halting style that suggests background without the narrator's having to give the complete back story. In this style of writing, the "flatness of tone" gives the reader all she needs to know about the character and his or her past (Herzinger 8). By using the way the story is told to present character, Cleage, like the writers of this style, rejected the traditional way to tell a story. This way of presenting character through a flat, matter-of-fact tone is one of the hallmarks of Dirty Realism/Minimalism. A good way to show how Cleage's style compares with the style of an identified Dirty Realist/Minimalist would be to look at the way each writer introduces a character in a similar situation. First, in Raymond Carver's story "Why Don't You Dance?" Carver utilizes the Dirty Realistic/Minimalistic style of writing to show the aftermath of the break up of a marriage. He writes about a man looking at his bedroom furniture, which he has placed out in the front yard. Carver writes:

> In the kitchen he poured another drink and looked at the bedroom suite in his front yard. The mattress was stripped and the candy-striped sheets lay beside two pillows on the chiffonier. Except for that, things looked much the way they had in the bedroom — night stand and reading lamp on his side of the bed, night stand and reading lamp on her side.
> His side, her side.
> He considered this as he sipped whiskey [3].

In her story "Christmas 1981," Cleage also writes about the aftermath of a failed relationship. Just as in the Carver story, the causes of the break up are only hinted at, but the tone, what Herzinger calls "deadpan" (7), indicates to the reader the causes of character trouble minus the narrator's explanation. Without being told, the reader has a good idea what the character is like and what her problems are. Cleage writes:

> Last night, we spent it together, me and him. We thought it was important to the kid. We thought we could make her think it meant something for us to be sitting there, opening presents and taking snapshots. I spent the night there, in the house where I used to live. And Christmas morning, I started smoking dope before it was ten o'clock [66].

To even greater effect, Cleage uses the Dirty Realistic/Minimalistic style of writing in the title story of her collection. In very few words, she explains the difference between the men of the family she writes about with the women of the family. She writes:

> The lineage runs through the women. Because of the children. And the bed. Or maybe that's saying the same thing twice. Or once removed. No matter. It was a lot of different things for the men. Mostly land. Sometimes gambling. But for the women, it was always because of the children that they made a move or didn't. Left a man, or stayed. Their choices were more limited [7].

Just as with the Dirty Realists/Minimalists of the Eighties, Cleage uses fragments of sentences to highlight the essentials of the backstory in order to set up the story proper. This "slightness of story" (Herzinger 11) style is one that, like the other writers of this style, Cleage employs to get at the essence of character and story. It is not a "trick" or a distraction from the story, as some have called this style (15), but instead a way to present character raw, to get to the heart of who the character is and the particular situation in which the character finds herself. This rawness of presentation is seen in "The Brass Bed" when the narrator introduces the reader to the spouses of the two main characters of the story, the sisters Abbie and Jennie. Cleage writes about Abbie's husband:

> After a few years [...], Abbie, in a fit of passion and defiance, married herself off to a riverboat gambler with a dimple in his chin and a cruel mouth who beat her, threw her children into the street and locked the door behind them [7].

Later in the story, we are told that Abbie's sister Jennie "had married a musician, presented him with two daughters and watched him die of stab wounds at a church bar-b-que that got out of hand" (8). In this story, and others in the collection, Cleage clearly establishes herself, stylistically, as a Dirty Realist/Minimalist. There is little doubt she is of this school.

However, there is more to Dirty Realism/Minimalism than just the style.

As mentioned earlier, this type of writing is *about* something. Kim A. Herzinger says that Dirty Realism/Minimalism is about

> tracing the collisions of the anarchic self and its inexplicable desires with the limitations imposed by life in the world, with special attention paid to that moment when the self confronts its limitations and decides to keep going [20].

In other words, Dirty Realists/Minimalists write about characters who are forced to acknowledge their own limitations when confronted by outside forces. To put it another way, these characters are often so self-absorbed that they are incapable of understanding where they fit in with others around them as well as the society they inhabit. At some point in these stories, these characters must decide how to react to circumstances that cause them to view themselves differently. In Richard Ford's stories, the protagonists often discover that their limited view of self conflicts with how others view them. In Tobias Wolff's stories, characters constantly try to impose on others their own sense of reality only to find that no one is interested. In Raymond Carver's stories, his characters spend much of their time trying to decide what to do about the problems they themselves created because of their "anarchic self and its inexplicable desires," as Herzinger says.

While Cleage's characters have similar conflicts in *The Brass Bed and Other Stories*, as an African American female, Cleage has created characters whose world view is somewhat different from the standard characters of the Dirty Realists/Minimalists. Her characters don't need to discover what forces hold them back and prevent them from obtaining their desires. They already know. That is where their "realism" springs from. In a Carver, or a Ford, or a Wolff story, because the characters are usually white and male, their vulnerabilities do not come from outside forces but rather from situations they themselves created. They, therefore, have the power to rectify the situation in most cases. On the other hand, Pearl Cleage's characters are black and female. Their vulnerabilities come from a society at large that puts woman, especially black woman, "under siege" (14), as Cleage says in her book of essays *Deals with the Devil and other Reasons to Riot*. Cleage goes on to say that black woman are "creature[s] oppressed by racism and sexism, buffeted from niggerhaters to womenhaters and back again with hardly time to take a deep breath and try to figure out what to do about it" (21).

This theme of the world as oppressor to Cleage's characters because they are female and African American, and therefore highly vulnerable, runs throughout *The Brass Bed and Other Stories*. In the story "Four From That Summer: Atlanta 1981," Cleage writes about how, even when little girls, black females learn about their vulnerability. The backdrop to the story is the Atlanta children murders of the late Seventies and early Eighties. When the story begins, the seventeenth body has been found. All the victims have been children and they have all been black. The narrator says about her daughter's vulnerability, "There is nothing in her six year old child's consciousness to account for random, calculated violence against her peers. It is like being a woman and first understanding what rape is" (30–31). Elaborating on this sense of vulnerability, which is imposed from the outside world, Cleage, in the same story, ties the Atlanta children murders to the beatings inflicted on Civil Rights marchers. She says:

> Being a black child in Atlanta now must be a little like being a Northern black person watching Bull Connor at work during the Sixties. We would sit in Detroit, or Chicago, or Philadelphia, and watch the Alabama police cracking heads, and feel for the first time a kind of vulnerability that settled on our chests like witch-trial stones and stayed there [31].

In the "Bus Trip," the narrator's sister explains that she missed her bus and ended up getting a car ride with a member of the Klan. Because the sister was light-skinned, the Klansman thought she was white and he proudly boasted of his membership. The narrator says about her sister's car ride with the Klansman:

> My sister's ride had simply picked her up thinking she was a white lady in distress, and had no idea that he was discussing his Klan membership with a terrified "blue vein" who at that moment was trying to throw race pride aside and concentrate on, as my sister said, "looking as white as possible" [46].

The sister's dilemma, as Cleage skillfully writes, had nothing to do with what her the sister did, but, instead, who she was. This theme is what makes her book compelling and what differentiates her from the other Dirty Realists/Minimalists, and, at the same time, is a reason to include her as a Dirty Realist/Minimalist. After all, as Cleage shows in this collection, what is more real or more "dirty" than the lives of African American women?

The answer, of course , is nothing. Her characters must live every day of their lives with this "dirty realism." And though they can't come to terms with what has been imposed on them, they must find a way to make some kind of sense of the cards they have been dealt in order to carry on and decide how "to keep on going," as Herzinger says (20). Here, in the story, "Them Changes," the narrator wonders how, given all the problems she and her daughter face, how she will carry on, how she will keep on going. This passage is as affecting and as powerful as anything in Cleage's collection. She writes:

> So I try to understand and analyze. I stroke my daughter's cheek while she is sleeping and meet her at the bus stop when she comes from school so she won't have to walk two blocks alone. The last time she tried it, a car full of men followed her down the street, sucking their teeth and offering her a

free ride home. I stop myself when I start snapping at men I love and hope I don't start crying on the telephone at midnight. I wish my mother was here so I could ask her to explain. As if she could. As if anybody could [54].

Tobias Wolff, quoted in the famous *Granta* issue, says that what sets apart and helps define the writers who are Dirty Realists/Minimalists is that "they are able to speak to us about the things that matter" (*Granta* 1). Pearl Cleage, in her collection *The Brass Bed and Other Stories*, speaks to us about things that matter. In Cleage's stories being black matters, being a woman matters, and being an African American woman *really* matters.

WORKS CITED

Carver, Raymond. *What We Talk About When We Talk About Love*. New York: Vintage, 1989. Print.
Cleage, Pearl. *The Brass Bed and Other Stories*. Chicago: Third World, 1991. Print.
_____. *Deals with the Devil and Other Reasons to Riot*. New York: One World Ballantine, 1993. Print.
Granta. *Granta* 8: Dirty Realism. 1983. 12 March 2011. www.granta.com/Magazine/8. Web.
Herzinger, Kim A. "Introduction: On the New Fiction." *Mississippi Review* 13–14 (1985): 7–30. Print.

The Blues, Psychosis, and the Black Arts Movement in *Bourbon at the Border*

LADRICA MENSON-FURR

The twenty-first century's list of historical moments will include the fiftieth year commemoration of 1961's Freedom Summer, its Freedom Rides and riders. During this volatile summer, hundreds of young people — college students, black and white, rich and poor — boarded buses and challenged Interstate Transportation Laws. Hundreds of these same activists continued their freedom work as they walked Mississippi roads encouraging and assisting African American men and women register to vote. It is this turbulent but imperative moment in American civil rights history and activism that Pearl Cleage dramatizes in *Bourbon at the Border*. Pearl Cleage's *Bourbon at the Border* (commissioned by the Alliance Theatre Company and premiering in 1997 under the direction of Kenny Leon) did not resonate well with her audiences (Cleage 188). She explains their response in an interview with Alexis Greene:

> Audiences felt betrayed when they saw it; they wanted *Flyin' West*. People always want you to write the thing they like. But in *Bourbon at the Border*, May and Charlie don't get over what happened to them in the South in the 1960s.... He figures he will get well again if he kills three white men.... At the end, the police start knocking on the door.
> Nobody in the audience wants that.... But these people have been destroyed by American racism. The audience wants a happy ending, but nothing good's going to happen once the police come [Greene 43].

Bourbon at the Border is a drama about love, trauma, violence, and disappointment. It is a painful play that does not celebrate heroism, but instead, as Cleage explains, depicts a troubled couple trying to achieve normality although their lives "have been destroyed by American racism" (Greene 43). The play centers on a married couple, Charles and May Thompson, who work together to love one another, and survive despite a shared and painful past experienced during the 1960s. They exist on the very edge of an enormous psychological fissure that racism, violence, and trauma have created in their lives. *Bourbon at the Border* interrogates their attempts to escape from troubled pasts and traumatic experiences and into safe spaces. Cleage further complicates this drama's plot as she separates the unified protagonists — Charles and May — as the play draws on and creates dueling protagonists who foreshadow a painful resolution for both characters, especially May.

Set in Detroit, Michigan, in September 1995, three decades following the 1961 Freedom Rides Summer, *Bourbon at the Border* opens at the dawn of a new day for Charles and May Thompson. The play's action begins as May anxiously awaits Charles's return from his most recent hospitalization at a mental institution. The reason for Charlie's institutionalization and illness is offered early on, as May explains, or rather defends his condition to her friend and neighbor, Rosa ("Rose"), and begins a lesson for both Rose and the drama's audience as, together, they attempt to understand the complexity of the Thompsons as individuals and a married couple:

> MAY: He's not dangerous Rose. He's depressed.
>
> ROSA: A lot of people get depressed from time to time, but Charlie is the first black person I ever knew who went all the way crazy.
>
> MAY: Me, too [200].

Charles's illness becomes a character in the drama. It is both an abstract and complex concept that is foreign to both women, and, in turn, to the audience who must try to understand what has catalyzed this black man's mental breakdown. Moreover, as Rosa comments that she never knew anyone who she could identify as "crazy" before meeting Charlie and May, she proves that the realities of mental illness are too often relegated to back rooms within African American culture. Rosa very well might have known someone suffering from mental illness if discussions of it were not so shunned. Further, Rosa does not demonstrate supportive friendship or tolerance of mental illness as she later admonishes May for her commitment to Charlie, saying "Most folks wouldn't a stuck like you have" (200).

During this same conversation, May offers Rose a more tangible rendering of Charlie's pre-insanity state by way of a sighting, a visual flashback, in the form of a photograph of Charlie and May in their "prime" (201) during the 1960s when they were young, revolutionary co-eds attending Howard University. Through this photographic sighting, Rosa sees Charles and May in stark contrast to their present visages to which she states, "You all look so serious" and May responds, "We were serious" (201). The Charlie who Rose knows as being fragmented and in some ways frightening is not the same Charlie she encounters in the photograph. He is the Charlie who May describes and further defends and explains as the pre–Detroit Charlie, the one who "got hurt in Mississippi a long time ago" (205).

May elaborates on her vague explanation of Charlie's mental illness as an injury when she locates the setting and source of Charlie's pain in 1960s Mississippi. Here, Cleage both encourages and instructs her audience to recall American history, specifically civil rights history, and revisit the events that can and did drive a man to insanity. However, the drama does not leave the audience long to ponder. After Charlie returns home, he offers his own accounting of his Mississippi memory to Tyrone, Rose's gentleman friend:

> CHARLIE: Yeah. Broke my leg in three places, threw me in a hole and waited three days before they called somebody to set it.
>
> ...
>
> CHARLIE: When they threw me in that hole, they looked at me and said, "We're going to be fair about this, nigger. You gonna leave your mind down there or your nuts. You can decide." (A beat) So whenever a muthafucker calls me crazy, I say, goddamn right! [229].

Charlie's version of the story is not only much more detailed than May's vague explanation, but it also concludes with a bit of humor that leaves one wondering if Charlie has finally accepted the tragi-comedy of his time. Reading this aspect of his recounting alone, one can imagine that he has processed his experiences during the movement during his previous hospitalizations and thus been cured of his insanity. His ability to make a joke out of a physical and psychological experience takes on a blues logic and, as Ralph Ellison explains, using this trope of the blues allows Charlie to relive the moment and "keep the painful detail and episodes of a brutal existence alive in one's aching consciousness, to finger its jazzed grain, and to transcend it, not by consolation of philosophy but by squeezing from it a near-tragic, near-comic lyricism" (Ellison as quoted by Gates and McKay in "Blues" 23). However, his version of the story is lacking because it silences both May's recollection and her shared experience as a victim of racialized violence.

By the end of the drama's first act, Charlie appears to have become a functioning member of society. In an offer of brotherly support, Tyrone helps him to find steady employment, and Charlie seems to have readjusted to society. But the drama's plot foreshadows the challenge to this semblance of "happily ever after." As Act One concludes, the two couples — Charlie and May, Tyrone and Rose — celebrate Charlie's success but then begin to discuss reports of random murders of white men in their sixties taking place within the city:

> TYRONE: They found another body. Throat cut like the last one.
>
> MAY: White guy?
>
> TYRONE: Yeah. Sixty-five years old. Had money on him, too. Nothing stolen.
>
> MAY: If he keeps going like this, ain't no white folks coming back downtown [239].

This discussion appears to be about current events between the friends, but the text leads one to question, as it does for Tyrone and May, who and why would someone target these men? However, it is Charlie's responses to May and Rosa, "Why'd you say 'he'? What if it's a woman ... or It could be something political" (239) that answers their questions. He does so while deflecting suspicion from himself by challenging gendered assumptions of who a murder suspect is likely to be. In so doing, Charlie cleverly hints at the emergence of the murderer, and anticipates the drama's conclusion.

It is not until later in the text when Cleage transforms the site of Charlie's pain into both physical site and literal or historical citation of memory when the complexity of Charlie's injury is unveiled and reveals that not only he, but also May, have both been harmed. Only after learning that Charlie is a suspect in the murders of the three White men does May offer her memory of that summer to Rosa and leads the audience, and herself, to the realization that Charlie is the culprit. She acknowledges that Charlie was given the impossible choice of either beating her or standing by while May was sexually assaulted.

May takes Rose to her rememory of that very day in order to make her understand and accept Charlie's crimes and his "innocence":

> MAY: Charlie said, "Stop! Don't touch her. I'll do it." I begged him not to. I didn't care what they did to me, but I was in love with sweet Charles. He was the only man I'd ever had ... they made him beat me half to death and then that one [deputy] who had told me to take my clothes off pulled my dress over my face and did it anyway.... Right in front of Charlie.
>
> But see, I knew that already. That's what I kept trying to tell him. I don't care what they do to me, but not to you. I can't take it from you [261–62]

Rosa's response is to note that, while her memory of Charlie's trauma is clear, Rose wonders, "What about what happened to you, May?" (264). This moment is just as climatic as May's full confession and explanation of Charlie's mental illness, for this is the point where the drama, like Charlie's anger, explodes. Rosa reminds May that though she, as she bravely asserts, "survived" that horrific night, it "doesn't make it right." She confirms for May that she is just as much a victim and martyr as Charlie.

May is forced to share this memory with Rosa in order to explain Charlie's murderous action and hope that her friend will understand his innocence. Yet it is also at this point in the drama that Cleage inserts another side of civil rights history, the history of black females in the civil rights movement, and encourages the audience and even May to recognize the scars that experience has inflicted upon her psyche. May's beating and rape reflect the history of abuse and sexual violation that black women endured during slavery, Reconstruction, and yes, even during the civil rights movement, but her story is further burdened by the insertion of her then boyfriend, Charlie, as one of her abusers. Thus, *Bourbon's* plot and the couple's marriage become even more complex because the drama's audience members fully understand that May and Charlie marry despite of, or rather because of, their determination to continue to love one another despite their past(s).

On one level, Cleage's aim is to tell a story of the horrors and repercussions of civil rights battles and Freedom Summer. But more importantly, Cleage insists on relaying the *entire story*, forcing her audience to analyze Charlie's actions (i.e., the murders) while also recognizing that he is not the only victim. More importantly, this point in the drama begs the question, "What about May?" While accounts such as the one that May shares with Rosa are housed within civil rights historical texts and legal documents, Cleage uses the dramatic form to more permanently engrave these narratives on to her audiences' minds as Charlie and May become conjoined and individual living citations or endnotes for the document that is known as Freedom Summer. Yet, while this freedom changed the world forever, as Rosa says in the text, it also simultaneously ruptured the lives and psyches of both of these young activists; Charlie is not the only victim.

Rosa responds to May's story with a sympathetic demand that May recognize that she was "hurt" also, "You always talk about what happened to Charlie. What about what happened to you, May?" (264), and illustrates the drama's dueling traumas and protagonists. As Rosa reminds May that even though she, as she bravely asserts, "survived" that horrific night it "doesn't make it right," and she demands that May and *Bourbon's* audience members acknowledge that May is also victim and martyr, in spite of her sane appearance. May suffers as much trauma as does Charlie. Instead of suffering publicly and demonstratively, she suffers in silence and as a willing martyr. She does not or cannot give in to insanity, for she claims to have "survived" that painful experience. While she has forgiven Charlie for the abuse that she suffered at his hands, one must wonder if she has forgotten that she was willing to sacrifice her body for him. After confessing to May that he murdered the men, Charlie explains his actions and admits that he is not "cured." Instead, he is haunted by guilt and by the belief that May resents his insanity and inability to heal:

> CHARLIE: All those years, I thought it was fear that was driving me crazy.... It wasn't fear I was running from. It was the anger, May, because I couldn't protect you. I couldn't forget and you couldn't forgive me for remembering [268].

Charlie thinks that May has moved on from this experience because she is the "sane" one in the marriage. But he fails to interpret her silence or recognize that her strength has not been for herself, but for him. She has to remain functional in order to protect their relationship and their love from the dysfunctionality that threatens to destroy it.

But, again, what about May? How has she managed to maintain her sanity? What has been her escape? Interestingly, Cleage locates May's survival technique in a dream of flight to Canada, an escape from both America's physical borders and the borders of her tragic memories. May tells Charlie, "When we first moved in, the thing I really liked about this place was I could wake up every day and be some place that wasn't here. I could just walk across the bridge and everything was different.... There was a whole country where not a living soul knew my name" (254). May's thought echoes the aspirations and actions of numerous African Americans — slave and free — who sought out places such as Canada for a place to be free of the vices of American racism and its violence. Yet, it also depicts a visage of May's own insanity.

Although set in 1995, *Bourbon at the Border* is a text influenced by the convergence of the ideals of the civil rights movement and the black arts/black aesthetic and black power movement, especially in the revolutionary violence that assuages Charlie's "hurt" and guilt, the serial murders. In the "Playwright's Note" to the play's text, Cleage notes that during the same 1964 Freedom Rides Summer, Leroi Jones's *Dutchman* was produced. Moreover, preceding the first page of the play's text, she quotes *Dutchman's* protagonist's, Clay, momentary revolutionary monologue in which he explains and offers a cure for the "neurosis" that plagues black American culture:

> A whole people of neurotics, struggling to keep from being sane. And the only thing that would cure the neurosis would be your murder. Simple as that. I mean if I murdered you, then other white people would begin to understand me.... If Bessie Smith had killed some white people she wouldn't have needed all that music. She could have talked very straight and plain about world. No metaphors.... Crazy niggers turning their backs on sanity. When all it needs is that simple act. Murder. Just murder! Would make us all sane.

Charlie, three decades later, finally acts on Clay's prescription by murdering three white men, but his act of vengeance does not lead to the calm or equanimity of the numerous lives destroyed and lost to the Civil Rights struggles.

Charlie admits to killing those men, but he realizes that his fear would have been more powerfully expressed as anger.

Ultimately, Charlie apologizes to May for not protecting her in that Mississippi jail and for not taking this curative action sooner, believing that it might have finally put him in his right mind. If they had crossed the Windsor Bridge into Canada, would Charlie be miraculously cured? Would May truly be able to forget her brutal beating and rape? Would Canada provide the safe space or utopia that she needs to be truly free and sane? These are questions that *Bourbon* challenges the audience to consider as they watch May appease Charlie's need to hear her describe the garden that they had planned to plant in Canada and hear the police officers' "insistent" knocking on the door (II. iv.).

In a departure from the ameliorative ending that many audiences have come to expect, Cleage situates Charlie's and *Bourbon*'s conclusions in stark reality—the sounds of police officers pounding on the door as May paints a visual picture, a sighting, and the new reality that she and Charlie dream of planting a Freedom Garden full of all kinds of tomatoes, fruits and vegetables just across the Windsor Bridge in Canada:

> MAY: We grow all kinds.
> We grow Red Plum. Green Zebra. Big Rainbow. Yellow Pear. Ultra Pink. Sun Gold. Super Sweet 100 [270].

But this dream is never meant to be fulfilled. The end of play also serves as the end of Charlie's freedom.

Cleage explains that *Bourbon at the Border* is a play "about one of those moments when love is not enough. The moment where black women realize that white racist violence has made our lovers, husbands, fathers, sons, incapable of loving us" (44). The drama is Baraka's "Black Art," and it is the commemoration and acknowledgement of the realistic barriers that prevent the Black Aesthetic movement's vision of black love, at least for this couple and their comrades, from fully existing. This drama also illustrates Cleage's contention and response to the question posed by Greene: "Do you think that love, then, is political as well as personal?" Cleage's answer is yes, that one's politics and relationships are intertwined in significant ways. *Bourbon's* love story is political and the act of loving, especially for fragmented beings such as Charlie and May is revolutionary.

While *Blues for an Alabama Sky* attracted an audience outside of Cleage's Atlanta Alliance Theatre productions, *Bourbon at the Border* did not. Cleage states, "After the Alliance did *Bourbon at the Border*, I said to myself, 'This is not going to be picked up on the white theater circuit that picked up *Flyin West* or *Blues*.' Those other pieces have a historic context, which maybe blunts their accusatory nature. It's difficult to find a black play without an accusation at the heart, which is, 'Y'all see what racism did' (Greene 48); the response to *Bourbon at the Border*, because it made white people nervous too, was quiet. The black audiences, because there's a lot of humor in the first part of the play, do what black audiences usually do, which is respond very vocally to what's going" (Greene 46).

Cleage grapples with her responsibility to tell the history of the Charlies and Mays of the world, but also reminds her audience members, primarily envisioned as African Americans, that Charlie's erroneous solution will not cure the neurosis he sadly has experienced at the hands of a racist nation. This is where *Bourbon* breaks with black aesthetic/arts ideology, for while Charlie is a martyr for the civil rights movement and poster child for black militancy, he remains a citizen of a nation that has laws that punish others for murder. Cleage cannot, as she further explains to Greene, appease the black audience's desire for "the black person to win" in *Bourbon* (43). Hence, witnessing Charlie act out his rage in his attempt to even the score is a lesson itself. Murder is not the answer. Moreover, while Charlie and his actions may appear to be drama's primary foci, *Bourbon at the Border* demands that we remember that Charlie's is not the lone victim. In the end, we cannot forget about May or about her blues.

Works Cited

Cleage, Pearl. *Bourbon at the Border. Flyin' West and Other Plays*. New York: Theatre Communications Group, 1999. 187–270. Print.

Gates, Henry L., and Nellie McKay, eds. "Blues." *The Norton Anthology of African American Literature*. New York: Norton, 1997. 23. Print.

Greene, Alexis. "Pearl Cleage." *Women Who Write Plays: Interviews with American Dramatists*. Hanover. NH: Smith and Kraus, 2001. 24–55. Print.

Social Mediation: Pearl Cleage and the Digital Divide

SHEILA SMITH MCKOY

I am invisible, understand, simply because people refuse to see me.—
Ralph Ellison, *Invisible Man*

The role of the revolutionary artist is to make revolution irresistible.—
Toni Cade Bambara

In 1997, after many years of writing essays, plays and for the press, Pearl Cleage published the first of what is — to date — eight novels set in the West End section of Atlanta, a place where the community is maintained by shared expectation of masculine responsibility and underpinned by reformative power of love. As is implied by her linkage of black male accountability with the humanizing force of love (albeit romantic and heterosexual), Cleage's work crosses genre boundaries. Her West End novels are shaped by constructs associated with several different types of fiction: the highly intellectual novel, romance fiction, and popular fiction, with each loci making it impossible for her work to be characterized in a single category. Cleage's fictional West End is also a part of a national history of racial divides. Established in the 1830s, it was once home to Joel Chandler Harris, a Southern writer known for his appropriation of and literary enslavement of stories told by enslaved African Americans which were published as his *Uncle Remus Tales*. By the 1960s, however, West End was a center for African American culture that was anchored by the historically black colleges and universities that it birthed, including Spelman College, Morehouse College, Clark Atlanta University, the Interdenominational Theological Center, and the now-severely troubled Morris Brown College. West End was also shaped by a history shared by many prosperous, majority African American neighborhoods in the 1960s with the expansion of the Interstate Highway System. When I-20 was established in 1960s, the West End about which Cleage would later write became an African American enclave defined by its own African descent traditions.

With the publication of *Till You Hear from Me* (2010), the sixth novel in this series of West End stories, Cleage presents the first realized portrait of a singularly African American community in post–Obama America. Cleage has undertaken what can be seen as an ambitious project of limning a "segregated" community within a culture defined by Obama-mic notions of multiracial America. Moreover, Cleage's West End is maintained as a community by the dynamic force of Blue Hamilton, who is so committed to reclaiming the area as a safe space for the women of the community that he is willing to kill for it. Cleage's West End, then, is a community in which this paradigm is embraced by, enforced by, and replicated throughout the community. Her West End is defined by its own language of commitment to these principles, is contained by a geography of recognized borders, and is supported by the community's embrace of the West End News where Cleage's characters gather to read the national and international news and, as importantly, to share in the news of the community.

While making the print media and communal in-group communication an important aspect of the novel, Cleage also engages in the debate about the digital divide. The novel opens, in fact, with a scene set in the West End News where the Obama presidency shapes the discussion. The central issue of the novel, though, involves comments made by the Rev. Horace Dunbar, whose derogatory, race-baiting comments about Obama have gone viral on the internet. Dunbar's daughter, Ida, who hopes to parlay her work on the Obama campaign into a job with the administration goes home to assist in silencing her father, a respected community leader, before he — like Jeremiah Wright both inside of and outside of the text — must be disavowed by the Obama administration. However, early in the text, Cleage uses her characterization of Ida to suggest that like Obama, those who will be most empowered in this community will need to use the internet in revolutionary ways, by adapting "old-school techniques to new-school possibilities" (35). The plot also revolves around a comparison of the Reverend Dunbar with Cleage's portrait of Wes Harper, a capitalist, motivated more by money than political affiliation or race. Though born in West End and mentored by the "Rev.," Wes plans to use the internet and other social media against the newly minted voters who became active during the Obama campaign. Rather than being stored digitally, a key set of Georgia voters' names have been archived on index cards stored in the Reverend Dunbar's closet. Intent on stealing the cards, digitizing the list and disenfranchising the new voters, Harper has no allegiance to the community nor to his blackness. He defines storing the data on index cards as merely a mistrust of technology (169). What Cleage asks her readers to consider in the scenario is a part of the wider conversation about race and how it shapes the "new school possibilities" of the digital world, the digital divide and African American community in a society in which — as I note in my review of the novel — blackness and black identity can no longer be considered to be monolithic, inclusive categories.[1]

In fact, Cleage's West End novels situate the reader within an exclusively African American community, an in-group with its own history of cultural reclamation and its particularized ways of disseminating information. One of the salient aspects of African American culture is the way in which this African descent culture engages in communication with the in-group. This, too, has a peculiar and double meaning in American racial ideologies, and to expand on this point, I will focus on the African principle, *ayan*, as means through which to provide a historical and cultural reading adapting "old school" and "new school" communication strategies within the closed community of West End that Cleage creates in *Till You Hear from Me*. *Ayan*, as I shall discuss further, describes both the language of and the *communitas* established by the "talking drum" in West Africa. My larger goal in this discussion is to establish how we might read the in-group, "old school" communications strategies alongside the possibilities of an internet system defined by a racial, digital divide. The concept of *ayan* provides a lens through which to understand how Cleage resolves the questions raised by the racing of the digital divide by exploring the divide's racial and cultural moorings.

An ancient term, *ayan* has its origins in many cultures in West Africa. *Ayan* is language and rhythm; it is understood only by those within a closed community. In the Akan cultures of Ghana, *ayan* refers to the language of the talking drum, the atumpane.[2] Within the Twi-speaking Akan groups, *ayan* resonates with the tones of the language so that those taught the *ayan* can translate the drum sounds into Twi. Nana Oforiatta-Ayim suggests that the language of the drum, the *ayan*, vocalizes what may not be spoken overtly.[3] Benjamin Kwabena Ankomah asserts that *ayan* is taught within closed groups and passed along descent-lines.[4] As well, Ankomah notes that the message of *ayan* is not defined by the drummer. Instead, the drum linguist, the *Okyerema*, translates the words of the community leader into ayan so that the message—in its entirety and verbatim — can be disseminated throughout the community. In Akan culture, as Catie Coe suggests, in *ayan*, language and rhythm are inextricably linked to the extent that one cannot teach drumming without understanding *ayan* is a language. Meaning and knowledge in *ayan* is created through a shared understanding of the message, the language, and the medium through which it reaches the members of the community. *Ayan* opens the pathway between the living and the ancestors and between life and the world of spirit. In short, the cultural work that *ayan* performs in the Akan tradition is to create meaning across space and time synchronously.

Ayan is also embedded in Yoruba traditions of Nigeria. Yoruba culture locates the communicative and amalgamate possibilities of *ayan* as an aspect of the divine. *Ayan* is not only the language of the talking drum, it is also the name of the deity who embodies the spirit of communication.[5] The followers of the orisha, *Ayan*, are empowered as drummers to communicate through the drum. *Ayan* as language is aligned with the Yoruba language; each note is believed to have it own vibrational power. *Ayan* is also the name of the tree from which the talking drum is traditionally made. In Yoruba culture, *ayan* is necessary to communicate with the Orisha as well as with community. *Ayan* is both divine and human; it is communication without boundaries and without limitation. As is true in Akan cultures, among the Yoruba, the *ayan* defies the limitations of space and time, opening channels of communication with the community, the ancestors and the divine.

Throughout West Africa, the talking drum embodies a communal message that is made manifest through rhythm and language. Those traditions migrated to the African Diaspora as a part of the transatlantic trade in humans. However, unlike in many other African descent cultures, Africans enslaved in the United States were not allowed to utilize traditional means of social communication through which to synchronously communicate. The possibility that African American enslaved people might communicate outside of a language accessible to slaveholders and those who aspired to slaveholding elicited the same fears as speaking in an African language in America and was, therefore, forbidden. Having no access to *ayan* as a means of synchronous, communal communication, African Americans created methods of in-group communication, both preceding the digital revolution and since.

In keeping with African traditions of the talking drum, African Americans developed a unique language and communications apparatus that enabled those "speaking" the cultural language to understand and, as importantly, prevented access to those outside of the culture. Simultaneously, the laws that prevented traditional forms of communication for Africans in America were accompanied by a view of African Americans as singularly monolithic and shaped only by the dominate culture. The monolithic view of African Americans held in the Western world, including those applied to modes of communication, does not easily admit the possibility of subversive communication strategies that define in-group communication in African descent cultures in Western world. My focus on *ayan* suggests that the technology of drumming, of sending distinct vibrational codes linked to language, is not unlike internet communication which can only be "heard" when one can access the technology. Yet, *ayan* allows for in-group communication that cannot be accessed by those outside of the community. Those who embrace racism and African American inferiority — like Wes and his partners — are unable to "hear" the message and are, instead, duped by their own insistence on race as a limiting, biopolitical concept. As Cleage demonstrates in *Till You Hear from Me*, the belief that racial stereotypes are reliable indicators of social literacy renders African American in-group strategies both powerful and viable. Moreover, part of the power of the *Till You Hear from Me* as an exploration of both perceptions about the "digital divide" and in-group communication strategies lies in her focus on racial beliefs held on "both" sides of the racial divide.

In contemporary studies about digital literacy in the United States — as is true of any disparities based in the biopolitics of American culture — race is one of the measures by which this kind of literacy is evaluated and through which biases about race are perpetuated. This position persists despite a large body of work on the construction of race and despite the growing body of work that links the digital divide to economic, rather than to racial, difference. Here, then, it is important to focus on understanding the ways in which racially marked audiences defy notions about the digital divide as well as on how perceptions about the "divide" operate within and outside of African descent communities.

The idea of the racial digital divide is rooted in the phenomenon that became today's internet as is clearly seen in the U.S. government publication, *Falling through the Net, I* (1998) which indicated that only 19 percent of households defined as "Black" used the internet.[6] However, numerous studies about the digital divide suggest plausible alternatives to the race-based discussion of internet accessibility and usage. In *Technology and Social Inclusion: Rethinking the Digital Divide*, Mark Warschauer asserts that African Americans are placed on "the wrong side of the digital divide" because studies do not accurately reflect the fact that in higher economic groups, the "divide" decreases. Further, Warschauer argues that these studies "serve to further social stratification by discouraging employers or content providers from reaching out to those groups" (7). While most explorations of the perceived digital divide focus on access to the internet in the household, under-privileged communities have access to the internet through alternative means; whether through public access internet resources or through mobile technologies, those perceived as digital "have nots" may access it at higher rates than their white peers.[7] This body of research, of course, indicates that our understanding of the digital divide is influenced by racial mythmaking. As Karen Mossberger, et al., suggests, "The question, then, is whether race is an independent (non-spurious) predictor of access to information technology or whether, for example, education is really driving differences in access" (17). Reading Cleage's novels in the context of the digital divide, allows us to assess the role of technology in African American society generally, more specifically, the role that technology plays in inter-cultural communication in the novels, and how *ayan* can be applied as a means to understand alternative spaces of in-group communication in the digital age.

Certainly, as Rudolph Byrd reminds us, "There is text and there is context" (Byrd). Of course, race-based statistics are grounded in both the prehistory and in the subtext of race in American culture. The prehistory most certainly originates in an American culture shaped by a belief in race as a biological, intellectual, religious and economic characteristic ascribed to "blackness" and other "others." Indeed, it would be difficult to separate "America" from the proscriptive and prescriptive definitions allied with race. As Derrick Bell suggests in *Faces at the Bottom of the Well*, racism may well be an "integral, permanent, and indestructible" component of American society (ix). It is also intimately tied to America's origins as a slave state, one whose wealth and existence is owed to the institution of black enslavement. Anchored as it is in American biopolitics, this notion of blackness and difference makes those racially defined as "black" ultimately impeachable because of their race and ultimately responsible for their own axes of disparity.

In its most benign form, the conversation about racial disparities generates advocacy for social justice and equality and supports movement towards universal human rights in the United States. In its most insidious form, however, the biopolitics of American racism re-writes our shared racial histories in ways that not only widen these disparities but that also trace the source of these disparities to blackness itself. A part of the mythmaking that underwrites whiteness in American culture, the revised histories shape contemporary discourse about race. We can learn, for example, from recent comments made by Michele Bachmann and the ensuing internet response in the following extended example. Michele Bachmann's assertion that African American children born into slavery had a better chance of growing up in a two-parent household than children of the current generation exemplifies the racial rewriting that is the outgrowth of white mythmaking in American racial biopolitics. My point is, perhaps, made clear when one notes that Bachmann, an aspirant for the presidency of the United States, not only lacks a clear knowledge of America's history of slavery, but she also demonstrates that her beliefs about contemporary African American people are defined by the stereotypes born in the period of American slavery. It is also interesting that, when pressed about her statements, Bachmann insisted that her comments grew out of her support of "The Marriage Vow—A Declaration of Dependence upon Marriage and Family" which links the necessity for the "dependence upon marriage" in which the first two premises are validated by the negative divides of blackness:

- Slavery had a disastrous impact on African American families, yet sadly a child born into slavery in 1860 was more likely to be raised by his mother and father in a two-parent household than was an African American baby born after the election of the USA's first African American President.
- LBJ's 1965 War on Poverty was triggered in part by the famous "Moynihan Report" finding that the black out-of-wedlock birthrate had hit 26 percent; today, the white rate exceeds that, the overall rate is 41 percent, and *over 70 percent* of African American babies are born to single parents—a prime sociological indicator for poverty, pathology and prison regardless of race or ethnicity. (http://www.thefamily leader.com/wpcontent/uploads/2011/07/themarriagevow.final_.7.7.111. pdf)

These points also elucidate my point about American biopolitics. Consider the fact that the Declaration relies on the 1968 Moynihan Report as a measure of black hyper-sexuality and indicates that the American founders—slaveholders all—were divinely endowed with the concepts of "human rights, racial justice and gender equality."[8] What is even more remarkable is that Bachmann's sentiments, like those of many Americans, continue to define African American identity and culture through the racial stereotypes that made slavery palatable to the slave-holding American public. Not surprisingly, Bachmann's comments went viral on the internet.

My point here is not to discount nor even to minimize the real impact of American racism on bodies of color; rather, the question I want to raise is how the definitions of the digital divide are grounded in these same racial biases that predate internet literacy. Simply put, it is clear that racial stereotypes created centuries and decades before the creation of the internet continue to have a suasory impact on American constructions of blackness and—as I shall make clear—of the racial, digital divide. Further, I am interested in the treatment of this paradigm in Pearl Cleage's *Till You Hear from Me*, the first African American novel informed by the election of Barack Obama and a novel whose storyline is made plausible because these notions of black disparity that now mis-define the digital realm are still suasory for those who embrace them.

In *Till You Hear from Me*, Pearl Cleage treats these beliefs about inbred African American inferiority as the historical and racialized relics that they are. In the process, Cleage also demonstrates that the unique racial and social terrain that define the biopolitics of African American culture also nurtured a specialized set of communication strategies that — in what might be considered a tribute to the notions expressed by Ralph Ellison and Toni Cade Bambara in the epigraphs — make these racial biases visible and they open a transformative space for resistance and social empowerment. In the community she creates in her West End novels, Cleage demonstrates that the digital terrain is a means through which to achieve social and political change. In the same manner in which her political essays presented the possibilities of social transformation beyond racism, digital and social media operate as transformational media in *Seen It All and Done the Rest (2008)* and is fully realized in *Till You Hear from Me* (2010). However, in *Till You Hear from Me*, Cleage demonstrates the principle of *ayan* at work within the in-group communications practices established in the closed community of West End. Further, she confronts how racial mythmaking contributes to the perception of the digital divide and, most importantly, how this same mythmaking enables *ayan* communication to be effective in an era defined by digital access.

As I have noted previously, *ayan* works within a closed community in which meaning and knowledge is created and disseminated through a shared understating of the message. Clearly, West End is a closed community where the residents embrace a particular set of values that are reinforced throughout the community. In all of her West End novels, Cleage opens that narrative space by insisting on the idea that the community is a distinct space, one set apart from other physical — as well as narrative and digital — spaces. In so doing, she emphasizes the fact that her West End is an empowered locale where all of the residents have a shared sense of a social meaning and social justice. When West End's "unofficial godfather," Blue Hamilton, set the tone and expectation that the area be defined by specific social codes including respect for women, respect for the neighborhood and male responsibility, he also established the tenets that would define West Ends' *ayan* (50). Hamilton is at the center of a community that he saw as a "peaceful oasis" (222) and rescued from urban blight. It is seen as "a place where things only change for the better," and as one that "cannot be replicated" (219). Interestingly, Hamilton is all but absent from this novel though he is a central figure in the previous ones. Thus, Cleage sets the parameters that are at work within the community for *ayan* to be effective: the community leaders set the message which is then transmitted and understood throughout the communal space. In West End, as in the communal traditions from which the concept of *ayan* originates, the mode of in-group communication defines the community where, though the internet exists and is accessible, communication in the in-group is dominated by personal contact.

Ayan is, in fact, operating in the text beginning with its prologue. In the opening of *Till You Hear from Me,* Cleage situates her readers in the aftermath of the Obama election, but she does so in such a way that Hamilton's ideas about social justice within the African American community of West End are maintained, even in his absence. As is clear in the text, the over-riding message of how to maintain and sustain the community originates with the community leader. The novel also offers an excellent example of how *ayan* is only possible when the protocol of using the o*kyerema*— the drum linguist — is followed. As the o*kyerema*, the Reverend Dunbar has, at least up to the point at which the novel opens, been a consistent force of communal support and uplift in his region. In contrast, when he speaks against Obama in the novel's open, it is clear that his community does not share in the message. Consider, however, the fact that in the West End community, *ayan* is created within the framework of personal communication by telephone, through oratory and through personal conversations with other community members. In the words of Cleage's the Reverend Dunbar: "We call them on the telephone. We send them letters in the kind of mail you put in a box. We place notices in their bulletins at church right beside the list of sick and shut-ins. We go knock on the front door and hope they invite us in for lemonade" (151). This difference between *ayan* and media that the "Rev." uses to deride Obama is clarified when Cleage reveals that the Reverend Dunbar was participating in a federal governmental operation designed to stop voter intimidation. The interview was intended to attract the attention of political operatives intent on dismantling a huge network of African American and other minority voters registered during the Obama campaign. As such, when the anti–Obama comments that are the center of the conflict in the novel are made, the Reverend Dunbar uses another medium of communication, knowing that the video interview will go viral on the internet. This communication is clearly outside of the *ayan* framework that defines West End culture and — by extension — it is not directed in the community. Indeed, the lyric to the Duke Ellington song from which the novel gets its name summarizes the importance of the personal aspects of this in-group *ayan*.

As an organizing principle of communications within the in-group of West End, however, all of the characters understand the protocol that defines *ayan* in the community. Note, for instance, that two of the most digitally connected people in the novel are Wes Harper and Ida B. Dunbar, both of whom are born in West End and both of whom now live outside of the community. Throughout the novel, Cleage emphasizes Ida's understanding and embrace of the *ayan* of the West End community. She appropriately recognizes her elders and she values the personal contact that defines the *ayan*. At the same time, she is a part of the digital world. Although she reads online, for instance, she is "old fashioned" about newspapers (115). She is a part of the tech-savvy world of the Obama campaign, yet she understands how to communicate within the *ayan* culture of Cleage's West End. In contrast, Wes Harper, ironically president of Wes Harper Communications, lost his understanding of West End *ayan* along with his ability to embrace blackness as a part of his identity. Though raised in the community and mentored by his godfather, the Reverend Dunbar, Harper's education at Phillips Exeter has made him more capitalist than black, and he has disavowed any connection to the *ayan* of the community. Cleage creates Harper as a man willing to tighten the yoke of racial oppression by agreeing to obtain the list of over one hundred thousand new voters registered by the Reverend Dunbar to assist in the effort to disenfranchise them. That he does so for financial rather than for political gain, is also a reflection of his self hatred and the fact that he is literally a "sell out," known for his ability to "break in to the lucrative African American urban market" (16). Like Ida, Wes has mastered life in the digital world. Unlike Ida, he can no longer speak within the communal parameters of West End.

It is perhaps because of the similarities between Ida and Wes that Cleage can so effectively use Wes to disavow both *ayan* and any allegiance to the community. That this disavowal is based on Wes' acceptance of the binary opposition of blackness and whiteness that grounds the conversations about the digital divide is telling. Situated between the oppositional *ayan* and the racial mythmaking that defines technology as having racial characteristics, Wes assumes that adhering to *ayan* in a digital world equates to being black and without access. In so doing, he fails to understand the modernist and complex ways in which those who embrace the West End *ayan* benefit from being judged inferior to those who embrace negative racial stereotypes. Put succinctly, it is only because *ayan* can mistakenly be defined as being inferior and irrelevant that Wes and his associates were so easily prevented from completing their plans to defraud newly registered voters.

When Barack Obama was elected to the presidency on November 2, 2008, images of many African Americans, like those of their high media profile counterparts, graced the pages of newspapers and captured the attention of America's visual media culture. And, while the Obama ascendancy certainly gives Americans a unique opportunity to dismantle the culture of race that has defined America since its inception, it also provides a similarly unique lens through which to dismantle the operative consequences of race for racially defined Americans and for those who embrace American racial mythologies as truth. Conversations about the digital divide presuppose that the category of African American refers to a single, homogenous unit. In fact, discussions about the digital divide can only be defined as part of this racial construct if they fail to consider age and economic status as the primary indicators that limit access and instead default to race as a relevant metric. Cleage's *Till You Hear From Me* provides an alternative reading of African American community and communication and offers a way of reading a community's relationship with digital technology access and usage without being constrained by racial mythmaking.

Cleage's fiction can easily be defined as a kind of theorizing fiction that incorporates theoretical constructions about blackness and contemporary black culture to explore the issues that define her West End: advocacy for male responsibility alongside gender equality; political agency and advocacy; and the primacy of communal and familial relationships; and the legacy and history that defines the non–fictional space of West End. Her novels provide readers with a dynamic means through which to connect with and position African American culture as a space in which alternative ways of communicating can create and sustain community. Perhaps her greatest gift, then, is in offering a way to reconsider how new technologies relate to old assertions about how race — even in the digital — divides American culture.

Notes

1. "Review, Pearl Cleage, *Till You Hear from Me*." *Obsidian: Literature in the African Diaspora.* 12.1:150–152.

2. It is worth noting that the Atumpane drum of Ghana migrated to Suriname as the Atumpan.

3. See Nana Oforiatta-Ayim. Abstract: "Revealing the Secrets of the Ayan: drum poems from the Akyem Kingdom of Ghana." "The Media Translation/Translation between Media" Conference. The British Comparative Literature Association Graduate Conference in association with the Centre for Research in the Arts, Social Sciences and Humanities, University of Cambridge, March 20—21, 2009. *http://www.crassh.cam.ac.uk/uploads/documents/abstracts_media_t_09.pdf*

4. Interview with Benjamin Kwabena Ankomah, October 26, 2011.

5. The Yoruba version of the talking drum is called the dun dun.

6. See *Falling through the Net, I, http://www.ntia.doc.gov/legacy/ntiahome/fttn99/InternetUse_II/Chart-II-3.html*). Since the original publication of this study, there have been studies about internet use in the United States, published under the auspices of the U.S. government.

7. See McCollum, p. 52.

8. See *http://thinkprogress.org/wp-content/uploads/2011/07/The-Family-Leader-Presidential-Pledge.pdf*.

Works Cited

Ankomah, Benjamin Kwabena. Interview, October 26, 2011.
Byrd, Rudolph. "Song Reflects Racial Pride, Never Intended as Anthem." *http://www.cnn.com/2010/OPINION/07/27/byrd.james.johnson/?hpt=Mid*. Web.
Cleage, Pearl. *Seen It All and Done the Rest.* New York: Ballantine/One World, 2008.
_____. *Till You Hear from Me.* New York: Ballantine/One World, 2010. Print.

Coe, Catie. *Dilemmas of Culture in African Schools: Youth, Nationalism, and the Transformation of Knowledge.* Chicago: University of Chicago Press, 2005. Print.
Ellison, Ralph. *Invisible Man*, 2d ed. New York: Vintage, 1995. Print.
"The Marriage Vow—A Declaration of Dependence upon Marriage and Family." *http://thinkprogress.org/wp-content/uploads/2011/07/The-Family-Leader-Presidential-Pledge.pdf.* Web.
McCollum, Sean. "Getting Past the 'Digital Divide': Educators Who Can Work Around Obstacles and Recognize the Promise of New Technologies Are Making a Difference." *The Education Digest* 77.2: 52. Print.
Mossberger, Karen, Caroline J. Tolbert, and Mary Stansbury. *Virtual Inequality: Beyond the Digital Divide.* Washington, DC: Georgetown University Press, 2003. Print.
Oforiatta-Ayim, Nana. "Revealing the Secrets of the Ayan: Drum Poems from the Akyem Kingdom of Ghana." "The Media Translation/Translation between Media" Conference. The British Comparative Literature Association Graduate Conference in association with the Centre for Research in the Arts, Social Sciences and Humanities, University of Cambridge, March 20—21, 2009.
Smith McKoy, Sheila. "Review, Pearl Cleage, *Till You Hear from Me.*" *Obsidian: Literature in the African Diaspora.* 12.1 (2011):150–152. Print.

In Context: Teaching Pearl Cleage in Southwest Atlanta

Tikenya Foster-Singletary

For the past two years, I have taught a special topics class at Spelman College, where we explore the work of Pearl Cleage work exclusively; we read all of the novels, two of the plays, and a number of essays.[1] The course evolved from a veteran professor's suggestion that in addition to the work of black women writers typically in the canon, students would benefit from reading the work of alumnae who had matriculated into the same academic experience as they. Thus, in its original manifestation, the class examined the novels of both Pearl Cleage and her classmate, Tina McElroy Ansa. When I joined the faculty, I used my previous scholarship on Cleage, narrowing the focus of the course to Cleage alone. We used the city of Atlanta, since Cleage herself does the same, as a key lens through which to read her work.

While many of her novels are set in or refer to Atlanta, where Cleage herself lives, she presents a version of the city that is not entirely recognizable; it is Southwest Atlanta, with a twist. The Krispy Kreme doughnut store is located in the text in its exact real life location (in fact, since it moved down the street between the publication of two novels, Cleage also moved it in the fictional West End). The signature bungalow houses that dot streets in the Southwest part of the city are featured in the novels as "gingerbreads." Often, Spelman College and local restaurants show up in the background. The history of the city reflects Cleage's intimate knowledge of its evolution. But it is also a place where she has famously and repeatedly placed a fictitious 24-hour hair salon where black women can walk down the street without harassment or fear. There are gardens that bring life to neighborhoods. And yet, during a semester when I was teaching this course, Spelman College suffered the loss of a student who was shot and killed near the Atlanta University Center library.[2]

There is an odd space between the actual West End and the fictive one. The characters in the novels emerge as people who would fit comfortably in their setting, and yet, they are surrounded by a space that is manipulated by imagination and fantasy. It is an interesting landscape for examining Cleage's work.

The students I taught entered the class excited about the work and somewhat familiar with Cleage — she is a frequent presence on campus as writer-in-residence, speaker, Women's Center supporter, alumna, and recent honorary degree recipient. Because the students were in the middle of their own Spelman experiences, they were eager to locate Spelman in the work. The college was in the background, coloring the setting in familiar ways. The idea of sisterhood, for instance, anchors a number of Cleage's stories and figures prominently the branding of Spelman College. There was an intimacy between Cleage and the students reading her work even before the first day of class. Because of these kinds of preconceptions, I set a goal of composing a picture of Cleage's identity as a writer, what she intends for her work to do, and how we as readers and scholars might use her work as we carve out our own places in the world. Spelman could be an interesting way into the work, but I wanted to ensure that we avoided the risk of becoming entangled by it. Similarly, Atlanta clearly is important for Cleage, but the purpose of her work is much more concerned with issues of human rights, pacifism, and community. Teaching this course has helped to fashion a framework for what a course on Pearl Cleage might look like. A focus on negotiating the themes, embracing the setting, and situating the texts in relation to each other create a full teaching sequence.

I made the decision to begin the course by assigning an essay, "Why I Write," that would ground the students in Cleage's definition of herself as a writer. The essay is featured in both the nonfiction collection *Deals With the Devil and Other Reasons to Riot* and Cleage's earlier nonfiction collection, *Mad at Miles*. The teaching structure for the class clustered the texts by genre, with an interdisciplinary approach. We relied heavily on class discussion to tease out the questions presented by the texts, and we used the nonfiction writing to give light to the fiction. In particular, the essay "Why I Write" is a striking introduction to Cleage's writing style. I often use it in composition courses as an example of the importance of words and language. In the context of Cleage's work overall, the essay is inviting and provocative. Students responded to the essay as if they are its perfect intended audience. They were affected deeply by the insistence to stare domestic violence right in the face, to name an enemy and confront it without apology. The evil is clear: violence, injustice, dishonor. Cleage clarifies in this essay that she sees racism and sexism as her dual foci. Importantly, she also presents women as her primary intended audience. She means to confront these ills in her writing. In every piece of creative work, this idea — that she sees her audience and priority as women and that she is grappling with race and gender issues — frames the narrative. Any full-bodied understanding of her work must acknowledge these ideas as crucial to the way the personal and socio-political intersect for Cleage.

We followed this seminal text with two other important ones. First, we moved to the poem written for Oprah Winfrey's Legends Ball, "We Speak Your Names." Her writing in "The Time Before the Men Came," in addition to "Why I Write" boils down the essence of her work so cleanly that even as we examined her work across decades, the continuum was salient. These texts become something of a primer for clarifying the way Cleage sees the world. I encourage students to refer to these foundational texts as a lodestone when trying to unpack other elements of her writing that we would later encounter. Violence against women, protection and nurturing of children, respect for and accountability of men, race consciousness — the threads that tie much of her work together — all show up in those texts. "Before the Men Came" demonstrates Cleage's use of her own created spaces as landscapes for very pointed plotlines. Her imagined community draws a portrait of Amazon women who are powerful and strong and who rely on each other; men in this community exist on the periphery. It creates a decidedly female space that favors the perspectives of women without apology. "We Speak Your Names" highlights the author's generational and aesthetic preferences in the world of popular arts. The poem is a testimony to Cleage's admiration for women, especially for women of color. She highlights the cultural contributions of artists who, like she, have made cultural commentary and artistic production their life's work. Together, these nonfiction texts inform our examination of the fiction and dramas, providing context and a useful framework. Even more, they point to specific themes in the fiction, expanding the ideas and offering a more thorough commentary.

With Cleage's essays as foundation, students more readily recognize the gravity of Cleage's concerns. Still, students also seem to experience a desire to look away, to fill their lives with the stuff of college life — parties, gossip, shopping, frivolity — instead of the uncomfortable realities of adulthood. Consequently, the insistence of Cleage's sometimes glaring language and uncomfortable themes forces readers' attention. Because of that, giving attention to what appear to be "lighter" elements of her work is important as well. It seems purposeful on her part. After all, many of Cleage's stories are love stories, despite the context of decidedly un-romantic circumstances.

As we begin to read the novels, applying the assertions of our introductory texts provide a palpable sense of the novels' mission. Also palpable is Cleage's primary mechanism for presenting that mission: coupling. The use of coupling is a thread that strings together all of the novels. That becomes even more clear because we read the novels in the order of publication; it was the first such experience for several students. Coupling is a thread that connects much of Cleage's work, both creative and essayistic. It is one of the more whimsical elements of her work. It is vital, though, to acknowledge and manage Cleage's didactic tendencies, noticing them as part of her activism rather than as aesthetic weaknesses. Her use of coupling is a solid example of that. As we began the class in which we discussed the first novel, *What Looks Like Crazy on an Ordinary Day*, one student enthusiastically commented that "It's like an updated Janie and Teacake!" This reference to such an iconic couple in African American literature was an apt one in many ways. Ava and Eddie, like Janie and Teacake, seem somewhat mismatched and socially stigmatized. Moreover, Cleage parallels Hurston in choosing to set her story in an African American utopian setting. Of course, Idlewild is more of a dystopia by the time Ava and Eddie arrive, but that fact only serves to underscore the ways in which Cleage signifies, rather than repeats, Hurston; in *Crazy* coupling is meant to shine a light on the communal ills that threaten to destroy romantic love itself. In doing so, love becomes the organizing principle that contextualizes the overall plot, a symbol for what a functional community would look like.

This focus on coupling and the all–African American community is central to all of the novels, and the plays also feature romantic relationships. The dynamics of these relationships, especially as related to social issues, also worked their way into class discussions by virtue of the fact that the class takes place on the campus of a historically black college. We explored questions about the sometimes hidden features that may only be visible behind racial "closed doors": homophobia, intergenerational tensions, epidemic rates of HIV infection, rampant domestic violence. Cleage demonstrates that an enclosed, homogenous community can be fertile ground for highlighting targeted principles. While her subjects and her audience are clearly defined as African American, coupling becomes a tool for a universal insistence on truth and justice and civility. It is a useful path into the stories. However, Ayana Weekly's essay, "Why Can't We Flip the Script? The Politics of Respectability in Pearl Cleage's *What Looks Like Crazy on an Ordinary Day*" argues that it is this persistent focus on coupling that interrupts the attention towards weighter issues. Weekly attempts to

> identify and highlight the politics of respectability in *What Looks Like Crazy* that influence the way the protagonist is able to negotiate HIV/AIDS, race, class, gender, and sexuality, arguing that these politics hinder full discussion of both black female sexualities in the U.S. and the impact of the HIV/AIDS epidemic on African American women ... and [critiques] the need to place black women in heteronormative relationships not only to save them, but to also save black communities [26–27].

The question, then, is whether or not these novels can be framed as coupling narratives, and how that aspect serves the activist tone of the work.

This question is a central one for class discussion, and perhaps, for writing assignments.

Weekly's focus on the conclusion of the novel points to the arguments of both Claudia Tate's *Domestic Allegories of Political Desire* and Ann duCille's *The Coupling Convention*, which see marriage in nineteenth and early twentieth century African American women's novels as expressions of political and social aspiration. Certainly, for Cleage the romantic relationships in her work are commentaries on the other issues she highlights. They are pathways for confronting the conflict of the text. The discussion it opens for students, though, is how much of a patriarchial norm they are willing to accept as readers. Many of the stories offer alternative sexualities and ways of knowing, and "millennial" students are constantly challenged with the contradictions of those alternatives. It can be fruitful to put pressure on those complexities. In *Baby Brother's Blues*, Brandi may be viewed as a sympathetic character with Horatio Algier-esque aspirations, but she may also be seen as an opportunistic Jezebel. Similarly, why does Ava marry at the end of the *What Looks Like Crazy on an Ordinary Day*? Is it an acceptable, believable conclusion? Or is it a means to endorsing "normality"? Students will need to ask, "What does the text invite readers to see?"

My student's initial connection to Hurston also invites us to join the wider literary conversation about what Hurston's text is actually about: a woman's quest, a feminist manifesto, a May–December romance. Hurston, of course, leaves *Their Eyes Were Watching God*'s Janie alone and wistfully remembering her lover at the novel's end; Cleage often plays matchmaker with her characters, especially at the end. Still, the stories don't seem to really be a*bout* the coupling, and it is worth noting that some of the stories end with tragic or unfortunate break ups to those coupling relationships. This is especially true with regard to the plays we read. The gender dynamics there lean more towards feminist readings that, like *Their Eyes*, leave the female protagonist without her stifling male counterpart, able to choose her own self-actualizing path. However, the novels begin with a woman in trouble (or at least in transition) who falls in love. *I Wish I Had a Red Dress* presents the complexities of Joyce's impending relationship as the protagonist, but it also explores the ways in which other women try and fail to navigate their desires for functional coupling. Undoubtedly, the play between romance and social commentary was the most enticing for my class of primarily female students. They certainly understood the dangers and the joys of romantic love. It was one of the most relevant themes and discussions returned to it again and again. Still, the other concerns were not lost on students, as they chose to discuss them at length in their discussions and in their writing.

While the love stories are perhaps the most inviting aspects of the novels, the social issues in those texts are also quite familiar. Young women and men in the twenty-first century are often forced into knowledge as a matter of survival. They have likely been discussing HIV and AIDS all of their lives. The statistics on infection rates and the devastating racial and gender demographics related to death have been thrust in the faces of young people in America early and often. Likewise, the phenomenon of "the down low"—men who identify as heterosexual but participate in covert sex with men—was part of their collective vocabularies long before reading *Baby Brother's Blues*, which features more than one male character who has sex with men but does not identify as gay. Another palpably clear way that students can find their way into the novels happens with *Till You Hear From Me*, with its references to the historic 2008 presidential election. The participation of students and young people across the country was key, so this novel resonates in the imagination of students who read it.

These contemporary references make Cleage's work, "relatable" (a word that students seem to like) and relevant to the in-real-time lives of students. Although my students' location in Southwest Atlanta enhances the flair of the course, even students not in Atlanta or at Spelman College will recognize the world in which the characters live. Interestingly, this also seems true for the plays; despite the specific historical settings, the issues are as concrete for students as the novels' more contemporary settings.

Cleage also represents her interest in social issues through gardening and a number of edenic landscapes. This presentation of nature may be read as a kind of pagan spirituality.[3] In *What Looks Like Crazy* ... and in *I Wish I Had a Red Dress* the fruit that Eddie feeds Ava from his garden and Joyce's moments of quiet, thoughtful serenity in the snow are examples of characters' connections to their deeper selves. Moreover, human-to-human connections also seem facilitated by these natural elements. The community gardens that make frequent appearances in the later novels, appropriately lead by Flora, further testify to Cleage's use of the land, nature, flowers, and gardens to bring her characters together. In *Flyin' West* the open land is what draws scores of African Americans to the West. As a result, a unique black community is formed and African Americans, as well as many women, are able to assert themselves economically.

Because my students are in Atlanta, they know exactly where the Atlanta-based novels are set and have their own relationships with the location. For this reason, acknowledging the experiential knowledge that students bring to the novels can be a useful tool. However, it is important not to allow it to overtake analysis of the texts either in discussion or in written responses. Similarly, because Cleage's work is so rooted in its themes, it can easily be snared by the themes alone. Class discussions could easily be consumed with how students experience domestic violence or race and gender issues. But the texts must be examined and questioned in the same way that other texts require, despite one's own intimacy with the subjects. Close reading is quite useful for students' individual study of the texts, and those moments are necessary to balance the handling of the larger looming issues (what one student called Cleage's "soapbox issues") that are gateways into each text. Supplemental texts also help to frame the treatment of thematic issues, and they help students unfold the stories. For example, a selection from James Cone's able work on black liberation theology can both fill in gaps about the ideology itself and invite full discussion of *Till You Hear From Me*. He writes, in 1975, that the "content of Black Theology is liberation, a theme that is derived from black religion's acceptance of the biblical claim that God discloses his presence in the struggle of the poor for freedom" (103). Because the contemporary cultural genesis of the novel is rooted in the complexity of this idea, having students properly define it is important. It helps to explain the significance of the real-life Rev. Jeremiah Wright and the fictional Rev. Horace Dunbar in juxtaposing racialized religious thought with mainstream perspectives on Christianity.

Ancillary readings also present opportunities to make discussions interdisciplinary. Cleage's writing is enhanced quite well by essays in Women's Studies, sociology, and popular culture. Feminism and its manifestations, for instance, inform most of her work. Students need a working understanding of the interplay between mainstream feminism and womanism, as defined by Alice Walker's *In Search of Our Mothers' Gardens*. What Cleage calls a free woman is an idea (and, perhaps, an ideal) that runs through nearly everything that she writes. Her list in *What Looks Like Crazy ...* offers one concise way to understand the concept. It is also useful to pair that idea, in the process of defining it beside feminism and womanism, with the nineteenth century concept of the Cult of True Womanhood. Other ideas that are clearly engaged need similar illumination. Examples might be the history of HIV/AIDS, "down low" homosexuality, or sex trafficking. Walker's text could also be useful in situating Cleage's repeated use of gardening as a sort of pagan spirituality. In *Till You Hear From* Me and in *Seen It All and Done the Rest*, among others, gardening parallels community healing and repair. It is another way in which the central ideas in the novels can be enhanced by outside texts. Per these models, additional readings may be gleaned from a wealth of sources, studies and newspapers as well as academic sources.

Carefully crafted assignments can help students find their own ways into the themes in the novels. A cultural handbook project, based on Eric Sundquist's *Cultural Contexts for Ralph Ellison's Invisible Man*, provides ample opportunity for students to explore the references in the texts. The projects require them to compose a handbook of short entries to supplement the creative works and offer greater context. This lends itself especially well to the Atlanta novels because the students were able to physically take their own photographs, etc. in addition to conducting research on the many cultural references. Again, while being located in Atlanta is useful, the texts are ripe for illumination in general. Place is a significant factor for much of Cleage's work, of course, and delving into the particulars of real spaces also underscores the author's geographical inventions. The other places — Idlewild, Michigan, Tybee Island, Georgia, and the District of Columbia, for instance — invite similar exploration through either concrete investigation or through research with documents. *Flyin' West* is also an example of how an assignment like the cultural handbook might be an inviting exercise. Students may delve deeply into the historical documents and evolution of westward migration in America as well as expand their knowledge about Paul Laurence Dunbar or early domestic violence law. This kind of learning activity allows for the creation of a unique lens through which to view the stories.

Perhaps the most distinct advantage to being in Atlanta is that we could actually invite Pearl Cleage to a class session. She has come to talk to students in the course each time it has been taught, and has been very open to answer students' questions, which sometimes reflect their challenges with the work. For example, one student struggled throughout the semester with the difficult presence of young black men in the novels. She was deeply concerned that so many of them (or "all of them," as she read it) were angry and lost and violent. There was, she said, no redemption for them. She posed that issue to Cleage during our class meeting and Cleage didn't hesitate to answer:

> So it was not meant to say all black men are doing business really terrible. It was to say these that we're looking at have come together in a way that for General and for baby brother, you know, baby brother was a person who just was not a positive guy. When you drop him into a circle, it's going to be a problem because he was a problem. General kind of lost his mind there because he was so in love and then he thought this was a reincarnation of the woman that was the only woman he'd ever loved. So his judgment was off. But it was really talking about the specific guys having a problem but not to say, you know, I'm optimistic about individual people so I'm never trying to say this means all black men are in big trouble, they're doomed, or this means all black women are doomed and all that. So I wasn't trying to say that at all [Cleage, Class Session].

Pushing that issue a little harder with follow up questions, Cleage describes a situation she observed in which a family was neglecting both their children and their property; when the county came for an official visit of some kind, the family launched into a tizzy of action, cleaning up the house and yard. Here we can see clearly how the world around her feeds the vision in her creative work:

> So how do you make the choice to live that way when you know it's wrong? And that's really what I'm always trying to get to with the problematic characters in these books. To say, of course we feel protective of baby brother [the previous question addressed Baby Brother from *Baby Brother's Blues* specifically]. We always feel protective of baby brother, but he's wrong. So what do we do? [Cleage, Class Visit].

We found that Cleage's personal stories could almost operate as an additional text for reading her work. She is so clearly interested in her audience, and their reaction to her writing, that talking to her personally (usually) confirms what readers see and feel as they are reading. Of course, having a visit from the author won't be possible for every class in which Cleage's work is taught around the country. The interviews on public radio, in arts publications, and the like are so prolific, however, that it will be possible to engage her own words as students and scholars study her work. These interviews are another layer to help untangle the mixing of activism, creativity, and social commentary. At this point, such interviews address many of the most apparent questions (why she made the switch from drama to fiction or the influence of her father's ideas [Albert Cleage] on her work, for example) and she continues to be very available to both individuals and groups who want to ask questions.

Pearl Cleage is a perfect writer for a single author course. Her artistic voice is carefully aligned with itself, even through multiple genres. Teaching it as a whole can push students to use both literary and critical thinking skills in ways that perhaps they have not previously. Included in this chapter is one example of student writing by Alexia Williams; this essay illustrates how students might ultimately demonstrate understanding of the aims of Cleage's writing and how it functions across texts. Further, it points towards the possibilities for students in a course like this. Whatever the space, Cleage's work invites serious discourse and inquiry.

Notes

1. Note that, while I have taught this class two times, here I will explicate my approach with a focus on the first time, with the idea that other people teaching Cleage's work may be able to use the suggestions and teach similar seminars or courses.

2. See Steve Visser's article in the *Atlanta Journal Constitution* website, http://www.ajc.com/news/atlanta/fatal-shooting-of-spelman-130776.html

3. Georgene Bess Montgomery's *The Spirit and the Word* offers extended readings of nature and spirituality through a diasporic African paradigm.

WORKS CITED

Cleage, Pearl. Class Visit. 18 April 2010
―――. Personal Interview. 23 April 2011.
Cone, James. "The Content and Method of Black Theology." *Journal of Religious Thought*. September 1, 1975: 90–103. Print.
Weekly, Ayana, "Why Can't We Flip the Script? The Politics of Respectability in Pearl Cleage's *What Looks Like Crazy on an Ordinary Day*. *Michigan Feminist Studies* 21. (2008): 24–42. Print.

Backtalk: Respectability as Repression and Pearl Cleage's Incitement to Discourse

ALEXIA WILLIAMS

Repression, or the process of implementing cultural, social or political conditions with the purpose of limiting the personal freedom of a group of members in society, shapes a community's cultural identity and controls the behavior of individual community members. In his book *The History of Sexuality*, Michel Foucault develops his "repressive hypothesis," or the process by which sexual repression has become a technology of power that constrains people's sexual identities (Foucault 3). Foucault insists that the only way to resist repression is through an incitement to discourse, which forces repressed people to initiate a discussion of sexuality that recognizes their own repression and allows for sexual liberation. Pearl Cleage's novels, plays and essays represent this incitement to discourse as she unveils the ways in which black American women are expected to compromise the development of their own free, sexual identities with the sexual repression required by black images of respectability including marriage, motherhood and community. In her novels *What Looks like Crazy on an Ordinary Day* and *Baby Brother's Blues*, Cleage's discussions of the HIV/AIDS epidemic, homosexuality, heterosexuality, and sexual liberation as an integral part of free womanhood provoke the conversations among black women that transgress from this system of repression and transform the mentalities that prevent their own sexual, social and cultural liberation.

According to Foucault, repression operates "as a sentence to disappear ... an injunction to silence, an affirmation of nonexistence, and, by implication, an admission that there was nothing to say about such things ... nothing to know" (Foucault 4). Therefore, an incitement to discourse "will be required

... [because] the mere fact that one is speaking about it has the appearance of a deliberate transgression" (Foucault 6). Here Foucault explains that repression inhibits the acknowledgement of inappropriate sexual behaviors (or all sexual behaviors according to Victorian social mores) as a means of denying the existence of human sexuality. The incitement to discourse dissolves the barriers that enforce repression by insisting that human beings possess sexual desires that are part of the human experience and cannot be considered inappropriate without encouraging cultural oppression. Specifically in the black American community, images of respectability serve as repressive technologies because blacks often refuse to acknowledge "indecent" issues plaguing their communities at times when white America might be watching. According to Evelyn Brooks Higginbotham, as cited by Ayana Weekly, "these politics [of respectability] are internally as well as externally directed with the intended purpose of elevating African American's social standing within the nation" (Weekly 31). In *What Looks like Crazy on an Ordinary Day* and *Baby Brother's Blues*, these images of respectability inhibit social progress by refusing to address the problem of the HIV/AIDS epidemic, the existence of homosexuality and drug culture in the black community.

In *What Looks like Crazy on an Ordinary* Day, community efforts to maintain an image of black respectability in Atlanta causes Ava Johnson to be marginalized and excluded from black society, until her departure finally allows black leaders in Atlanta to act as if Ava and her illness never existed. Ava's HIV diagnosis does not cause any disturbances in the social order until she publicly acknowledges her illness by contacting the men who she may have infected. When the wife of one of Ava's sexual partners approaches Ava in the salon, she effectively silences Ava when she slaps her in her mouth (Cleage 9). This woman literally stops Ava from speaking because she specifically hits Ava in the mouth. The other women in the salon are also shocked to the point of silence by this accusation and the salon is instantly quiet (Cleage 8). This pattern of rendering sexuality nonexistent continues in Idlewild as Joyce demonstrates the correct way to use a condom to the women of the Sewing Circus. When Mrs. Reverend Anderson, the ideal image of black respectability, sees this explicit acknowledgement and acceptance of female sexuality, "the power of her outrage brought an immediate silence" (Cleage 94). Mrs. Anderson is most outraged when Joyce insists that her efforts to impart truth to the girls will save their very lives (Cleage 94). Joyce's active discussion of sexuality demonstrates the fulfillment of Foucault's assertion that discourse inspires liberation. Mrs. Anderson refuses to acknowledge this discourse; instead, she upends the table of Joyce's teaching paraphernalia, rendering the necessity of sexual education nonexistent through her adamant endorsement of abstinence (Cleage 95). Ayana Weekley claims that the politics of respectability impact African American discourses of race, gender, sexuality, as well as their engagement with discourses of the HIV/AIDS epidemic. This argument obviously applies to *What looks like Crazy on an Ordinary Day* as efforts to preserve black respectability silence any discourse pertaining to HIV or AIDS.

Similarly, in *Baby Brother's Blues* discussions that acknowledge the existence of homosexuality and drug culture are silenced. Baby Brother, or Wes Jameson, uses his heterosexual appearance to overpower his homosexual experiences. He reasons that "[h]e didn't look gay ... his classic hip-hop style ... screamed 'straight' as loud as if he'd had it tattooed on his stomach" (Cleage 255). This image overpowers his homosexual identity as when he asks other men why they approach him for sexual favors, "they would just mumble something about a certain feeling" (Cleage 255). This lack of specificity causes the remnants of Baby Brother's homosexual identity to disappear as it cannot even be clearly articulated by his male sexual partners. A lack of specificity continues throughout the narrative as Cleage refers to gay night at the club as "DL night," or simply by saying, "Tonight, Club Baltimore was all about *the brothers*" (Cleage 255). Her refusal to clearly state that Sunday night is gay night at Club Baltimore reflects the attitudes of her "Down Low" characters who do not openly acknowledge their homosexuality. Parts of the narrative are therefore silenced by Cleage as she attempts to recreate the repressive atmosphere of her characters for her readers.

Cleage also identifies the ways in which respectability causes repression through the extreme violence that occurs when a small-time drug dealer is murdered. When the mother of the murdered teenager goes searching for clues about her son's disappearance, she is effectively silenced when his murderers "sent her his dick home in a show box [and] ... dropped his dickless ass body on the steps of his mother's church" (Cleage 159–160). This horrifyingly explicit act of violence preserves the technology of power that represses conversations of indecency. These murderers do not send this woman her son's penis to incite sexually deviant ideas in her, rather they castrate him to assert their own manhood. They leave his mutilated body on the steps of her church not to desecrate the center of black respectability, but to warn respectable, churchgoing members of society that any discourse of inappropriate behaviors, including accusations of the presence of the drug trade in the black community, warrants severe punishment and immediate repression. These murderers punish, "niggas [for] always talkin' about shit ain't none a they business" (Cleage 163). This explicitly violent act highlights the power of repression to inhibit liberation. As an advocate for free personhood, Pearl Cleage immediately begins to unravel the institutions that preserve these systems of repression and technologies of power.

Although his incitement to discourse requires the acknowledgement and discussion of human sexuality in order to insure liberation, Michel Foucault also describes the development of a repressive discourse to, "take charge of sex, tracked down as it were, by a discourse that aimed to allow it no obscurity, no respite" (Foucault 20). Religious confessions, particularly in the Catholic Church, caused people to "confess to the acts contravening the law ... to transform your desire, your every desire, into a discourse ... .meant to yield multiple effects of displacement, intensification, reorientation, and modification of desire itself" (Cleage 21, 23). Cleage acknowledges the power confession has to further repress sexuality in her novels as her characters' confessions and refusals to confess either devastate or empower them.

In *What Looks like Crazy on an Ordinary Day*, Ava recognizes the power confession has to classify women, particularly black women as sexual deviants. She realizes that having HIV means that she is almost required to lay to bear her personal sexual and drug history, play-by-play; this behavior is immediately classified as sinful and dirty. Women who are infected with HIV or AIDS must confess every detail of their sexual experiences in order to receive any sympathy or compassion from other people. They are not allowed to cherish the memories of any of these sexual encounters as each detail is converted into proof of their deviance in this repressive discourse. According to Jacqueline Bobo, "representations of black women in mainstream media constitute a venerable tradition of distorted and limited imagery [as they] ... have been presented as sexually deviant" (Bobo 1). Ava refuses to accept the community's declaration of her sexual deviance as she states, "I'm not buying into that shit" (Cleage 4). Although confession can have repressive purposes, when Cleage's characters confess on their own terms, they are able to find happiness.

Confession becomes an incitement to discourse when Eddie tells Ava why he was sent to prison. There is a sharp contrast between the confessions of the white AIDS victims and Eddie's confession to Ava as this discussion is not obligatory. Eddie initiates the conversation by telling Ava that he wants to tell her why he went to prison (Cleage 128). At the end of his confession, Eddie actually thanks Ava for listening and suspending her judgment as she absolves him. She comes to the conclusion that, despite the fact that "[p]eople died," she now knew him as a good and decent man (Cleage 131). Ava is able to forgive Eddie because he acknowledges his own deviance and discusses the problem of drug culture within the black community. Ava incites her own discourse by confessing to Eddie that she is HIV-positive. Despite this, she does not force her confession or describe every detail of her previous sexual experiences. She simply states, "I'm HIV-positive ... I've known it for a year and I feel fine.... I just wanted to tell you because ... *(because I want to make love with you)*" (Cleage 139). She is rewarded for initiating this discussion of HIV because Eddie does not judge her at all. This suspension of judgment allows the confession to unravel its repressive purposes as Ava and Eddie both assert their sexuality into a realm of not only acceptable, but appropriate human behavior.

In *Baby Brother's Blues*, confessions only further repress the characters as these confessions are not made willingly. Kwame only confesses that he has been participating in homosexual relationships outside of his marriage, and that he was involved in the murder of Wes Jameson, when Lee Kilgore threatens him. The conversation is similar to the traditionally repressive confession as Lee presents, "a stack of snapshots" with incriminating evidence regarding Kwame's relationship with Baby Brother as well as Baby Brother's living arrangements in Kwame's loft. Unlike the exchange between Eddie and Ava, Lee refuses to suspend judgment and instead uses these pictures to demand silence from Kwame's mother Precious Hargrove; in fact, Lee demands that Precious not seek retribution for her crimes (Cleage 300). Furthermore Kwame refuses to accept responsibility for his role in this disorder. His first response is a desire to run away from the entire situation (Cleage 300). The photographs allow every detail of Kwame's relationship to be documented and become part of this repressive discourse while Lee's threats demand silence from Kwame as well as his mother Precious. Kwame's confession to his mother is unsuccessful because he does not immediately incite this discourse. Rather, his mother demands every incriminating detail as she insists, "Now tell me everything" (Cleage 306). However, Kwame is not even able to articulate a response. His confession further represses him and he faces the loss of his job, his marriage and his child — the images of respectability that confirm his manhood.

In *Baby Brother's Blues* the characters cannot simply incite discourse to challenge respectability, but they must clearly acknowledge their own sexuality to be liberated. When Blue Hamilton's friend and bodyguard General chooses an array of sixties style, shapeless, sheath dresses for his lover, the stripper Brandi, he combats both the sexual desirability which opposes the image of respectable womanhood, as well as the skin tight, low-cut, transparent clothing that characterizes Brandi's personal style. Brandi is physically exposed as she sheds her already transparent dress, allowing General an unobstructed view of her naked body. Despite this, while it seems that she has internalized her oppressed role as both a hypersexualized black woman and a prostitute, Brandi actually portrays her sexual independence through her refusal to accept her body as a source of shame or an object that should be constantly covered, hidden or disguised. The clothing General has chosen for her is more oppressive than the exposure of her naked body because it requires her to repress her own sexuality to fit into General's idea of respectability. This explicit refusal to accept repression is Cleage's own incitement to discourse which forces her readers to question their own definitions of respectability.

According to Foucault's article "We Other Victorians," an individual's sexuality becomes an issue of public concern because, "at the heart of the economic and political problem of population was sex: it was necessary to analyze the birthrate, the age of marriage, the legitimate and illegitimate births ... the effects of unmarried life ... [and] those notorious "deadly" secrets" (Foucault 25–26). Repression, therefore, becomes a community problem as sex influences population and therefore the wealth and power of a particular community. In her novels, Pearl Cleage allows her characters to exert their own sexual independence as a means of encouraging free personhood and developing stronger individual identities. Her characters are able to combat the issues plaguing black communities as Joyce begins to educate young women on sexual responsibility and domestic abuse, Ava educates community members on the HIV/AIDS epidemic and Precious Hargrove acknowledges the drug culture within black neighborhoods. Cleage does not allow her characters to liberate themselves in order to allow for sexual promiscuity or irresponsible sexual behaviors, but rather to give voice to her community members and strengthen these black neighborhoods. She uses these novels to "talk back" to people who sacrifice the common good of the community to preserve an image of black respectability, and uses this backtalk to redefine respectable personhood.

WORKS CITED

Bobo, Jacqueline. "Black Women as Interpretive Communities." *Black Women as Cultural Readers*. New York: Columbia University Press, 1995. 33–60. Print.
Cleage, Pearl. *Baby Brother's Blues*. New York: One World/Ballantine, 2007. Print.
_____. *What Looks Like Crazy on an Ordinary Day*. New York: HarperCollins, 1997. Print.
Foucault, Michel. "We 'Other Victorians'" and "The Repressive Hypothesis." *The History of Sexuality*. Trans. Robert Hurley. Vol. 1. New York: Random House, 1978. 1–35. Print.
Weekley, Ayana. "Why Can't We Flip the Script? The Politics of Respectability in Pearl Cleage's What Looks Like Crazy on an Ordinary Day." *Michigan Feminist Studies* 21. (2008): 24–42. MLA International Bibliography. EBSCO. Web. 22 April 2011.

A Conversation with Pearl Cleage

TIKENYA FOSTER-SINGLETARY and AISHA FRANCIS

A note on context: This interview is one of several formal and informal conversations the editors have held with Pearl Cleage over the last two years. This conversation was conducted in April 2011 on the campus of Spelman College, where Cleage had just completed meetings with two student groups, one a class session with Tikenya Foster-Singletary's English course, "The Works of Pearl Cleage," and the other a lecture-style presentation with a group of theater students in the Atlanta University Center.

The Editors: In the early 1970s, you were here at Spelman with several other creative types Tina McElroy Ansa, Varnette Honeywood and I think LaTonya Jackson was also here then. So do you think there was something specific about the Spelman ... area sort of colliding with that time period that fostered this many artists who are successful?

Pearl Cleage: Sam [Jackson] was here, too. She [LaTonya Jackson] was a little bit behind us. Sam was in my class but they were both here, Sam and LaTonya. I think the art department here and the drama department always had very strong faculty. The Morehouse-Spelman players were active for years before I got here doing plays by blacks. I mean they did very radical kind of things and it wasn't that they were young radical faculty, these were like older people. But they were very much involved with national and international ideas about theater. So I think the department here was always very strong.

But why there ended up being like a bunch of us at one time — Andrea Flagg was here a few years before I was, so she's a Spelman person — I don't really know. I think that part of what was happening was that there were more outlets available, more professional outlets available for people at that time.

So that Sam and LaTonya could go to New York and there were places where they could go and work. When I started writing plays there were theaters in New York that would be interested in the work that I was doing in a way that hadn't really happened before. In prior years, people were much more confined to whatever area they were in hoping they could find a small theater in their city that would do it.

And same thing with publishing ... it was just beginning to open up a little bit. So I think it was part of the end of the 60s, beginning of the 70s and all that protest, all that youth energy and all that from the 60s, you know. Now we're 25 years old, we're ready to actually produce something. I think that same spirit made people take themselves seriously and actually figure you could make a living as an actor, you could make a living as a writer, and try to pursue it thinking that that might be possible.

The other thing that struck me, I was reading the other day, there's a new book that's a memoir and the author's first name is Ann Rophe called *Art and Madness* and it's talking about the whole period of the women right before me, like people who were moving around in the 50s and how unwelcoming the environment was for women. She was talking about her teachers at the college where she was saying women can't write fiction because they don't have expansive enough ideas to write fiction. Their idea was young women who were writing should not put forward their own writing but become the muse of some of these genius men, many of whom were the alcoholic kind of guys who were drunken and philandering. But they were convinced that they were geniuses and they would marry women who were convinced that they were geniuses. So there was a whole society that grew up around that kind of role for women and role for men as artists. And my generation of women who came after that, who came of age in the 60s and all that, we were certainly not looking to be anybody's muse. We wanted to be writers and when I read that, I'm thinking wow, the 50s was not that far from when I came of age in the 60s. But it was another world.

The idea that they would not be allowed to think of themselves as writers, even in a college-writing program, is just beyond me. I mean I can't even imagine it because by the time I got to college, we were all writing, we were all protesting, we were all doing everything. So that whole idea that within my class with Tina and LaTonya and Varnette and the rest of us, I think that we were very much a part of that moment in history when women were stepping forward, whether or not we were doing it in an organized way as a part of something called the American women's movement — because most of us weren't — we were still in the flow of that in the same way that folks who weren't involved in the civil rights movement still had the advantages that were coming about because other people had been marching and doing all those things. So I think it's partly this, that there were spaces for us to step into that hadn't been there before.

AF: I'd like to ask about your relationship with publishers. You've talked in the course earlier today and in some previous conversations about what parts of the written text are yours as a writer, and what parts you separate in terms of the marketing of the book in order to have the work exposed to large audiences. And you've had a relationship with Random House for a long time at this point. The first question is: How did you come to have your work placed with Random House? Then as a follow up question, I'd love to find out how you first began to publish. We hear of so many people who were first writing in the late 60s and 70s and were self publishing, or publishing with Third World Press or other black presses. Were these an entrée into publishing for you too?

PC: Yes, I did all of that. Certainly I think many of us started off with the 60s idea of if it doesn't exist, we can make it; if we don't have a press, we'll start one; if we don't have a theater company, we'll start one. So we did a lot of that starting up things because we wanted a place to do the work that we were doing.

A. F.: And now in the same lifetime you're with Random House. Could talk a little bit about that process of moving from self publishing to Third World to being at Random House?

PC: Early on I published with Broadside Press in Detroit. I'm from Detroit, so Broadside was the press I thought of when I had a book of poetry. I knew Dudley Randall, so I sent my poetry to him because I was from Detroit and I knew that press, and I knew him. And they published my first book of poetry which was, *We Don't Need No Music*. He was very encouraging to young poets. So he was always looking for us, looking for people to send work.

Yeah, he was passionate about that work. As for Third World, I also knew Haki [Madhubuti], too, who was Don Lee at that time. And there it was the same kind of thing where they were starting out and they wanted to talk to me about publishing and I wanted to talk to them about publishing. These were all people in the community of poets and writers that I knew. So I sent things to them and knew that someone would read it. The terrible problem that young writers often have, and it's especially true now I think, is that they don't have personal relationships with other writers and writers who are starting presses or other directors and directors who are starting theaters. They're sending their stuff in blind to a big publisher like Random House or like Harper Collins and it never gets past the bottom shelf of somebody's office. Especially since many of them don't have agents, it never even gets to the bottom shelf. They throw it away because they're not going to take unsolicited manuscripts.

My path to those big publishers came in a way that's very interesting to me. I have lots of cousins and when I was writing and trying to figure out about publishing, I was doing mostly theater at the time. I had done a lot of the *Mad at Miles* pieces as theater pieces. But, I wanted to publish them together because they got a great response. My daughter had been Xeroxing these pieces to give to her friends, just as I was talking about this morning. So I wanted to be able to publish them but I didn't really feel like it was something that Third World Press was going to be interested in. Haki was not a radical feminist kind of guy at that moment so I wasn't looking for that. And I also knew Dudley Randall wasn't looking for this kind of stuff. So then I went to my cousins who had "straight jobs." [Laughter] You know, one was a lawyer, one was a doctor. There might have been another — I can't remember — but it was primarily those two who were doing well, making good money. I said to them, 'I've got a book and I think there's a market for it, will you all help me to publish the book?' They were excited about it so they did. My cousin Earnest Martin and my cousin Warren Evans, who went on to become the police chief in Detroit, put seed money in for me to publish *Mad at Miles*. They published it beautifully. I mean it still looks pretty.

Then I did some touring around with it. And someone got a hold of it and sent it to a black woman editor who had been given an imprint. At that moment, several of them had gotten imprints within the big publishers to publish black authors. So this woman wrote me and said that she had gotten a copy of *Mad at Miles* that someone had sent it to her, and that she was very excited about it and wanted to know if I was interested in expanding it and then publishing it. I said, 'Absolutely! Are you kidding me? Sure!' So we did and that became *Deals With the Devil and Other Reasons to Riot*. I didn't go in search of a publisher, they'd found me because someone had found *Mad at Miles*. So that one, *Deals With the Devil* did well. They sent me on a book tour, which shows how long ago that was since that hardly happens anymore, and it did well. It got good reviews and people talked about it — that was wonderful.

Then they asked me, would I like to write another? Absolutely! So they wanted to know what I wanted to write. I said I wanted to write a novel. They said fine. So I started. That became, *What Looks Like Crazy*. They had given me an advance to write it. I wrote What *Looks Like Crazy,* sent it to them and didn't hear anything back, didn't hear anything back, didn't hear anything back. I mean for months. So I'm saying, "Do you hate me? Do you want me to work on it? Is it the worst thing you've ever read?" I'm driving everybody crazy down here [in Atlanta], wanting them [the publisher] to tell me what's going on.

Finally the phone rings, and it had to be like four or five months since I had heard anything from her. The phone rings, I pick up the phone, she said, "I want to tell you something and I have been really struggling with how to tell you." So you know that it's not good if someone's been struggling for four months. I said, "Okay, it's fine, just tell me." I'm thinking she's gonna say you need to work on it. I mean it's a first novel, I understand, she's an editor, that's what they do. But she said to me, "It's the worst book I've ever read. The characters are unlikable, the plot is unbelievable, the subject matter is unacceptable. No one is going to like this book and if I were you, I would just throw it away. Don't try to send it to anyone else because if this book makes the rounds in the world of publishing, you'll never work again." It's like that joke where people say you'll never work in this town again. She actually said that to me.

I'm sitting in Atlanta shocked, saying, "Wow!" I had read from the book at Club Zebra, which was a thing my husband and I used to do, and it had gotten a great response there. People loved it. So I was crushed. I said to her, "Well, can we work on it?" She said, "No, it cannot be salvaged, it's totally a wreck, it's just bad. Maybe you could write a book of spiritual guidance for black women?" I said, that wouldn't be good because I am a maniac. I am not a peaceful centered person. I don't know what the hell I'm doing. I'm trying to meditate ... but I'm not that calm girl, I don't have words of wisdom. What would make her even think to ask me that? But she was just kind of casting around because she didn't know what to do with me. So I said, "Okay, let me just think about that and call you back."

So I called the late Bebe Moore-Campbell who was a good friend of mine. I miss her so much. I called her and was just telling her my tale of woe and how there's an editor that hates my book and all that. So Bebe, who was in California, listened to everything I had to say. And then she said, "What did your agent say?" And I said, "I don't have an agent." And Bebe said, "What do you mean you don't have an agent?" And I said, "Well, when the woman called me [the editor], she was a black woman from Detroit, I'm a black woman from Detroit, so I figured she would look out for me.' Bebe read me the riot act all the way from California!

She was like, "That is the stupidest thing. You should not do that. That is not how you do it. She works for a publisher. She works for them; your agent works for you. How could you possibly do that? Did you sign contracts?" I told her yes, I had signed contracts. So Bebe said, "You can't do that. This is terrible; I haven't read the book but I know it's not that bad. I don't know what's wrong with her. But you can still do this." She gave me three agents' names: Marie Brown, Faith Childs, and Denise Denson who was another black woman from Detroit. So I called Faith Childs first. She intimidated the hell out of me. I was just freaked out. She was just so on it and intense. I thought, this is not going to be good for me; she was too New York high power for me. Then I couldn't get Marie Brown on the phone. I had met her but I knew she was busy.

Then, I called Denise who was very welcoming and listened to the story about what had happened with this editor. And Denise said, "Okay, first of all that's not the way she should have done that." And being an agent, she said this would not have happened if I had an agent. So she asked me to send the book, and said she'd read it immediately then call to let me know what she thought. I was on the road in Boston, I think, but I called my husband and said, "Get the manuscript; send it to her [Denise]. She's promised to read it." He sent the thing overnight mail. And she read it, and called me the next day and said, "Don't listen to your editor. This book is going to do great!"

So I knew I wasn't crazy. But the publisher had given me an advance and now wanted me to write this spiritual book about how to be a good Buddhist black woman. And since I wasn't going to do that, I was going to have to give them back the money. Now you know writers don't have the money to give back an advance. I explained all this to Denise, who said "No problem, I can sell this book by the end of the week." But, I was still gonna owe them $40,000, or whatever. And Denise said not to worry about it. She got me a bigger advance so that I could pay back what was owed them and still have some money. So I signed with Denise and she explained how it all works.

She called the publisher, told them that I was not going to write the book about how to be a peaceful spiritual girl and that if they didn't want [*What Looks Like Crazy*] we wanted to buy the rights back. They said well, you've gotta pay back the advance. Denise said no problem, "We'll have a check to you next week." They were like, what, does she already have another publisher? She told them well, that's really not any of your business, but we'll get you the check by next week.

Denise sold that book in three days! There were three offers and she took Avon's bid for it. She sold it to Avon, and they gave me a big enough advance to pay back Ballantine and publish it. I don't think Avon made any changes at all. They just published it and then it got picked by Oprah. How's that?! All my girlfriends called me and said, I hope you called that woman up and said, "You see? I told you it was a good book." But, I didn't. Except in my mind of course! [Laughter] To this day, I don't know what it was in *What Looks Like Crazy* that struck her as so wrong that she hated that book. And of all the books I've written, that's the book that people love the most.

I always tell young writers don't believe it if somebody tells you something you love is not good. They could be wrong, or it could be just not the book for them. So I stayed there, of course, at Avon. I wrote *I Wish I Had a Red Dress* there, then that contract was up. It was a two-book contract, and they were kind of dragging their feet about what they wanted to do next. And with

Denise being my agent she said, "Okay, we're free agents now, she's finished the contract, let's see who else is out here."

Now, true, I had had an Oprah book that was on the *New York Times* Best Seller list for nine weeks and sold like a million copies and all that. But, the publishers are so naïve about that. They think that that means every book you write after that is going to sell Oprah numbers. Which almost never happens, and it drives publishers crazy. If the writer buys into that, then it drives them crazy, too, because then they'll say things to you like, well, you know the book "only" sold 250,000.

The Editors: Incredible!

PC: Right. But if the last one sold 850,000 they're so disappointed. And I know several writers who were chosen [for Oprah's Book Club] who had a real problem after that because they felt like they were failing because they didn't do Oprah numbers anymore. I'm always very clear that that's *her* audience. She just lends it to the books for a minute. Then after that, that audience goes on to the next thing.

Denise had talked to the people at Harper Collins. I think Harper Collins is where I went after that and they offered me a wonderful advance based on, I think, those Oprah numbers. So I took it, of course! I left Avon and went to Harper Collins and was there for awhile and then went back to Ballantine which is an imprint under Random House. I had another black editor when I first went back to Ballantine who got a very nice advance for me. But then she took a principled stand because they had published Malcolm X's daughter's book and they weren't promoting it at all. So she quit in protest because it was a shame and disrespectful to the memory of Malcolm X if you won't even give his daughter's book a reception to launch it. They called her bluff and she quit. But she had just signed me, so I still had to go there. Then, suddenly I had no advocate and it was kind of a difficult thing for me.

But I've been fortunate—after that first one anyway—that there has never been an editor who didn't like my work. I've never had a book rejected and I've never had an editor who looked over my shoulder a lot. That was a good thing for me. Part of that is because they figured it was a niche kind of book and it wasn't going to be Stephen King so they didn't need to spend a lot of time with me, which was all right by me.

You know, Bebe [Moore Campbell] had an editor once that made her send in something like 30 pages a month. I can't even imagine having to do that, and then having the person make notes in the process and send it back to you. I've been very fortunate that I never have had that. But there are lots of transitions. My editor currently, who is a black woman, is leaving, too. But I just finished my last book on that contract we'll see what's next.

The Editors: Has the rise of e-books impacted you at all?

PC: There's a lot of upheaval in publishing now because of the electronic stuff that's happening. They're very nervous about that but they don't really have a clear idea what it is that I'm doing and how it should be marketed. So it just doesn't get marketed. So I'm just going to let that sit for a minute because I'm writing plays again, too. I don't really want to write a play and a book at the same time; it's not good for me. I tried it once because I had a great idea for a play and I couldn't wait for it, but I also had a book deadline. So I wrote the play and then I was very late getting the book in. I know it's not good for me to try to do two things like that at one time. It's like asking for madness.

Publishing is a weird thing and the difficulty that you have as an artist is to keep the business separate in your mind from what you're doing artistically. It's difficult to do that because when they ask you the kinds of things that the publishers will ask if they don't really understand what you're doing, it will guide you in the wrong direction if you're not already clear about what you're doing. But I've always been really clear about how I was very grateful for those Oprah numbers. But, I always understood those were Oprah numbers and it didn't make me think I needed to start trying to write another way to get those numbers again.

AF: One of the other things that you mentioned that I think is interesting is that you knew your audience. At the Zebra Lounge you had been reading from What Looks Like Crazy *and people loved it. So you knew that there was somebody, probably many somebodys out there, who would have a positive response.*

PC: Actually my husband is the one who reminded me of that because I was so distraught by that first editor's reaction. I had spent a year of my life writing this book and I really loved it and I was very proud of it and then to have the woman tell me you'll never work in this town again ... I was weeping and all that stuff. And he said, "You have better information than that." I thought, what do you mean? And he said, "Didn't you just read that in front of a hundred people at our place who stood up and cheered at the end of it?" I said, "Well, yeah." So his point was, then why don't you go with what they think rather than this woman sitting in her office in New York thinks? I said, okay, that makes sense, let me cling to that because it's true and I know that to be true.

But, I can get 800 great reviews, wonderful response from an audience, and one bad review is what I remember. That's when you obsess about that one that didn't love it, and I've really learned how not to do that. I mean I don't read everything. I read some of the reviews of things that I do and I try very hard to look at the audience. You know, what do the people who are reading the book say, what do the people who are coming to see the play say, rather than what do the critics say. And if you go with what the folks that you can actually see and hear have to say, most of the time they're the ones that are going to support the work that you do. So I'm very conscious of not being swayed by someone who thinks the marketing plan is going to be able to tell them better than what I know from having sat in the room with the people and listened to them respond to what I'm doing.

TF-S: You mentioned your relationship with other writers and artists. I'm wondering if in those relationships you read each other's work before it's published or if you have any sort of collaborative working relationships with other writers or audiences.

PC: I have working relationships with directors, but you don't mean that, you mean like in terms of actual writing....

TF-S: Yes, with other writers....

PC: Oh no, I don't do that. I don't find it helpful to let people read things in draft form and I think that that's a product of being the youngest child. I mean I only have one older sister but my family is very opinionated, very demanding. And my father was always a larger than life figure for me — very demanding about everything so that I was always obsessed with pleasing my father. And I knew he wanted a boy and he had gotten two girls. You know how people tell you your birth story as you go through life? My birth story is when I was born, they went out to tell my dad that I was there and my father says, "Oh, another girl." Now why would you tell a child that? Why would you tell me that? But then they would laugh and I would think, that's really not a good birth story...

But it made me very conscious of trying to please my father. And in my work I find that when I used to try to show people things in draft and they would react, I would immediately shift into that kid trying to please her dad and be trying to make it what they wanted it to be, which is of course the worse thing that an artist can do is to let somebody else's opinion sway you one way or the other.

I can't take the criticism and filter it through. I immediately am knocked off where I'm going by trying to please my dad who is not even with us, but all of that kind of vibe comes forward to me. I've never been a person who was good at workshops where everybody reads their work and then critiques it and all that stuff. I want everyone to love everything I do instantly and if they don't, it's like okay, I need to do to fix it so that they'll love me. It's not a healthy part of my brain so I try not to activate it if I can. And I've never really had a relationship with another writer where I would read their work and critique it. As many writers as I know — and sometimes I feel like everybody I know is a writer — I don't think anybody who I would consider a peer has ever asked me to do that.

My husband is always the first person that I let read it once it's done, and we talk a lot in process because he's a writer and we both work at home so we have like an incessant conversation all the time and I really respect his opinions. He's much better than I am about structuring a craft and plot and all of that, so that we talk a lot about things as I'm working. But I don't ever show him pages and say, "Is this working for you?" Once it's done, then I show it to him and am interested in what he has to say. But by that time it's already done. I mean truly done to the point of you can read the galleys, or the play is opening tonight, and you may come to see it. [laughter]

TF-S: You mentioned your father [Albert Cleage] is intentionally and a lot like Rev. in Till You Hear From Me...

PC: A lot like my dad, totally.

TF-S: What parts of your father did you want us to see in Rev?

PC: That character actually came about because of Jeremiah Wright when they took that incendiary 20 second [video] where he was saying instead of saying God Bless America, goddamn America and all that. I had certainly known about Jeremiah Wright before that and I knew he was a radical theologian and that he believed in black liberation theology because my dad was one of those people who started black liberation theology. So I knew all of that but I remember watching the little section on TV of Jeremiah Wright's sermon that people were going crazy and thinking to myself, this is like any Sunday morning in my dad's church. This is not new; this is not wild. This is a part of what goes on in black churches. The people who were making a big deal about it may not have known. But also the people who were making a big deal out of it were doing it because they wanted to beat Barack Obama, not because they were shocked at Reverend Wright.

But I felt like he was put in an impossible position because he had been so close to Barack and then on the morning when Barack was going to announce and Jeremiah Wright was supposed to be at the prayer and they told him he couldn't attend because they had an inkling that this stuff was gonna come back around. You know he was crushed. I mean, black ministers have tremendous egos. To do that work, you've got to have a big ego. You're talking to God, so you definitely do. And I think that every time I saw Jeremiah Wright after that, like when he was speaking at the Press Club, he was just like beside himself. I just kept saying and thinking that it was only because he feels like his son turned on him and he can't stand it.

I've watched so many of the old civil rights guys who live in Atlanta who I know really struggle with Barack specifically because they're old now. You know, they're old but they don't feel old. They don't want to be the old guys in the room only when everybody talks about Black History Month and says, "Thank you so much. You did great. Goodbye." They still think of themselves as the warrior group but they're old men. I think Jesse [Jackson] was very competitive and jealous of Barack because he ran and didn't win.

I'm looking at all of that and really feeling sympathy for them because getting older is hard enough. But if you feel like you were the warrior and now you're the little old man at Pascal's and nobody even knows who you are and you did everything, how difficult. I remember being at a Quick Copy place in Southwest Atlanta and C.T. Vivian came in to make a copy. I love C.T. Vivian. I just love him and I'm always in awe of him because I remember that scene in "Eyes on the Prize" when they're in Birmingham and he walks up to the sheriff who we all know has been killing black folks and beating them in the head forever. And he's talking right back in the man's face, and the man does not want to let them in to the courthouse to register to vote. And C.T. is talking, talking, talking. The sheriff says "You're just an outsider, you're not from here." Then C.T. says, "But these people want me to speak for them. Don't you want me to speak for you?" And everybody behind him says, "Yes!" You know, they were really afraid to speak. So the sheriff finally got so mad that he hits C.T. in the face with a club and C.T. falls to the ground. Then he turns over, gets up, with blood running down his mouth, he had never stopped talking. Never missed a beat! Stood up with his beautiful suit on, brushed himself off, wiped that blood off and never stopped talking. So I loved him for that.

Well, he walks into the copy place. And we had a nice little exchange and all. There was a young man behind the counter, and another person in there, too. So when C.T. left, the guy behind the counter said, "Who was that?" I said, it was C.T. Vivian and he did this and he did that and told them everything I loved. And the guy who was on the copy machine said, "Oh yeah, well that was a long time ago." And I wanted to smack him, you know? I wanted to say, "That's the wrong answer. Even if you don't care, why would you say that?"

I feel protective of those guys in that way. And I felt very protective of Reverend Wright because I knew he that could have been my dad. And I knew how crushed my dad would have been if one of his parishioners who he had really helped and raised in faith and married and baptized his kids, and then at a certain point he said, "You're just too radical, Rev, we can't take you on this part of the journey." Now, we all wish that at that point Reverend Wright had said, "You know what? I totally get it, Barack. I think you're going to be a great President, I'm going to go to the beach for about three months. I'm gonna take Jesse with me and we're just gonna chill and take this all in because every time we talk to the press we put our foot in our mouths. So do a good job. Win, then invite us to the inauguration, and we'll be there." But of course he [Jeremiah Wright] can't do that.

So I wanted the Reverend Dunbar character to be a part of that tradition, but also to be somebody who was still very actively involved in what was going on. He's like those who are very conscious of the enemy in these days the same way they were in the old days because the Republicans never stop. That part of what the book *Seen it All and Done the Rest* is saying is: Don't get so happy celebrating that you forget that the people on the opposite side of what we're talking about are relentless. It was very much an opportunity for me to talk about what it feels like to be the daughter of a guy like that.

You know, the part about [the character Ida] riding around with the reverend to register people in South Georgia to vote? I used to do all of that. I mean, anywhere my dad was going, I wanted to go. So I spent a lot of time doing that and listening to him. And if your father is a minister, you are sitting in the congregation looking up at your father talking to God every week. So it's kind of having that built in hero worship thing because of the role that the person plays. And my dad was playing such a big role in the movement that it even intensified all of that.

I wanted the young woman in the book to be able to have the scene where she gets to introduce her father on Father's Day and say, "I wanted him to be at my dance concerts but he was, you know, out saving the race." I had to come to terms with all of that because when you're a kid, you want your dad to come and see your little ballet concert and my dad would be picketing at the police station. So writing that book really gave me a chance to think about that and to write about it because I really came to terms with it and had a real good conversation with my dad about that before he died. It was wonderful and I could write it without feeling like I had missed something. Because I understood that he didn't do the traditional dad things, but instead he gave me such a big idea about the world and what I was supposed to be doing and all that. It was like, okay, I wish you had been to the ballets but if it was a choice between a concert when I'm nine years old and a way to look at the world now, I'll go with the latter.

TF-S: Well, since we're talking about Seen It All and Done the Rest *one of the things that I noticed in teaching your texts is that some of the names show up again and again. There's a Dunbar who is the protagonist in one of the novels we were just discussing and then also in the "Nacirema Society" there are also Dunbars. There are also a couple of Eddies in some of the books.*

PC: That really wasn't intentional. There was a prominent Dr. Dunbar in Detroit and I think that's probably where I had the Dr. Dunbar idea in the first place. It's funny because somebody else said that to me and I hadn't really thought about it before ... that I had two Eddies and Avas in different pieces. And I thought to myself, could that be the same Eddie? Could that be the same Ava?

I think it could be the same. Because the Ava in the play [*Late Bus to*

Mecca] was coming to Atlanta to open a beauty shop. And the Ava in *What Looks Like Crazy* had opened a beauty shop. And you know, the Ava in the play had been working as a prostitute. So, for the other Ava to have contracted AIDS many years later and before she became a successful business woman could have been a by-product of the lifestyle since it was before we knew as much about prevention. But I wish there was a real reason why these things do this way.... But I just really like the name Ava. There's always been a big joke in our family about Ava Gardner being a black person because somebody in my family saw Ava Gardner somewhere and said, "You know, you can really tell if you look at her hair up close by the edges." So we're always laughing about Ava Gardner.

AF: I do that all the time.... There are plenty of people whose ancestors passed and they just don't know it. So, I'm always looking at people's edges and claiming them as black. [laughter].

PC: When I got to Howard, my first roommate was so happy to get to a black college. She had been in all white environments — you know, maybe there were 2 or 3 black people in her high school. She was so excited to get to Howard. And she got there the day before I did. And I had my hair straight at that time. I had bangs and a flip. So here I come into the room and she later told me she went straight across the hall to the other woman who had already been in the dorm and just burst into tears. She said, "I came all this way to a black school and I got the only white girl in the whole dorm as a roommate!" But it was D.C. in August so I had my hair down and straight when I got there. But then I put it up because it was too hot. So, when I leaned over the desk to sign up — you had to sign up in the dorm back then — and she saw the back of my hair and she was relieved and said, "Oh, yeah! She's a black girl!"

TF-S: Speaking of hair, I love that scene when Aretha is having her hair cut in Crazy *when she says, "Only free women can wear their hair like this."*

PC: I love that scene, too. It's funny because there are some scenes that you plan, plan, plan and then there are some scenes that just kind of evolve with the people. And that one where she cuts her hair and says all that about free women wearing their hair like this [evolved]. And Aretha is the character that has come forward, I think, the most of any of the others in *What Looks Like Crazy* because she's introduced in that first scene where she gets her hair cut low when she's 16 years old in Idlewild, Michigan and then [in another book] she comes to Atlanta and meets Blue Hamilton and goes on to have a husband on the down low and all that. She shines through because of that.... People keep trying to get me to bring Eddie Jefferson to Atlanta, too. Eddie Jefferson does not want to be in Atlanta. He is somewhere growing tomatoes....

The Editors: We've been thinking about moving in terms of black women and travel. There's also a piece in Deals With the Devil *about how activists who are really engrained in working need to be able to check out at some point and that can be through international travel. You know, you need to be able to go somewhere to kind of relax and take a break. For you, what are those experiences and the moments because you talk about being so passionate about political issues and you're active in political campaigns and there are things and causes that you're very involved in. What do you do to keep that balance?*

PC: I don't know. I do work a lot. I love the work that I do. My husband always teases me. He says "It's like you can't sit down for five minutes with you because it turns into a meeting. Whenever I sit with you and I'm thinking it's a long day, we're gonna drink a glass of wine and then you have a meeting on me." It's like I'm always working in that sense, so I try to be conscious of it. I love the beach. I love Tybee Island which is off the coast of Savannah, a little island off the coast. I probably would like to do more international travel but I'm definitely afraid of airplanes. I did a lot of flying for a long time but I just don't like it at all. So at this point I'm very focused on trying to see as much of the country that I live in as I can see.

I grew up in Detroit, went to school at Howard and then came here [to Atlanta], so I'm very much a city person. I've never lived in the country. And I've never had any relationship to the nation that would have made me want to go see my country because I never felt like it was my country. You know, growing up in a strictly black nationalist household on the West side of Detroit, it was like a little black nationalist world, and people from Detroit don't tend to leave Detroit a whole lot. We're kind of like New Orleans. You know, where people born in New Orleans, they stay in New Orleans. People born in Detroit stay in Detroit and they stay on whatever side they were born on, east side or west side. It's like you do not cross, you stay where you are. And I was very conscious of being a person who was comfortable in a city and comfortable in the black neighborhoods within a city. But then when I started traveling more, I was still traveling from city to city so I didn't have any idea of what happened once you got west of Chicago until you got to California. All that in the middle was mysterious to me and I was not interested because I always assumed that there would be ... a lot of people who did not like black folks in all that space between California and Chicago.

Also being very aware of what I look like, I'm always conscious of driving around in places that I don't know in the middle of the country with my husband and having people think we're in an interracial relationship and get mad about that. When people are mad about that, you can't stop and say, "Hey, look at my hair! I'm really a black girl; it's okay." So I was conscious of that. But then he had driven across the country many times, my husband, and was always trying to get me to do it and said, "You would really love this." So I finally got over the race part and thought okay, maybe it's not just the Klan that's out there. But still it's scary. You know, mountains and all the vast open space. I mean ... what do you do in the Great Plains? People think that I've been all over Nicodemus, Kansas because I wrote about it. I've never been to Nicodemus. But I'm going this summer.

I finally said, "Okay, I will take a train with you across the country and if that feels okay, then we can drive back." So we took a train. To get there from Atlanta you have to go to New Orleans first and then go across the country to LA. Most of that is Texas. Texas is the biggest part of what you do on that trip. The train goes across kind of the middle so you go to sleep in Texas and you wake up in Texas. And you're in Texas for a long time, and then you get to California, so you don't see much. But it was like, you know, I saw no crosses burning in the distance. And it was beautiful...

So coming back he said, "Okay, let's drive back. We'll take Route 66 because you love that song." So we had the music and stuff and all that and we started driving from LA back to Atlanta and it was a life changing experience for me. The first time we did it and we've done it several times since, was in 2005. We were coming from [Oprah Winfrey's] Legends Ball, where I did the poem, "We Speak Your names." And Barack Obama was there with Michelle, but he was a senator then from Chicago. He had just made that wonderful speech to the democratic convention, so at the ball that night he got to say a few words and he was so wonderful and fabulous and everybody was like, "He's gonna be the President!." So I'm saying, "Okay, well that's good, if he's gonna be the President then I need to at least look at the country."

So I was feeling kind of connected to the country in a way that I hadn't before. And we came into Arizona, we were driving, and my husband said, "When we come around this curve there's gonna be a mountain so look for it. You'll love this; it's gonna be beautiful." ... So we come around the corner and of course there's a giant snowcapped mountain. I just wept my way through Arizona because it was so beautiful all the way into New Mexico, and wept my way through New Mexico all the way into Amarillo, Texas.

I had never had any idea about how beautiful the country was, and as a person raised in the city when you first see a real snowcapped mountain, when you first see the Grand Canyon it's beautiful!.... Once I kind of got myself together and said, "Okay, maybe I do have a feeling for the country I was born in, maybe I can embrace the country as an American citizen." It took me three more years to really do that. Barack had to get elected before I would actually let down my guard and say, "Okay."

I remember watching the primary and he carried South Dakota and I'm thinking to myself, what I know black people thought all over the country, which is, "That can't be possible. How many black people are there in South Dakota? How many are there in North Dakota, how many in any of these places?" And then you have to realize, okay, that means somebody other than us is voting for him which means all that pushing we've been trying to do to make this country do right has had some affect on people because they're voting for the best guy, not for the white guy. So this means something good about the country. Now by that time [2008] we had driven across the country another couple of times.

Every single cross-country trip I'm awed by the land and we've never had a bad experience with people on the road. We stop anywhere we want. We've run into all different kinds of people, Native American people, Mexican American people, European American people, black folks. Everybody that we run into, everybody's been lovely. It really made me feel grounded in the country in a way that I never had before. And I know that that's having an affect on the work that I do because thinking of yourself as an adversary always on the outside as a radical feminist, as a radical black nationalist, you're always standing outside shaking your finger in somebody's face. If you actually feel like a citizen of the country, it's a different relationship. It doesn't have to be adversarial because it's my country, too. There's nobody who has more right to it than me so there's no reason to shake your finger in everybody's face.

They're a citizen, I'm a citizen. So it's a different feeling and I'm still trying to figure out how it will manifest itself in my work. But it's wonderful because I've claimed the civil rights movement, which I was born into, the women's movement which I adopted myself, and now I've got trying to figure out what it means to be a citizen as a basis of the work that I'm doing according to my understanding of the world from which the work comes.

All of this is really wonderful to me. I figure it's gonna take me at least another 10–20 years to figure out what that means to be a black woman citizen of the United States.... When I was thinking about working at the Alliance Theater and I'd fussed at them and written them indignant letters over the years about when they were doing wrong things and how black folks weren't on the stage or any of that, and now we have new artistic directors, Susan Booth, who's wonderful. What does this mean? [Booth] directed the *Nacirema Society*, is just a wonderful artistic director, very good person and all of that. And when she asked me about directing a play, I was very nervous about that because, you know, August Wilson always said, "No, only black directors can direct black plays." and all of that. So I'm trying to figure out what would I say if August came down from heaven and said, "What did I tell you, what did I tell you?" [Laughs].

I'm thinking, "I'm an independent black play writer going to work at the big white theater, how is this going to be?" And my husband said, you're thinking about it wrong. Instead of saying "independent black playwright, big white theater" describe it as you're an "American artist," this is an "American theater," and see how different it sounds. So I said, okay, "I'm a major American major theater artist going to work at a major American theater." That *is* completely different than saying I'm the independent black artist going to work at the big white theater! Now I have an exercise for myself. Whenever I'm talking about something and I hear myself getting ready to say black and white, I ask myself if I can say American and it would be the same, I would be saying the same thing. Is it really race that I'm talking about or is it class that I'm talking about? Is it something other than race even though I am totally trained from birth to think and talk and interpret everything as being about race. What if it's not about race? What if it's class, which is a big unspoken thing in this country these days? More often than not it's class they're talking about and not race. So that's very exciting to me just to be able to know that there's a whole new batch of stuff for me to explore as an American writer.

The Editors: You're reframing from a different perspective.

PC: Yeah, it's new so I'm like, okay.

The Editors: That's great seeing that in yourself.

PC: This is good. So then I look at what's going on in Washington. Even when I'm angry at Barack I can't fuss at him like that. But it's funny because it's just good to have more energy to push the work that you do to make you do it.

There's so many stories that I think are yet to be even touched in the work that we do as Americans but specifically in this case as women, black women. We just have so many stories that are going to be wider as our frame of experience gets wider, as our acceptance of who and what we are and the wider scheme of things get wider, we'll make our stories be a little bigger, too. This is why I loved writing about Josephine being in Amsterdam. I can let them be in the bars and smoking and drinking and all that because I've been to Amsterdam and thought it was like a great place to live. But it also gives people who read the books a sense that there's a bigger world and someone just like them chose to move around in that world. Josephine went there, fabulous, and didn't care where in the world she was. She was gonna be fabulous anywhere, just like Josephine Baker. But there are so many people who don't know that there are people like that. So if I can sneak them in for people who don't know anything about Josephine Baker or that don't know Paul Robeson, who don't know that black folks have been traveling internationally and doing stuff for a long time, I can.

TF-S: Well, the major question I wanted to ask was about one of the rea-

son I came to What Looks Like Crazy, *which is because I was writing my dissertation on romantic love. I'm always thinking love is sort of a central idea for you. I don't know if you would identify it that way.*

PC: I would.

TF-S: So I wondered (A) how do you write about love and (B) how do you write about love when you're not — or when you haven't been — in love?

PC: I've never had that moment. I've been in love with somebody since I was six years old. I remember the little boy who used to sit in front of me in second grade, Turner Crooks, and I was madly in love with him [laughter].

I think my mother was a very romantic person. For her, romantic love was very important. When everybody in our black neighborhood in Detroit is playing Motown, my mother is weeping to "Madam Butterfly." It was blasting out of our house and people were like, "Tell your mother to turn that down!" But, of course, you know, I wouldn't have had the nerve to tell her to turn anything down and she wouldn't have done it anyway. But I think that that kind of big operatic feeling about love and how important it is came from her. I remember my mother and my stepfather arguing about something one time. And my mother was not happy with what my stepfather was saying and I couldn't figure out what she was so mad at. And she stood up at the dinner table and said, "What about love and all of that?" And she stomped off. I said, "Wow, this is great. But what is she talking about?" It was that kind of household where my mother was always reading these passionate stories and thinking about love.

So I grew up in an environment where my mother validated romantic love as being very important. My mother also was very progressive and ahead of her time in terms of being very frank about sexual love. I remember — and I asked my girlfriends about this once because we were all sitting in somebody's kitchen — and they were talking about all the things their mothers had said to them when they first got their periods. They said you know, "Keep your dress down. Don't have sex. Don't do this. Don't do that." So I said, "Okay, but when did your moms talk to you about the other stuff?" And they said, "What do you mean 'the other stuff?'" Never. Not one of my girlfriends had a mother who ever talked to them about sex and pleasure at all. And I remember my mother saying specifically, "Sex is really wonderful. It's gonna be a big part of your life. If you love the person, it's even better. So hold out for love *and* sex if you can. But if you can't, sex by itself is also a powerful thing in your life." My friends all looked at me like, "Where was your mother when we were 16?"

I think that my father is such a big influence on my politics but my mother is the one that put that idea about love in me. And I observed her in a very passionate relationship with my stepfather where they were.... You know, when they were happy, they were happy; and when they were arguing, they were both so intense about it. I grew up with that and I have been a person for whom that was important and I think really not in a joking way I have been in love with somebody for most of my life. Whether or not it was unrequited love, you know, whether or not it was someone I was longing for who didn't give me the time of day, or whether or not it was someone with whom I had an intense relationship with and then moved to something else, it was still love. There have been very few times in my life when I haven't had a one-on-one intense kind of love, romance, passionate kind of relationship.

I mean I had one that was really a bad one which is the stuff in *Mad at Miles*. That was really bad. But other than that I've had relationships where the people weren't perfect for me and we would realize it and there'd be that moment where you wish they could change and you could change and you can't. But just really very intense long term relationships with people and I think that shows up in my work. My husband and I met in 1971. I was married to my first husband then, but we met and kind of recognized each other in a way that I haven't ever done before. Zaron is my husband's name — when I met him we started talking and I felt like we were picking up in the middle of a conversation. We were having dinner with some other people. I don't even remember who the people were. People say, "Oh, I was at that dinner when y'all met." But, I thought it was the two of us. I actually don't remember the people being there. When I came back to Atlanta he was doing alternative service because he was a conscientious objector and we didn't see each other for five years.

Then he moved here and we ran into each other again and became very, very good friends and then both of our marriages dissolved and we stayed good friends, and stayed good friends. Then there's that moment when you look at the person and say, "Oh, I think I love you." And he was feeling it, too, so it was wonderful. And my relationship with him is a very active part of my life and the fact that we do the same kind of work and we live together and work together in the same space means we're real close all the time. I mean in physical proximity, yes. But we're also very much involved in conversation about everything all the time. We love to talk to each other. So that's why it shows up in the books that the person is talking to the man and trying to figure out things and they're madly in love and running down the beach and all that stuff, because I feel like my life is like that. So people tell me, "Oh it's so great that you can write like that." And I say, "I think it's great that I can write like that, but the even greater thing is that I actually live like that." Because I don't think I could write that or that it would show up in my books every time unless that was something that was actually a part of what my real life is like. So I'm lucky.

The Editors: Very.

PC: Yeah, very. My husband is the one who started that past lives stuff that's in some of the books. That's why Blue Hamilton has past lives. We were driving from New York to Philadelphia, I think sometime early in the morning and he was talking about remembering past lives. And I said, "right, yeah, okay." But it was so specific what he remembered, and of course I teased him and then I used almost the same kind of thing in the book where the woman who is Regina responds when Blue first says things about his past life.

You know, it's funny when men remember past lives they're always kings and emperors and stuff, and when we remember we're just out there. But I thought it was so interesting because he [Zaron] is not a mystical kind of guy but he was so straightforward that I took it in and gave it to Blue, who was a very down to earth guy but he has these past lives. I just thought that was interesting to put in there because how wonderful would that be if you could remember? Not only could you remember but that it means you're coming back. I would love to have great confidence that that was true. I want to believe in reincarnation but I really don't.

AF: OK, this is a purely nosy question. You said earlier today that you're working on a play set in 1973 in Atlanta partly about the political scene here then. And you talked about the fact that you'll be working on that for the next year. How far out do you start thinking about other things? Do you already know what it's going to be after that? Do you have a series of ideas?

PC: In this case I do because I'm going to write the play and I'll be done with the play probably by the fall, certainly by the end of the year. And then I want to do something with my journals because I've read a bunch of them and once I got over saying, "Oh my God! How stupid! How young were you and how careless were you?" [laughing] No, I had to really get over it.

I first tried it about a year ago and I just was appalled at how stupid I was. So I was like, "Ugh, I don't want to know this." But now I want to do something with it. I hadn't looked at the journals for many years and I've got a big old trunk full of them. After I read them, I said to my daughter that when her oldest daughter, who is now seven, when she was a kid I said — "When Chloe gets to be 16 — that's my granddaughter's name — I'm going to box all these up and give them to her so she can have all this." And my daughter said, "Absolutely not!" I said, "What do you mean?" She said, "Chloe doesn't need to know all that." I said, "But you haven't read my journals." Then, she said, "I don't need to, I was there." So I didn't even want to know what that meant!

But *I* want to look at them and I want to kind of look at what in there is valuable because we [women in the 1970s] learned a lot. I mean I'm 62 so my generation of women went through a whole lot of stuff and now we arrive at 62, so it's like okay, let's try to tell people what we learned.

The Editors: Now, there are "The Pearls of Wisdom" that your first editor wanted you to write! That seems like a perfect place to end. Thank you so much for your time. It was a pleasure.

About the Contributors

Rhonda M. **Collier** is an associate professor of English at Tuskegee University, where she specializes in teaching English and writing through service-learning. A recent publication is "From Hip Hop to Hip Hope: Art and Public Theology in South Africa," and her book in progress is *Women and Words: Rewriting the Nation with the Voices of Black Women.*

Kelly **DeLong** is an assistant professor of English at Clark Atlanta University. His short stories and personal essays have appeared in many literary magazines, including *The Sun, Evansville Review, Palo Alto Review,* and *Roanoke Review.*

Sandra C. **Duvivier** is an assistant professor of English at Bronx Community College and an adjunct assistant professor of English at Queens College. She was a scholar-in-residence at the Schomburg Center for Research in Black Culture, where she wrote *Beyond Nation, Beyond Diaspora: Mapping Transnational Black American Women's Literature.*

Tikenya **Foster-Singletary** is a faculty member in the Department of English at Spelman College. Her work has been published in *The Hip Hop Encyclopedia, Black Magnolias Literary Journal, Obsidian* and *The MAWA Review.*

Aisha **Francis** is vice president of Institutional Advancement at Crittenton Women's Union in Boston. Her publications appear in *Obsidian, The Encyclopedia of African American Literature,* and *The Encyclopedia of Black Studies.*

Margaret T. **McGehee** is an assistant professor of English at Presbyterian College in Clinton, South Carolina, where she also directs the Southern Studies program. She has published in *Southern Spaces, Cinema Journal,* and the *American Writers* series edited by Jay Parini.

Monica L. **Melton** is an assistant professor of women's studies in the Women's Research and Resource Center at Spelman College. She has published essays in *Many Floridas: Women Envisioning Change, Multicultural Reflections on Race and Change,* and *Race, Gender, & Class.*

Ladrica **Menson-Furr** is an associate professor of English at the University of Memphis in Memphis, Tennessee. Her writing appears in *Mosaic* and the *College Language Association Journal.* She is the author of *August Wilson's Fences,* and has published articles, chapters, and scholarly entries on Wilson, Zora Neale Hurston, and Walter Dean Myers.

Shanna L. **Smith** is a doctoral candidate in the American Studies Department at the University of Maryland College Park. A member of the Affrilachian Poets, she has published poetry in several regional publications including *Artists in Revolution*.

Sheila **Smith McKoy** is an associate professor of English, director of the Africana Studies Program and director of the African American Culture Center at North Carolina State University. She is the author of *When Whites Riot: Writing Race and Violence in American and South African Cultures* and editor-in-chief of *Obsidian: Literature in the African Diaspora*.

RaShell R. **Smith-Spears** is an associate professor of English at Jackson State University in Jackson, Mississippi. She has published essays and creative works in *Icons of African American Literature*, *Encyclopedia of Hip Hop Literature*, *Short Story*, *Black Magnolias*, and *A Lime Jewel*.

Ama S. **Wattley** is an assistant professor of English at Pace University in Pleasantville, New York. She has published essays in *Topic: The Washington & Jefferson College Review*, *The Journal of Intercultural Disciplines*, *The Critical Response to Ann Petry*, and *Obsidian III*, and on writers Alice Childress, P. J. Gibson, Toni Morrison, Ann Petry, and Aishah Rahman, and Amiri Baraka.

Alexia **Williams** is a senior English and Spanish language double major at Spelman College. She has studied racial politics and identity formation in African American and Afro-Peruvian literature. As a UNCF Mellon Mays Undergraduate Fellow, she has analyzed Afro-Peruvian poetry and folklore to understand experiences of slavery and racial discrimination in Peru.

Index

African American women writers 7–8, 34, 40, 41, 16
Ansa, Tina McElroy 166, 182
Atlanta 15–36, 37–48, 49–62, 69, 80–81, 99, 111–112, 118–119, 130, 133, 137, 143–144, 152, 154, 166–175, 177, 185–186, 191–192, 194–196, 200–201; Alliance Theater 10, 15, 146, 152, 197; West End 11, 13, 16, 52–53, 56, 59–60, 80, 92, 106–107, 154–156, 161–164, 166–167

Baby Brother's Blues 7, 14, 16, 20–22, 26–27, 30, 53, 170–171, 173–174, 176–178, 180
Babylon Sisters 16, 20, 24, 26–28, 53, 92
black church 12, 65–71, 114–117, 122–125, 191–192
Blues for an Alabama Sky 152
Bourbon at the Border 13, 34, 64, 146–153
The Brass Bed and Other Stories 13, 140–145

citizen/citizenship 31, 38–39, 49–62, 196–197
Cleage, Albert 22, 174, 191; *see also* liberation theology

Deals with the Devil and Other Reasons to Riot 4, 9–10, 24, 32, 72, 128–129, 139, 143, 167, 185, 195; see also *Mad at Miles*
Detroit 2, 23, 80, 130, 133, 137, 147–148, 184–186, 193, 195, 199
domestic violence 4, 9, 14, 24, 32, 64, 73–74, 78, 82, 98–99, 104–108, 131, 136, 167–169

feminism 10, 12, 14, 19, 73, 95–109, 128, 133, 172
Flyin' West 7, 9–10, 23, 51, 146, 152, 171, 173
Free womanhood 9–10, 37, 47, 59, 72, 74, 83–91, 176

gardens 22–23, 43–45, 53, 56, 58, 171

Harris, Joel Chandler 117, 154
HIV/AIDS 9, 30, 63–70, 75–76, 111–114, 117–121, 124–125, 169, 171, 177–181
Hughes, Langston 46, 64, 76, 86
Hurston, Zora Neale 37, 40, 44, 51, 169–170

I Wish I Had a Red Dress 7, 10, 12, 15, 63–64, 68–69, 72–76, 78–93, 81–91, 95–109, 170–71, 187; *see also* Sewing Circus
Idlewild, MI 23, 51, 64, 69, 79–83, 92, 98, 111–117, 120, 169, 194

Jones, Tayari 3–5, 33–34
Just Wanna Testify 7, 16, 21, 28

Late Bus to Mecca 13, 68, 127–139, 194
liberation theology 16, 172, 191
Lorde, Audre 41, 117–118

Mad at Miles 4, 64, 167, 185, 200; see also *Deals with the Devil and Other Reasons to Riot*

Seen It All and Done the Rest 7, 11, 13, 16, 21, 27–31, 37–48, 49–62, 161, 172, 193
Sewing Circus 66–68, 70–74, 81–91, 95, 98, 112–117, 120–124, 177
Shange, Ntozake 8, 39, 41, 45–46
Some Things I Never Thought I'd Do 7, 12, 16, 20, 22, 28–29, 53, 55, 59–60, 95–100, 102–108
Spelman College 3–4, 9, 14, 15–17, 33–34, 42, 154, 166–171, 182

technology 11, 43–47, 57–58, 154–164

What Looks Like Crazy on an Ordinary Day 7, 10, 12, 14, 15, 63–77, 79, 110–126, 169–175, 176–181, 185–187, 189, 194, 199

www.ingramcontent.com/pod-product-compliance
Lightning Source LLC
Chambersburg PA
CBHW032058300426
44116CB00007B/795